RELIGION AND EXTREMISM

Also available from Bloomsbury

EXTREME RIGHT WING POLITICAL VIOLENCE AND TERRORISM,
edited by Max Taylor

RELIGION, NGOS AND THE UNITED NATIONS,
edited by Jeremy Carrette and Hugh Miall

STEREOTYPING RELIGION,
edited by Brad Stoddard and Craig Martin

THE WRITING OF VIOLENCE IN THE MIDDLE EAST,
Jason Bahbak Mohaghegh

RELIGION AND EXTREMISM

REJECTING DIVERSITY

Douglas Pratt

Bloomsbury Academic
An imprint of Bloomsbury Publishing Plc

B L O O M S B U R Y
LONDON • OXFORD • NEW YORK • NEW DELHI • SYDNEY

Bloomsbury Academic
An imprint of Bloomsbury Publishing Plc

50 Bedford Square
London
WC1B 3DP
UK

1385 Broadway
New York
NY 10018
USA

www.bloomsbury.com

BLOOMSBURY and the Diana logo are trademarks of Bloomsbury Publishing Plc

First published 2018

© Douglas Pratt, 2018

Douglas Pratt has asserted his right under the Copyright, Designs and Patents Act, 1988, to be identified as Author of this work.

All rights reserved. No part of this publication may be reproduced or transmitted in any form or by any means, electronic or mechanical, including photocopying, recording, or any information storage or retrieval system, without prior permission in writing from the publishers.

No responsibility for loss caused to any individual or organization acting on or refraining from action as a result of the material in this publication can be accepted by Bloomsbury or the author.

British Library Cataloguing-in-Publication Data
A catalogue record for this book is available from the British Library.

ISBN: HB: 978-1-4742-9225-2
PB: 978-1-4742-9224-5
ePDF: 978-1-4742-9227-6
ePub: 978-1-4742-9226-9

Library of Congress Cataloging-in-Publication Data
Names: Pratt, Douglas, author.
Title: Religion and extremism : rejecting diversity / Douglas Pratt.
Description: 1 [edition]. | New York : Bloomsbury Academic, 2017. |
Includes bibliographical references and index.
Identifiers: LCCN 2017036884 | ISBN 9781474292252 (hardback) |
ISBN 9781474292245 (pbk.)
Subjects: LCSH: Religion and politics. | Radicalism–Religious aspects. |
Religious fanaticism. | Violence–Religious aspects.
Classification: LCC BL65.P7 P726 2017 |
DDC 201/.7–dc23 LC record available at https://lccn.loc.gov/2017036884

Cover Design by Catherine Wood
Cover image © iStock

Typeset by Newgen KnowledgeWorks Pvt. Ltd., Chennai, India

To find out more about our authors and books visit www.bloomsbury.com. Here you will find extracts, author interviews, details of forthcoming events and the option to sign up for our newsletters.

CONTENTS

Preface	vi
Acknowledgements	viii
1 Introduction	1
2 Accommodating Diversity: Paradigms and Patterns	13
3 Diversity Resisted: Exclusion and Fundamentalism	31
4 Texts of Terror: Scriptural Motifs for Extremism	49
5 The Jewish Experience of Extremism	65
6 Forms of Christian Extremism	81
7 Trajectories of Islamic Extremism	99
8 Mutual Extremism: Reactive Co-radicalization	117
9 Extremism and Islamophobia	133
10 Conclusion	149
Notes	161
Bibliography	180
Index	191

PREFACE

The twenty-first century has ushered in a sea change with respect to religion. Whereas the twentieth century opened the door to interfaith engagements, the new century is thus far an age of extremism. Since the early twentieth century there has been a burgeoning of inter-religious dialogue and, with respect to the world's largest religion, Christianity, the advent of ecumenical détente. Inter- and intra-religious engagement has aimed at the breaking down of barriers of antipathy and rolling back histories of mutual hostility. By contrast, the current century is witness to a disquieting new phase: the predominance of aggressive, even exclusionary, religion and a rise of impositional religious extremism. To be sure, the relational openness, advances and cross-religious rapport that have been the fruit of quite momentous developments happily continue. They may, indeed, prove to be the one source of hope at a time of an otherwise bleak and seemingly hopeless outlook. For to the extent religion is part of the problem – which it undoubtedly is – its critical contemporary challenge is to be part of the solution. I firmly believe it can be that, and there are very good reasons for thinking so.

However, this book is not about solutions as such. Rather, it is about coming to grips with the problem, albeit focusing only on three historically and theologically related religions – Judaism, Christianity and Islam. For these three arguably form *the* dominant set of religions impacting much of the world today. While extremism may be found, to a greater or lesser degree, in all religions, it would be fair to say it is the extremisms of these three which currently garner the most attention, especially in the West. It is their extremisms that lie at the heart of very real global concerns. Religious extremism drives upheavals in respect of refugee crises. In some parts of the world it is a prime factor in respect of immigration pressures and reactions thereto. And it can play a significant role in international relations and border control policies. Religious extremism, including religiously motivated terrorism, is one of the most pernicious and troublesome issues which confronts us all in today's world.

This book argues that the rejection of diversity is what underlies religious extremism. How societies, and their religions, deal with religious diversity is a critical factor in whether or not extremism flourishes or is contained. The curtailment of diversity, to the point even of outright rejection, is a marker of the predominance of an exclusionary ideology operative within a society. This may be an outright anti-religious ideology, as was and is the case with classic expressions of communism. Or it may be an exclusive religious ideology at play, as with a nation that identifies itself as a religious state, one premised on the exclusivity of its own religion. In such cases, other religions may be varyingly allowed for, but in a role of grace and favour dependency, or in other ways curtailed in terms of form and function within the society. Or they may be rejected – excluded – outright. A liberal and open secular democratic state is one that values and upholds diversities of many sorts, including that of religion. A fear-filled society in retreat from openness to the wider world and inter alia manifesting hostility towards one or more religions is likely rejecting other human diversities as well and is certainly on a path to closed, fascist insularity. If it is a religious perspective driving, or significantly influencing, such a society, then it is likely that the society is in the grip of a religious extremism.

In this book I bring together various threads of research and reflection I have worked on for some twenty years, spanning a wide range of interests in respect of contemporary religious issues. These include interfaith matters on the one hand, and questions of diversity and extremism on the other. This book concentrates on the latter and has taken me into new areas of research, as well as deepened those already familiar to me. It is by no means a last, or even a particularly full, word on this very complex and vexed subject. But hopefully it offers something of a fresh perspective and helpful insight as we try to figure out the whys and wherefores of what is going on with religious extremism today – and thus arrive at a way to deal with it.

ACKNOWLEDGEMENTS

As with any book, it takes more than just the author to bring an idea to published fruition. While in some respects I have had the advantage of drawing upon and adapting earlier material, reworking and interweaving that with new research in order to create a wholly new work has been no walk in the park. Much of this book has been previously tested in the classroom. However, it has been to my great advantage that the entire manuscript was read through by my colleague Dr Todd Nachowitz, who cut his teeth in the study of religion under the tutelage of the late and internationally respected Professor Huston Smith. Todd's own wide-ranging knowledge and editorial acumen are duly acknowledged and greatly appreciated. Associate Professor Pete Lentini, of the School of Social Sciences at Monash University, Caulfield, Victoria, Australia, kindly read and usefully commented upon Chapter 9. Both scholars have been warmly encouraging of my approach. Any remaining infelicities and errors are entirely my own.

My previous association with the Global Terrorism Research Centre at Monash University, Melbourne, Australia, and my long-standing associate relationship with the Centre for the Study of Religion and Politics at the University of St Andrews, Scotland, are part of a wider academic context in which I work. Both of these have contributed to the shaping of this book, and in particular I am most appreciative of the collegial encouragement and support of Professor Mario Aguilar of the University of St Andrews, and of Professor Angela Berlis of the University of Bern. I am deeply grateful to Lalle Pursglove of Bloomsbury Press who made an initial approach following my keynote lecture to the 2012 annual conference of the British Association for the Study of Religion. Lalle, together with her assistant Lucy Carroll, and the Bloomsbury publication team have proved to be a wonderfully supportive group for an author to work with. I am also grateful for the support I have had from the University of Waikato, and especially Professor Robert Hannah, my former faculty dean, to undertake periods of necessary research and writing. Finally, I am very grateful for permission to cite from a seminal article by Gideon Aran and Ron E. Hassner ('Religious Violence in Judaism: Past and Present', *Terrorism and Political Violence* 25, no. 3 (2013): 355–405).

CHAPTER 1
INTRODUCTION

Religious extremism is perhaps one of the most pernicious and troublesome among the many challenges with which we human beings, in our diverse societies and nations, are confronted. This is particularly so in light of the accompanying phenomenon of religiously motivated terrorism that is often a feature of this extremism. In a widely reported radio address just ahead of Christmas 2016, Britain's Prince Charles voiced a concern felt by many.[1] Some seventy years since his (and my) parents' generation 'had fought, and died, in a battle against intolerance, monstrous extremism and an inhuman attempt to exterminate the Jewish population of Europe', we are witnesses to new waves of persecution and militancy in parts of the world where 'even more insidious forms of extremisms' have now appeared. And in some ultra-extreme cases, this includes the staggering goal of eliminating 'all types of religious diversity'. The Prince, noting the persecution of religious minorities in the Middle East – Baha'is, Jews, Yazidis, among others – reported in particular on the persecution of Christians in parts of Syria and Iraq, persecution which is repeated elsewhere and which involves more than just extreme Muslim antipathy towards Christianity. 'The scale of religious persecution around the world is not widely appreciated', the Prince opined. I suspect he is right. Further, I suggest that the underlying issue of the rejection of diversity – of both religious and other kinds – which lies at the heart of the impositional exclusivism that drives religious extremism is also not well understood. It is this which drives the extreme ideologies that manifest in deadly terrorist acts. This book aims to address such issues and to attempt to throw some light of understanding on them.

The effects of religious extremism are clear for all to see. The mass migrations of the last few years are not the result of natural disasters such as fire, flood and famine – though there are examples enough of those. Neither are they simply an expression of economic privation and the desire for 'something better', though that motive is certainly found. No, the plight of the massive migratory flows of suffering peoples in recent times is attributable to but one – albeit complex – phenomenon: the outworking of extreme religious ideologies. Syrians and Iraqis are exiting their countries en masse not because of economic hardships or the effects of famine that might be the case elsewhere. They are fleeing the imposition of extreme religion. Many of the problems that puzzle the world today are nothing less than the manifestation of impositional religious absolutism of one sort or another. And, as Prince Charles notes, 'the ripple effect' is immense. But neither is it a simple matter of one-way traffic. While the so-called 'Islamic State' has been – and is still – at the epicentre of much of today's violent extremism, extremism is by no means the province of Islam or Muslims alone. For there is also increasing evidence of the contemporary rise of populist right-wing – in some places now referred to as 'alt-right' – groups whose very extremism is, in effect, a mirror image reaction to the extremism, whether real or perceived, of an 'other' – most often religious other – labelled as a threatening 'extremist'. And the world can hardly forget the words of American president Donald Trump when, as a presidential candidate, he articulated the question reflecting the concern of many: 'What the hell is going on?' His response, namely to advocate the shutting down of immigration in order to exclude those he regards as suspect in some way, or to erect barriers of protection – in effect to retreat into fortress America – is no more than a reactionary mirror image to the driving ideology of Islamic State of Iraq and Shams/Syria (ISIS) which aims to create a fortress Islam – the 'Caliphate' – wherein true believers can live in peace and harmony provided, of course, they abide by the rules and laws of the ISIS form of Islamic faith and life. So, in effect, one form of extremism begets its reactionary polar parallel. And each form is premised on an ideology of impositional exclusivism with the result of a 'clash of fundamentalisms', to use Tariq Ali's phrase.[2] The contemporary phenomenon of what I call reactive co-radicalization is increasingly evident, and we will look at this more closely below.

Even as in England Prince Charles was broadcasting his reflections, in Germany a young first-time mother, in her Christmas 2016 and New Year 2017 greeting to friends and family, expressed her joyous anticipation of showing her child 'all the beautiful things there are to do with us in the world' and, at the same time, expressed her real fear 'that hatred and violence could spread still further and humanity is lost'.[3] She articulated an anxiety widely felt by her generation. Wherein lies hope today? How do we deal with the rising level of threat that grows daily around us? The lived reality of human existence is often a mixed bag; goodness and beauty contrasts with evil ugliness. One action evokes dramatic reaction. Prince Charles reminded his listeners of the flight of the Holy Family – Joseph, Mary and the infant Jesus – to escape violent persecution that was both political and religious in form. And he added: 'We might also remember that when the Prophet Mohammed migrated from Mecca to Medina, he did so because he, too, was seeking freedom for himself and his followers.' The first Muslims fled persecution at the hands of pagan Meccans. And today there are many Muslims, especially those of minority or heterodox varieties of Islam, who are suffering at the hands of those who claim the sole right to represent this faith. Furthermore, in some parts of the world it is Muslims who are suffering persecution and violence at the hands of peoples of other religions, such as the case in parts of Southeast Asia where Buddhist extremists have attacked and killed local Muslims. And we have all been witnesses to the great acts of vandalism undertaken in the name of a particular religious ideology: the destruction of ancient heritage sites, the trashing of artefacts of antiquity, the sheer elimination of human artistic and architectural accomplishment simply because they do not fit a mould of an austere religious aesthetic. Material diversity and all that it signifies is as much at threat by the imposition of an extreme religious ideology as is human life. Such iconoclastic destruction – the elimination of material symbols and signs of that to which the iconoclast objects – has happened before, but has perhaps never been so widespread, never so immediately apprehended by so many, and never so threateningly present to the global community. In today's globalized and economically interdependent world, this is the context of us all. We all see this, even if we do not directly experience the effects of religious extremism today. We need to understand what the hell is going on.

At one level there appears a simple answer: humanity prefers homogeneity. Deep down we don't like difference. We are most comfortable when we are among our own. We like, maybe, a little spice of diversity – but, really, on our terms. We need to be in control, to ensure the diversity of 'otherness' does not overwhelm. Too much variety threatens. Recognize the theme? Feel like saying: 'Yes, but …?' There is something here that we instinctively know makes sense, yet at the same time we know it is no real answer. It is, indeed, but a simplistic response to the question of what is going on. And it is a misleading one. For variety, difference, diversity – of so many sorts – is the very stuff of life. A garden is praised not because it consists of the same plant repeated, but because it contains a rich variety, a profusion of colour, a diversity of shape and form. The garden that is any human society is made up of a rich diversity of individuals – and nowadays in many places also of an increasing diversity of subgroups. Ethnic, cultural, racial, linguistic and religious differences are often the markers of internal diversity within a given society, along with otherwise long-standing dimensions of social, economic and political diversity. This rich mix is the hallmark of a contemporary postmodern society. To the extent such diversity is affirmed, valued and societally supported, it makes for a vibrant and inclusive community. Such a community prizes peaceful coexistence and prosperous harmony. To the extent diversity is called into question – let alone actively rejected – disharmony, discord and disunity reign. And a violent rejection of various 'others' ensues.

Today there is increasing evidence of violent reactions to diversity, including religious, ethnic and cultural in many cases, all too often grounded in religious ideology and a presumption of competitive identities. While by no means the only causal element, religion, or rather religious ideologies, especially when taken and applied in what can only be described as an 'extreme' fashion, is undeniably a major component. It appears in many situations of conflict and strife. It is not my task to enumerate and survey the many instances of religious extremism or narrate the particularities of any given application of it that abound in the world today. Specifics are constantly changing – one only has to think of the rapidly shifting situation pertaining to the phenomenon of ISIS and its Islamic State, which is but a recent expression of one religion's propensity to produce an extreme ideology, to realize that a book which goes into the detail of such a phenomenon today will be out of date by tomorrow. Rather, what I shall seek to do is to identify, reflect upon, probe, question and critique the ideological thinking that produces what we name as 'religious extremism'. For the action of religious extremists – crusaders, jihadists, terrorists or whoever – arises out of a particular understanding and application of a religious worldview. The phenomenon of religious extremism encompasses not just action but also thought: the motivating drivers for behavioural outcomes. Also, while aspects of what I analyse and discuss may apply across many religious contexts, and potentially other, non-religious contexts as well, it is not my intention to address a full range of religions but rather a particular historically and theologically related set: Judaism, Christianity and Islam. These three share a common heritage of key theological motifs, scriptural orientation and ethical imperative. They all proclaim the ultimate value of peace – *shalom, pax et bonum, salaam*. As well, they share also a history and heritage of violent imposition, both internally and externally applied, that is granted divine sanction and, in some instances, even explicitly expressed warrant.

Christianity and Islam between them represent over half the population of the globe. Judaism has ever been a backdrop and foil for both. While the record of the religion of the ancient Hebrews has provided a source of motifs and models of extremism and allied violence that have informed all three faiths, the rabbinic Judaism that emerged from the ancient heritage is a religious tradition in its own right. It has been ever apprehended by its sister Abrahamic faith traditions as varyingly a religious competitor or an irritant, if not illegitimate, 'other'. Thus Judaism has known a history of rejection, especially at the hands of an extreme Christian prejudice towards Jews. Today the flashpoint of Middle East politics is where the three faiths simultaneously coincide and conflict. As has been famously said, there can be no peace in the world unless there is peace among the religions. And the biggest threat to peace among and between these particular three religions today is the presence of a deepening extremism evident in each of them.

How, then, might we understand this extremism? Extremism can mean many things and take many forms. One of the more obvious is violence. Violent behaviours and actions emanate from extreme beliefs and opinions. Religious violence is an outcome of an extreme religious perspective. There is a long history of investigation into the relation of religion and violence, some of which I will touch upon in the pages that follow. There are three views which have tended to predominate. The first is that of violence being inherent to religion.[4] This, however, is a reductionist position that 'trivializes historical circumstances and leaves actors with little to no agency'.[5] The second holds that certain religions have within them a violent core; thus while some religions are inherently peaceable and peace-loving, others are inherently the opposite. Advocacy for this perspective abounds today when, for example, some Christians identify their religion with the former while declaiming Islam as evidence of the latter.[6] A third view is instrumentalist – that is, religion is used ('instrumentalized') – to bring about non-religious ends, using violence if need be. Such a reductionist view regards religion as not the true or 'real' driver of behaviours; rather it is 'at the disposal of rational agents who engage in violence for practical reasons' and thus it 'is epiphenomenal, a medium for strategic or materialist motives'.[7] In contrast to these otherwise standard perspectives, Gideon Aran and Ron Hassner take a more dynamic and dialectical approach whereby religious agents 'engage in a constant evaluation, selection, and reinterpretation of religious ideas from an ever-growing reservoir and in so doing contribute to that reservoir'.[8] Religion presents opportunities for the inculcation of extremism and violence, and also provides checks and boundaries. The key, then, is the interpretive framework that is brought to bear. Invariably that framework is based upon recourse to the relevant sacred text. As J. Harold Ellens remarks: 'From the Talmud in Judaism with its layers of commentary to Christianity with its creeds, affirmations of faith, commentaries and liturgy, to Islam with the Hadith, sacred texts are never found in isolation.'[9] Indeed, relevant scriptural texts 'provide a particularly potent tool for supporting aggression and hostility to others due to the significant role sacred texts play in developing group identity and setting group boundaries'.[10] Ideologically grounded in scriptural narrative and motif, religious violence and extremism is the behaviour of those 'individuals or groups who self-define and are identified by those around them as religious' and who 'account for their violence in a religious language, invoking religious symbols and referencing religious norms and values'.[11]

Religious extremism is a particular, but also complex and multifaceted phenomenon. It cannot be reduced to just one thing, or one line of explanation. There is no simple answer to 'what the hell is going on?' As we begin to probe this complex phenomenon, there is a useful distinction to be made. On the one hand, there is the extremism of the margin (the 'radical') and on the other, the extremism of the centre (the 'fanatic'). The ordinarily religious person or community does not engage in violence as a matter of course; but some religious people become 'extreme' and engage in violent behaviours, whether from the perspective of the radical at the margins or a fanatic at – or claiming to rightly represent – the centre. Religions normatively espouse values of peace and harmony even in contexts of challenge and contestation. But religions may also – and do – produce fanatical and radical extremists. Religious extremism is an ideologically and theologically based phenomenon requiring to be critically understood in order to be resisted and ameliorated.

On the one hand, as indicated, 'extremism' can evoke a sense of being at the margins, of existing on the boundaries, of functioning at the edges; in other words, extremism naturally suggests extremities, by definition. And any organization or group that is, in this sense, extreme will tend to manifest a tenuous link to whatever is the appropriate 'centre', or give evidence of a loose connection to the relevant normative tradition. In this respect, extremism expresses heterodoxy or heresy in contrast to an orthodoxy. On the other hand, extremism can refer to something else altogether, even, indeed, the opposite of being 'at the margins', and that is being at, or claiming, the centre. Here the term connotes degrees of intensity or sharpness of focus; extremism suggests fanaticism. In this case an extremist ideology or group will claim the relevant central position exclusively and, in so doing, will proclaim the apropos normative tradition intensely. Extremism in this sense takes group identity – its religion or tradition – 'to an extreme', not by a move away from the centre, but conversely by intensifying its self-understanding and self-proclamation as representing, or being, the centre. Here, in contrast with whatever is the relevant orthodoxy, extremism expresses an ultra-orthodox perspective. It is important to note, I suggest, that either way extremism belongs to a 'tradition'; extremism, by definition, has to do with the extremity or centring of an existing tradition, or religion, with which the extremist is concerned. A religious extremist requires specific religious identity as the primary reference for self-legitimization. Religious extremism is specific: it is a particular religion's extremism. There is no generic religious extremism as such. The term rather names a field of religious ideology and phenomena that, while displaying certain family resemblances and dynamic commonalities, in each case is something very specific. To understand 'what the hell is going on' with any given religious extremism requires a nuanced understanding of the religion whence it arose and that provides the ideological oxygen.

By contrast, religious cults, certain sects and other radical alternatives, which are sometimes regarded as manifestations of religious extremism, do not belong to any given religious tradition as such – by definition they are *other than* a normative tradition or religion.[12] These are more properly understood as new religious movements (NRMs) and are to be distinguished from the religious extremism which I am here discussing. Phenomenologically there are three forms of NRM. An interactive NRM is the product or outcome of an encounter of, usually, a major world or missionary religion with a local tribal or primal type of religion. An exoteric NRM is an outgrowth of, or from, a single tradition. An esoteric NRM comprises an eclectic compounding of multiple traditions. Thus a cult is an esoteric NRM and a sect is an exoteric NRM. But religious extremists are the extremists of a religion. They ought not be construed as representing a cult, sect or other form of NRM and so be regarded as 'not belonging' to a religion as such. They cannot be ignored or excused as not being the putative responsibility of the religious community that they claim to represent.

If the war on terror derived from religious extremism is a war of ideology – in particular, a war against the dominance of certain religious fundamentalisms – how are we to address the challenge of religious extremism and related terrorism? The primary component in any strategy aimed at countering such extremism and terrorism, I suggest, has to be in respect of identifying, and addressing, the ideological rhetoric and elements within communities from which potential terrorists are likely to appear, and by which they are likely to be nourished. But to do that, to make sense of any potential data or evidence, we need a framework of interpretation, a lens of perspective. It is in respect of this which, I suggest, a paradigm analysis of religious fundamentalism offers a way of understanding the origin and dynamic structure of religious extremism and so of religiously motivated terrorism. This is inherently different from situations of terrorism motivated by other factors such as economic pressures, political hegemony, social conflicts or whatever, where religion as such is not a key player, if indeed it features at all. In such cases a form or element of what I call the 'fundamentalist paradigm', which we shall examine shortly, may indeed apply. But not the religious modality of it. Our focus here is with religious fundamentalism and what an analysis of that might yield. Further, it needs to be noted that the involvement of religion as a driver of a diversity-rejecting extremist ideology need not necessarily manifest in violence, even though the religious viewpoint is forcefully made. For example, on the occasion of the meeting of a government-sponsored multinational Asia-Pacific Regional Interfaith Dialogue in New Zealand in early 2007, the leader of the ultra-conservative Destiny Church proclaimed his church's opposition to the promotion of religious diversity. Although resiling from advocating an outright exclusion of other religions, he nonetheless asserted they should not have any status that would rank them as equivalent with Christianity, regarded by such fundamentalists as the default religion of the nation.[13] This represents an extremely conservative view that identifies 'opening the door to a diversity of religions' with 'dismantling our own

Christian heritage'.[14] In its dynamic essence, such sentiments parallel those of so-called 'Islamic fundamentalists' who advocate an impositional Islamic State upon an otherwise majority, largely traditionalist, Muslim society.

Broadly speaking, the term 'fundamentalism' today names a religio-political perspective found in most if not all major religions. At the present time it is associated with various expressions of religious extremism and, most worryingly, with religiously motivated terrorism. However, the term 'fundamentalism' is contentious. Its origin is within the orbit of Christianity, it does not necessarily translate well or meaningfully to other religions. Close analytical and critical work on the underlying phenomenon that has been named 'fundamentalism' highlights 'absolutism' as perhaps a more apposite common phenomenal dynamic across religions, and certainly across theistic religions. We shall explore more of this below, along with a closer look at the phenomenon of religious diversity.

Diversity names the dominant context of contemporary life; it names the present situation of religion in society. Religious diversity is a fact of our time in a way that, arguably, is qualitatively different from almost anything hitherto. Indeed, an affirmation of diversity is a hallmark of so-called 'postmodernity'. As sociologist Gary Bouma remarks, 'Being consciously multifaith is part of being a postmodern society'.[15] Individual freedoms today juxtapose with accommodating the presence of otherness: that which was formerly 'other' in the sense of being not present, of being 'over there', is now on our doorstep and down our street. Today, in just about all quarters of the globe, the religious dimension of any given community is pluriform. And this raises many issues, not the least of which is the manner of interrelating across religious identities. The question of inter-religious dialogue is not merely theoretical. People of different religious allegiances are neighbours who must talk with each other, live together in our communities, and together address concerns held in common. Dialogue is the route to the antidote for extremism. While most, if not all, religious traditions have unity – or internal uniformity and coherence – proclaimed as a sine qua non, the lived reality of many religious people today is the context of, and contention with, difference of viewpoint, experience, cognition, interpretation and hence competing claims for allegiance and identity. And yet, even though there are positive modes of comprehending and engaging diversity – via the paradigms of inclusivism and pluralism, for example – there is today an apparent increase in recourse to exclusivist paradigms. And it is in contexts where inter-religious and intercommunal dialogical engagement breaks down that extremism flourishes and violence too often ensues.

It is thus imperative to attempt to understand critically any potential – let alone real – relationship between religion and extremism. It is, I suggest, *the* contemporary religious challenge, without equal. International travel, national economies – the price we pay for our petrol – are all impacted today not so much by the convolutions of foreign policies and international relations, or even by global economic and political power plays, significant as they are. Rather it is impositional religious ideologies, taken to extreme and at times clashing competitively, that presently impinge upon all our lives and constitute a defining feature of our times. Extremism is manifested in rhetoric, attitudes and behaviours. It is at the very end of the extremism scale that violence, bloodshed and terrorism ensue. It is only relatively recently that the phenomenon of religious terrorism has been analysed and understood within a broader framework of terrorizing violence. Since the late nineteenth century, according to David C. Rapoport, terrorism has occurred in 'four successive waves'.[16] These are identified as anarchist terrorism, anti-colonial terrorism, the terrorism of the new Left, and religious terrorism. Whereas the first arose from the perceived failure of democratic reforms, the second was a manifestation of national self-determination and the third emerged in contexts aiming to bolster democratic reforms. However, the religious terrorism wave seemingly takes aim at both liberal democracy and secularism. While al-Qaeda was identified as the prime example of the fourth wave, that dubious honour would now perhaps go to ISIS. And while it is Muslim – Islamist – extremism which is currently the most pernicious and persistent manifestation of the fourth wave, there are nevertheless terrorists from other religious groups and movements also involved, 'including Sikhs in the Punjab, the Aum Shinrikyo group in Japan, and members of the Christian Identity movement in the United States'.[17]

Contemporary Jewish violence, which we will discuss shortly, is reckoned as having emerged also during this wave – wherein religious motifs and drivers become much more pronounced, if not predominant. Indeed, as with the case elsewhere, 'Jewish terrorists combine religious motivations with political and territorial goals'.[18] It is salutary to note that today in Israel, with respect to the construction of settlements in the West Bank area of Shiloh, a tourist centre features a video 'in which the biblical figure Joshua commands the Jewish people to settle the land promised to them by God'.[19] A biblical motif emerges as the absolute religious support for an otherwise 'secular' activity. Is this an example of religious extremism in the fanatical mode? It is also salutary to note the observation that Jewish extremism has tended to emerge and increase 'in parallel to attacks initiated by other religiously motivated terrorist movements'.[20] Do we see here evidence of the reactive co-radicalization that we will explore further below? And it has been observed that, given the commonality of the theme of promoting the common good and with that a shared ethical code that threads throughout the so-called 'Abrahamic' faiths, extremist Muslims are 'as much at war with mainstream Islamic thinking as with mainstream Christian thinking and enlightened secular thought'.[21]

One of the key elements that needs to be addressed in a study of religious extremism is the use of relevant scriptures. Within the biblical and Quranic texts there are references to and models of violent behaviour and extreme attitudes, which we will examine further in Chapter 5. Keith Ward notes of such texts, or rather the use made of them, that: 'The real question to ask is what makes people pull them out and make them decisive texts to be literally applied in very different circumstances of the modern world.'[22] What Ward seems to be alluding to is the propensity for religions that are premised on the notion of an absolute reference point for existence and value to subvert any hint of relativity, such as contextuality for example, and so make of the notion of this 'absolute' an ideological 'absolutism'. In so doing, a selective process is at work. It makes of certain texts, and the reading of them, to be an overriding absolute that, paradoxically, then relativizes all other texts which could suggest a different perception or outcome. One classic example is that of supersession and abrogation: the later text in respect of its understood temporal origin is treated as superior to, even replacing – and so negating or abrogating – the earlier text. Christianity has inclined to this technique with respect to its Bible superseding the earlier Jewish texts, and Islam had done this with respect to the Qur'an superseding both the Jewish and Christian texts. Also, within the Quranic corpus where, for instance, early Meccan verses that are positive and open towards people of other faiths – Jews and Christians in particular – are regarded as superseded by later Medinan verses that are varyingly hostile towards, or dismissive of, these religious others.

On the one hand, then, positive scriptural affirmations of diversity do exist. But on the other hand such positive regard is more often than not negated by way of an assertion of apparently later texts as being normative in so far as religious value, attitude and belief are concerned. Yet, as Keith Ward rightly observes, 'Each tradition has developed sophisticated ways of overriding those texts with other and usually later interpretations that stress what is quite clearly more basic – the command of God to have compassion and mercy.'[23] Here the effect of religion seeking and affirming an absolute core value and belief can be seen. For the core orientation of these theistic religions involves positive and life-affirming values such as compassion, peace, love, mercy, fellow-feeling and so forth. But overriding them with negatively oriented values of rejection, denial, exclusion and elimination occurs when such values and attitudes that are certainly found within the religious texts and would typically be contextually read, and so 'contained', are instead elevated to the status of overriding and ideologically governing absolutes. This is the hallmark of religious absolutism at work. As we will see, this is also the way of fundamentalism. And while it may be Islam in the frame today, the reality is that it is Christianity that led the way, and Judaism that has provided many models and motifs from out of its ancient sacred text. But in particular,

> Christians have tortured and killed people for having the 'wrong' beliefs, and that is because of the view that having correct beliefs, or belonging to the true church, is necessary for eternal salvation. Christians have regarded Jews as responsible for the death of Christ, and have discriminated against them. Christians have regarded infidels as 'enemies of God' and have fought against them, most spectacularly in the Crusades. And Christians have attempted to impose their beliefs on whole societies, repressing all other forms of worship.[24]

We will examine more of this below.

As John Shepherd has remarked, 'religious commitment can conduce rather readily, and apparently logically and as a matter of principle, to religious extremism'.[25] And he notes Jewish, and subsequent Christian, claim to territory as a divine right that both requires and excuses genocidal ethnic cleansing of previous inhabitants or their utter subjection in the course of their salvation. The biblical record is replete with many relevant examples. And both Jews and Christians have at times made much of the biblical motif of 'The Chosen People' to effect policies and actions that in other contexts would be deemed abusive and abhorrent. Christian application of anti-Jewish exclusions and eliminations throughout later centuries and down to the horror of the Holocaust, together with Muslim visceral 'hatred of idolatry' that has been more recently manifest in the action of some Islamists, give further evidence of extreme religious ideology being no fringe or occasional matter. Such extremism is not something that is outside religion, to be dismissed when it arises as 'not really religious'. And, as Ward has remarked, 'religion cannot be exempted from the almost universal human tendency towards hatred of and violence against others'.[26] The pernicious persistence of religious extremism is because it is grounded in a specific religious belief system. The particularities of any given religious extremism are, of course, dependent on the actual religion of which it is extreme. However, 'it is historically incorrect to say that most violent conflicts have religion as their cause, or that the worst cases of violence are religious'.[27] In many instances it has been ethnic and tribal conflicts through the centuries that have provoked violence. It was 'Communist and Fascist pogroms in the twentieth century' such as Stalin's Russia, which killed many more people than the wars of religion in Europe, for example.[28] Although religion has often 'been implicated in violence, especially where it becomes a marker of identity in situations of social conflict', yet also 'religion has often been a voice of moderation and reconciliation'.[29] Arguably, 'as the scriptural documents of all the great world religions clearly state', this is the proper role of religion.[30]

According to Karen Armstrong, 'nationalism has been far more productive than religion' as an inspiration for terrorism.[31] And when nationalism and religion combine, the result is a potent force for an absolutist ideology that is often impervious to any self-critique and certainly reacts hostilely to external criticism. The combination of jingoistic nationalism and religious fervour and corresponding ideological outlook gives the context for extremism to move from the margins to the centre. Arguably, we see this phenomenon today emerging in the otherwise secular heartlands of northern Europe and North America as well as in Australia and elsewhere. This may yet constitute one of the greatest challenges of the early twenty-first century. Indeed, John Shepherd notes it is 'the Orthodox and ultra-Orthodox yeshivas of Judaism, in the Bible institutes of American conservative evangelicals, in the conservative and ultra-conservative madrasas that multiplied, for example, in Pakistan' where the challenge of this extremism is found.[32] It is in such institutions that attitudes and values foundational for extremist ideologies are nurtured. What such institutions hold in common is that their pedagogical approach is 'one where to each question there is presumed to be a safe, orthodox answer. Thus there can be no real rocking of the boat, given the absence of that open-mindedness that is its necessary precondition.'[33]

Against the mid-twentieth century's prediction of the triumph of Western secularism, Gilles Kepel notes the rise of militant and strident religiosity, and this continues to be the case.[34] As remarked already, and to be discussed in more detail below, one key element in this is religious fundamentalism. By and large it generally indicates 'a certain intellectual stance that claims to derive political principles from a timeless, divine text'.[35] Choueiri also notes that 'ideological pronouncements of fundamentalism reveal a hostile attitude towards both traditionalism and official religious institutions. In other words, it is neither tradition-bound, nor a literalist transcription of the statements of a divinely inspired book. This is true of Jewish, Christian and Islamic fundamentalism.'[36] And as Ron Geaves rightly remarks: 'Any informed discussion of "fundamentalism" … must endeavour to go beyond both the popular usage of the term by the public and the closely connected media depictions of certain typologies of religion which are seen as anti-modern, traditionalist, intolerant and reactionary.'[37] Geaves further notes the diversities within and of fundamentalism: religious fundamentalism across different religions may display some form of family resemblance, but each religion produces its own forms of fundamentalism. Following Kimball,[38] Jonathan Matusitz notes five key principles of fundamentalism, namely the 'means to justify the end, holy war, blind obedience, absolute truth claims, and the ideal times'.[39] Thus religious fundamentalism

> is the belief that religious doctrines or texts contain the fundamental, straightforward, intrinsic, absolute truth about humanity and deity; that this essential truth is diametrically opposed to forces of evil, which must be fought until the end; that this truth must be embraced immediately (based on the central, rigid practices of the past); and that those who have faith in these fundamental teachings and adhere to them have a special connection with the deity.[40]

Furthermore,

> Religious fundamentalism is a dimension or kind of religiosity that is theoretically present within any belief system.… Religious fundamentalists profess strong commitments to their beliefs and are regarded as unbending and resistant to change. Due to their religious commitments, there is no prospect for any compromise or other types of negotiation. The statements of many religious-based terrorist groups seem to validate such inflexibility.[41]

While I believe Matusitz is broadly correct, my own analysis will provide a more nuanced understanding of the nature and range of fundamentalism, and its link to extremism and terrorism. Certainly, as has been observed by many, extremism and terrorism that is 'motivated by religious fundamentalism can be persistent and lethal'.[42]

Following the discussion of religious diversity in Chapter 2, I will outline in Chapter 3 an analysis of fundamentalism and its reactionary response to diversity. Religious extremism may be understood as a particular outworking of what we name as 'fundamentalism', which, I argue, varyingly expresses forms of an ideology of absolutism. It is the absolutism of 'fundamentalism' which is at the core, and it is manifested in an exclusionary stance that rejects the diversity of other religions and often also diversity within a religion, especially that of the 'fundamentalist'. In other words, an absolutist mindset with an accompanying ideological framework leads to forms of extremism that can, and do, manifest in violent rejections of that which is different, which is 'other-than', a rejection of that which confronts the absolutism of an exclusive singularity with the relativity of diverse alternatives. The religio-political fundamentalism that underpins much right-wing and 'alt-right' sociopolitical movements today drives the ideological rhetoric of rejection of any sort of challenging diversity, especially that of a critical 'other'. Both these chapters are theoretically oriented. Although I include some limited examples and references in these chapters, it will be an interesting challenge for the reader to see to what extent, where and how, known religious groups or individuals align with the analysis that is presented.

From Chapter 4 onwards I pursue a more empirical tack wherein I explore something of the specifics of the three religions and their engagement in extremism. This is at the heart of this study, and I commence with a review of scriptural motifs for extremism. All three religions are grounded in their holy texts, and these include elements that can, and do, feed an extremist interpretation and ideology. Three chapters – 5, 6 and 7 – traverse, in turn, Jewish, Christian and Muslim forms and examples of extremism. I then turn to the emergence of two recent and, arguably, as yet either little recognized, or else quite contested, issues. These are, first, mutual extremism, which I describe as 'reactive co-radicalization' (Chapter 8), and second the contemporary and contentious phenomenon of Islamophobia (Chapter 9). A concluding chapter will draw out some key findings, critical observations and suggestive reflections.

CHAPTER 2
ACCOMMODATING DIVERSITY: PARADIGMS AND PATTERNS

Difference, diversity, multiplicity – in whatever sphere of human life – has ever been the lot of humanity. Religion is no exception. Today diversity rules in virtually all things. But diversity can also be highly contentious, and that is certainly the case in some religious quarters. In this chapter I discuss religious diversity with respect to the contemporary context of Western postmodernity and the cultural reaction to modernity, and the ways in which religions respond to the very presence of this diversity, especially in contexts where religion was once a cultural marker of homogeneity. This involves, on the one hand, examining the positive response to diversity by way of paradigms of affirmation and, on the other, the more conservative tendency to maintain at least a semblance of overriding homogeneity by way of relativizing the impact of diversity through paradigms of incorporation. The third response, outright rejection, will be discussed in the next chapter.

The Australian sociologist Gary Bouma speaks of our Western 'twenty-first-century postmodern and secular world where spiritualities are rife and religious diversity is an accepted feature' as the contemporary temporal locus of 'a seriously multicultural society'.[1] It is the present experience of plurality, especially in the form of religious diversity, which sets the scene for a critical analysis and discussion of religious extremism. This requires some understanding of 'modernity' and the response of 'postmodernism', for it is these terms that denote key cultural constructs and underlying worldview concepts – often not articulated – which influence our thinking, perceptions and conceptions, thus the way we approach and contend with the myriad of phenomena we encounter in the course of our daily lives. Religious diversity is one of them. And the chief factor leading to a fresh approach to diversity, at least within Western societal orbits, is this broadly cultural shift that is presently underway. Some would say it has happened already, others disavow the process and categories altogether. The cultural shift from modernity to postmodernity is accompanied by a cognitive shift from modernism to postmodernism. If 'postmodernity' names the contemporary context wherein the fact of plurality is accounted for and understood in terms of the hermeneutic of pluralism, then complementarily 'pluralism' may be viewed as denoting the postmodern interpretive response to the contemporary encounter with the fact of plurality. The phenomenon of modernism, or the fact and concept of modernity, arguably emerged in the West during the eighteenth century with what is known as the Enlightenment project, or the Age of Reason. This heralded the rise of scientific methodology, literary and philosophical analysis, and critical thinking. Such intellectual tools were applied to all spheres of human endeavour. This intellectual project produced objective science and promoted ideas of universal morality and law. Its watchwords were rationality, autonomy and liberation from all narrow, impositional and prejudiced thinking. The enlightenment 'promised to use the light of reason to shatter all residues of superstition and ignorance. It became the intellectual foundation for the modern world'.[2] Religious dogma was dismissed as a distraction.

> The idea was to use the accumulation of knowledge generated by many individuals working freely and creatively for the pursuit of human emancipation and the enrichment of daily life.... The development of rational forms of social organization and rational modes of thought promised liberation from the irrationalities of myth, religion, superstition, [and] release from the arbitrary use of power as well as from the dark side of our own human natures. Only through such a project could the universal, eternal, and the immutable qualities of all humanity be revealed.[3]

The premodern consciousness that dominated the West up to the sixteenth century invoked a fatalistic acceptance of history and nature 'as reflecting God's immutable ordering of the world'.[4] Modernism, in the West, held out the prospect of freedom from fatalism: 'It promised to break the religiously legitimated constraints of classical Catholic tradition and its authoritarian institutions. It promised a new vision, entered in secular science seeking freedom and progress for all the world'.[5] The Enlightenment project thus provides the foundation for the Modernist project.

The religious and theological worldviews that had been forged in the preceding centuries were forever disrupted. Human capability, especially in regard to reason and investigation, now took centre stage; cognitive coherence by way of assent to dogma was removed to the wings. The quest for truth – rationally grounded – and a demonstrable coherence to nature eclipsed the appeal to divinely given revelation, and also ecclesial determinations of the limits of understanding. To quote Harvey again: 'Modernism from its very beginning ... became preoccupied with language, with finding some special mode of representation of eternal truths'.[6] Reason supplanted revelation as the bearer of truth; nature was seen as the source and arena, and natural law the proper mode of expressing the timeless veracities contained therein. Alongside the elevation of the principles of reason and nature there also emerged new notions of autonomy and harmony supplanting external decrees and arbiters. The prior sense of 'order' within 'Creation', as a religious motif, was reinterpreted in stoic-like logos (rational) fashion as the assumption of an undergirding and reliable natural order, inherently reasonable and amenable to empirical uncovering. The intellectual icing on the cake of Enlightenment and the subsequent Modernist project was the principle of progress believed naturally to inhere to the cosmos.

Ironically, the theme of unity – or 'comprehensive coherence and cohesiveness' – that was part and parcel of the religious mentality of Christendom was not itself displaced. To be sure, the underlying religious mentality was dismissed, or at least significantly sidelined. But the ideal of an intellectually apprehensible unity remained. For the French philosopher René Descartes, reckoned to be one of the 'Fathers' of the modern period, this rested on the human mind – the reasoning subject – in concert with the application of rigorous critical doubt as representing the proper cognitive process, and the profession of dualism as representing the nature of reality. Although the Enlightenment gave way to the scepticism of David Hume and the critiques of Immanuel Kant, its essential themes nonetheless undergird, and are incorporated into, the modern age. Yet, through all, the quest for the certainty of an intrinsic underlying unity of being – the Kantian *ding-an-sich* (thing as such; thing as, or in, itself) – remained. The essence of the modernist response to the fact of plurality – against which postmodernism reacts – was to propose a mode of comprehensive and unifying embrace wherein understanding reality as inherently singular 'had to be constructed through the exploration of multiple perspectives'.[7] The embrace of multiple perspectives and of relativism as the epistemological route to uncover and understand the reality of 'unified, though complex, underlying reality' was the order of the day.

Stanley Grenz remarks that the modern perspective assumes that knowledge is certain, objective and good. It presupposes that the rational, dispassionate self can obtain such knowledge and that the knowing self 'peers at the mechanistic world as a neutral observer armed with the scientific method'.[8] The modernism which emerged out of the Enlightenment held that 'the goal of the human intellectual quest has been to unlock the secrets of the universe in order to master nature for human benefit and create a better world'.[9] This in turn produced the modern Western technological society driven by 'the desire to rationally manage life, on the assumption that scientific advancement and technology provide the means to improving the quality of human life'.[10] Modernism is about conformity and control: ameliorating the effects of diversity, fomenting a culture of uniformity, countering the clash of differences. Postmodernism is the counter – it values diversity and celebrates difference. Modernist thought, in whatever field, tends to systematize, to formulate overarching constructs of understanding into which the diversity of detail can fit and find its place. However, in general, postmodernism rejects all such formulation of guiding principle and governing mythology as arbitrary and/or inauthentic tools of control, cognitively delimiting and narrowly interpretive of 'all the diverse forms of discursive activity in the world'.[11]

Postmodernity: The contemporary context of religious diversity

Postmodernist thought constitutes a way of comprehending the extent of change, the persistence of flux and the constancy of novelty across the full spectrum of human life and societal being. Postmodernist understandings of contemporary existence range from positive prospect about, to nihilistic rejection of, culture and cultural institutions in the so-called 'postmodern' age. Postmodernism celebrates the *dissonance* as well as the diversity that constantly eclipses any ideal or programme of uniformity and conformity, in whatever sphere of human endeavour. By contrast modernism, against which postmodernism reacts, pursues an undergirding quest for *coherence* and unicity of action and comprehension. This has been a prime motif guiding intellectual activity as well as sociopolitical action during the recent 'modern' period of Western history. A catch-cry formula – 'suspicion of metanarratives' – introduced by the French scholar Jean-François Lyotard is a useful and widely held key to unlocking the mystery of the interpretive lens of postmodernism.[12] Lyotard's work is credited with having put postmodernism firmly onto the Western intellectual agenda. 'Fragmentation, indeterminacy, and intense distrust of all universal or "totalizing" discourses ... are the hallmark of postmodernist thought' as also is the 'rejection of "meta-narratives" (large-scale theoretical interpretations purportedly of universal application)'.[13] David Ray Griffin comments that '*postmodernism* refers to a diffuse sentiment rather than to any common set of doctrines – the sentiment that humanity can and must go beyond the modern'.[14]

The term, 'postmodernism', which came into use during the 1950s and 60s, thus refers to a particular way of describing and understanding the contemporary world, and in particular that of Western cultural life. The cultural phenomenon of postmodernity, however, may be deemed to have started earlier, the actual dating rather dependent on one's point of view. Stanley Grenz gives a later point of reference: postmodernism for him began on 'a July afternoon in 1972', although the particular urban event in St Louis, USA, that he refers to, namely the dynamiting of a postwar 'modern' massive impersonal box-like housing complex, is more an illustration that as a sociopolitical-cultural phenomenon postmodernity was in fact underway already. Certainly the concept of 'postmodernism' emerged with increasing vigour, if not clarity, during the 1970s. Thus while, arguably, the twentieth century saw the full flowering of modernism, it also ushered in the eclipse of modernism. As the century drew to a close, many commentators on Western culture utilized the term *postmodern* to describe the nature of that cultural reality in its broadest sense, and the term *postmodernity* to refer more directly to the conditions and factors that predominated many areas of Western, or Western-oriented, civilization: from architecture, art and literature, to economics, philosophy, theology and religion. The dominant defining element of postmodernism is, of course, the nature, extent and increasing rapidity of change. Alvin Toffler's *Future Shock* is today's commonplace experience.[15] So, as Frederic Jameson has remarked, postmodernism, as the expression of a postmodern consciousness, is a self-reflective theorizing 'which consists primarily in the sheer enumeration of changes and modifications'.[16] In this regard, postmodernism refers to the interpretive framework, or theoretical understanding, of articulating the way things are in a constantly changing world. Factors that have led to this new way of thinking about the nature of the world and the society we live in include direct philosophical challenges to key Enlightenment notions and ideals that have held sway within so-called 'modernist' thinking – for example the very concepts of the 'self', of 'truth', and the even concept of 'values' – together with a rethinking of the nature of language.[17]

Postmodernism, as noted, is suspicious of all metanarratives. 'Whatever else postmodernism may be, it is a rejection of the Enlightenment project, the modern technological ideal, and the philosophical assumptions upon which modernism was built'.[18]

Postmodernism is an intellectual vector, a direction of reflective expression and critical appreciation, rather than a developed theoretical construct. Indeed, arguably, the predominant ideas of postmodernist thought would count decisively against the possibility of a coherent articulation of a postmodern philosophy, theology or hermeneutic system – such a task would itself be inherently 'modernist'. This has led to some scathing rejections of the postmodernist approach, and to abjuring postmodernism as a valid cognitive enterprise.[19] Postmodernist thinking can issue in a sort of dilettantish silliness, a dalliance with difference, a surfing of the superficial.[20] Others, however, hold a more appreciative critical stance.

Diversity: Plurality versus pluralism

Plurality is not the same as pluralism. The former denotes the fact of diversity, the latter names a response to the fact. Often the two terms are used synonymously to refer to the generic idea of 'many-ness', which can be confusing. However, there are a variety of ways in which a religion (such as Christianity, e.g.) can and does respond to and so contend with religious diversity – both within and without. Diversity – in whatever sphere of human life – has always been the case. Interfaith scholar Kenneth Cracknell once put the theological issue of religious plurality – the sheer fact of there being a diversity of religions – somewhat succinctly by asking: If there is but one God, how is it there are so many religions?[21] He went on to tease this out into other pertinent questions: How are Christians to relate to peoples of other faiths – and, indeed, to other faith- or belief-systems as such? Are we caught in a context of perpetual rivalry? Is the only peaceful option that of mute coexistence at the level of mere tolerance? Are we called to a life of cooperation with people of other religions? Are we not all fellow-travellers in some sense? Situations of religious diversity effectively demand dialogical engagement in order to resist a slide into exclusivism or the encroachments of an imperial inclusivism.[22] Where religious people choose to ignore the other and reject dialogical encounter, this 'can only lead to a closed particularity which feeds on itself and in the process impoverishes the community'.[23] Furthermore, 'it is important to recognize not only the plurality of religions but also the plurality *within* religions'.[24]

The context of religious plurality in which, today, more and more people live in consequence of demographic, socio-economic and other changes, and the upsurge of sociopolitical activity involving religion, suggest more, not less, external impetus for inter-religious dialogical engagement. While most, if not all, religious traditions have promoted unity – or internal uniformity and coherence – as a sine qua non, the lived reality of religious people everywhere has been the context of, and contention with, difference of viewpoint, experience, cognition, interpretation, and hence competing claims for religious allegiance and identity. In an age of heightened awareness of religious plurality as the lived context for a great number of peoples, and with it an enhanced appreciation of attendant tensions and issues, the question of inter-religious engagement – or, more broadly, the promotion of interfaith relations and dialogue – is no theoretical nicety. People of different religious allegiances are neighbours who, with varying degrees of necessity, must talk with each other and together address concerns held in common. And today, of course, the need for cross-religious communication is increasingly urgent. It is religion – or more accurately, religious ideologies and ideals – that is so often the prime context of many current situations of geopolitical concern. If, in response to such situations, inter-religious engagement is to be authentic, it must necessarily involve dialogical partners committed to their own religion *and* to the cause of dialogue. Yet such dialogical engagement is rejected by some – indeed possibly many, if the global resurgence of religious 'fundamentalism',[25] in a myriad of forms, is anything to go by – as too threatening to their religion's fundamentals, or too potentially disruptive of a secure religious identity. But whereas significant difference – as opposed to allowable variance – was coped with, as it were, by way of denial or dismissal, largely through the erection of cognitive and experiential barriers, today it is both harder to erect and maintain such barriers and, more to the point, the advisability and need for them has come under question. In many respects the world is no longer as barrier-dominated as it used to be. The Berlin Wall has fallen, the Iron Curtain has come down, apartheid is no more – although there are yet other, even new, barriers and border walls nonetheless.

It is certainly the case today that modern communications and interpersonal interactions of all sorts allow for levels of contact and exposure to any 'other' such that it is harder to maintain a singular identity by blissfully 'ignoring' the other and, concomitantly, to depreciate the presence of diversity. Plurality as a particular element of our time and our worldview cannot be avoided. But neither can it be factually acknowledged then cognitively shunned, except by enacting a most obtuse denial. Indeed, plurality may be responded to cognitively in a number of ways, given its acknowledgment as fact. Pluralism, broadly speaking, is the stance that embraces the fact and gives it a positive interpretation with a self-reflexive edge. Inclusivism is the response of regarding all other religions as in some sense subsumed within, or under, one dominant or 'superior' religion. Exclusivism, as the word suggests, regards only one religion as correct, true or valid, with all others necessarily 'excluded'. I shall briefly explore the first two of these – pluralism and inclusivism – below. I discuss exclusivism, in conjunction with fundamentalism, in the next chapter, for it is with these two that the propensity for religion to manifest as extremism will be seen.

Pluralism: Paradigms of diversity affirmation

Today, in just about all quarters of the globe, the religious dimension of any given community is pluriform. Pluralism not only affirms plurality, it asserts that any unitary or singular identity within the plural mix needs to view itself as an integral *part of* that mix, not something which contrasts with, or stands diametrically opposed to, the rest of the mix. Hence any unitary identity, of whatever sort, that sits within a plural milieu is to be conceived on the basis of its necessarily being within a pluralist context. Therefore its very conceptuality must take account of that context. This is the situation for Christian denominational identity within the context of ecumenical plurality, for example. The World Council of Churches is an ecumenical fellowship comprising some several hundred churches that regard each other as equals, even though there is considerable diversity of ecclesial (church) culture and even belief, or at least the interpretation of beliefs, among them. At the very least, the hermeneutic of pluralism signals some measure of an equalizing of value and cognitive status across the substantive items that make up a plurality. It does not require the abandonment of distinctiveness and uniqueness of particulars within that plurality; it does however require openness to relativity and relationality, including openness to interactive responsiveness as fundamental components of the identity and being of singular items within the diverse mix. Plurality, or diversity, names much of the context of contemporary life; it names the present situation of religion in society. Arguably, however, religious diversity is a fact of our time in a way that is qualitatively different from almost anything hitherto. This diversity can pose great challenges to contemporary societies and any religious tradition that has been an integral part of their identity. Diversity disrupts a status quo homogeneity.

The affirmation of diversity is a hallmark of 'postmodernity': 'Being consciously multifaith is part of being a postmodern society'.[26] The essential idea of pluralism, as an ideological or hermeneutical response to the fact of plurality, is to posit a multiplicity of particular expressions of that which is deemed to be universal in opposition to the idea that there can only be but one valid or fully valid expression of the universal. This means that different religions are equally valid expressions of some universal 'religious reality', whatever that may be; or that religions are co-equally valid expressions of some universal notion of 'religion' as such – howsoever this may be defined, and certainly not implying any necessary notion of singularity of 'religion as such'. Further, both difference and equality are affirmed. Religions are not all the 'same' – their differences are important, yet religions are no better or worse than each other as equally valid expressions of a universal sense of 'being religious'. On this basis, no one religion can lay claim to an objective superiority, or superlative congruence with the universal (singular) religious reality, in respect of other religions. Of course, the moment we engage in exploring the possibility of a pluralist response to religious plurality we run into a number of critical issues: To what extent, and in what way, can the notion of 'value equivalence' be applied? Is not an affirmation of plurality the beginning of a slippery slide into relativism and reductionism? Does this not reduce religion to a matter of indifferent alternatives? Is commitment vitiated? These are fair questions, but should not be taken as fatally dismissive rhetorical criticisms of pluralism, for rightly understood pluralism affirms commitment, counters indifference, and neither reduces nor relativizes.

> Some versions of the pluralist response focus on truth, affirming that all religions are equally true. Other versions focus on salvation, affirming that all religions are equally valid paths to salvation. Yet others focus on the notions of religious experience and encounter, affirming all religions to be equally good means of encountering a divine transcendent reality.[27]

Religion and Extremism

I take this recognition of the diversity of pluralist perspectives a little further, however. Indeed, I suggest there are a number of discrete paradigms of pluralism. Some are more obvious and well-known, others are somewhat novel. By way of a development upon the variants that I have discussed elsewhere,[28] I now group the variant paradigms of pluralism into five subset categories – *Standard, Radical, Interdependent, Ethical* and *Comprehensive*.

Standard pluralism

The first subset comprises the standard definitional paradigms of pluralism, namely *Common Ground* and *Common Goal* pluralism. These two tend to predominate any discussion of religious pluralism. The subset they constitute is the default position on pluralism that is most often discussed and the basis upon which religious pluralism, as an ideological response to plurality, is most often criticized. *Common Ground Pluralism* views religious differences, or the variety of religions, as contextualized variable expressions of/from a universal source. The fundamental idea is clear – there is a 'common ground' of religious 'reality' from which the different religions of the world derive. John Hick, a leading representative of this view, has argued that since the middle of the twentieth century a new consciousness of human existence set in one world with many world religions has arisen. New conditions and contexts demand new thinking. If our neighbour is someone with whom one can engage in conversation and dialogue and, in so engaging, make discoveries about the relativity of values in respect of religious identities, then, Hick asks, are members of one religion, Christianity for example, demonstrably any better (morally or behaviourally) than members of other religions? He draws the conclusion that 'it is not possible to establish the unique moral superiority of any one of the great world faiths'.[29] All religions contain examples of great good and of great evil. Says Hick: 'We need to compare apples with apples'. Hick viewed his own work as a kind of 'Copernican revolution' for it 'involves a shift from the dogma that Christianity is at the centre to the realization that it is *God* who is at the centre'.[30] Indeed, 'the different encounters with the transcendent within the different religious traditions may all be encounters with the one infinite reality, though with partially different and overlapping aspects of that reality'.[31] He reminds us that the great world religions, seen in historical context as movements of faith, 'are not essentially rivals. They begin at different times and in different places, and each expanded outwards into the surrounding world of primitive natural religion until most of the world was drawn up into one or other of the great revealed faiths'.[32] Hick's approach is one of reconciling aspectival relativism so as to embrace complementary diversity. The variant expressions of divine reality contained within the different religions are not necessarily or automatically mutually exclusive but rather necessarily limited, yet complementary, images or manifestations of the divine reality, 'each expressing some aspect or range of aspects and yet none by itself fully and exhaustively corresponding to the infinite nature of the ultimate reality'.[33]

The second variant within the standard paradigm of pluralism, closely allied to the first, is *Common Goal Pluralism* which holds that religious differences reflect the variety of salvific paths leading, or drawn to, the universal goal. In this view, the key idea is that there is a transformative goal that is the endpoint of all religions, even though it may be differingly expressed (in concert with the narrative tradition within which each religion dwells uniquely) and differently attained (again in keeping with the unique transformative or salvific narrative of each religion). As Hick remarks, 'different religions have their different names for God acting savingly towards mankind (sic)'.[34] Hick further suggests that the variant salvific paths of religion indicate that religions themselves may be regarded as but 'different manifestations to humanity of a yet more ultimate ground of all salvific transformation … the possibility that an infinite transcendent reality is being differently conceived, and therefore differently experienced, and therefore differently responded to from within our several religio-cultural ways of being human'.[35] Ground and goal, though complementarily linked, are nevertheless two variant paradigms of the pluralist hypothesis forming the 'standard' paradigmatic subset. The fundamental ideas are clear – there is a 'common ground' of religious 'reality' from which the different religions of the world derive, or a transformative 'goal' that is the endpoint of all religions, even though it may be differingly expressed (in concert with the narrative tradition within which each religion dwells uniquely) and differently attained (again, in keeping with the unique transformative or salvific narrative of each religion).

Radical pluralism

The second paradigm set consists of two relatively extreme definitions of pluralism. The first, *Radically Differentiated Pluralism*, holds that religious differences denote irreconcilable differentiation of religious identities. That is to say, there is no reasonable ground to assume a link across religions. Their individual, particular identities militate against any such linkage as inferred by the predominant standard paradigm-set of pluralism. For what are conveniently called 'religions' cannot be said to be variant examples of any single category named 'religion' in the first place. The difference between them is of such a nature that, strictly speaking, it is illicit even to consider that there is any point of meaningful conceptual contact among the religions. A leading example of a proponent of this variant is the American theologian and philosopher John Cobb.[36] He may be identified as a 'pure pluralist' for whom religions are not mere variant expressions of the one divine reality, but are genuinely plural in respect of the realities they represent. Thus, for example, the outcome of dialogical encounter may well be mutual transformation as opposed to mutual reinforcement.[37] Cobb shows himself to be an open-ended, non-common-ground pluralist who is suspicious of any organizing or categorial terms that might prejudge or limit dialogic conversation. He raises objections to the notion of 'universal theology of religion' and sketches difficulties that he sees with the term 'religion' as a denominating label. Cobb asserts the need for all traditions, including the Christian, to affirm their unique centres of meaning. He protests 'that the pretense to stand beyond all traditions and build neutrally out of all of them is a delusion' and clearly asserts the uniqueness of his own religious tradition – Christianity – but eschews any suggestion that this implies any necessary superiority: he argues for 'the Christian the rejection of all arrogance, exclusivism, and dogmatism in relation to other ways'.[38] The attractiveness of this paradigm lies in its clear assertion of the individual identity and integrity of the various religions themselves: none can be adequately interpreted in the terms of another; none can be viewed as in any sense subsumed within another. To that extent there is no confusion of dialogical motive. But it still rather begs the question that there are some religions – Judaism, Christianity and Islam, for instance – where historical, if not theological or ideological, linkages militate against this paradigm as the most apposite context for the conduct of any sort of dialogical relationship.

The second of the Radical Pluralism set is *Eschatological Pluralism*, a relatively new paradigm suggested by Mark Heim.[39] He proposes a hypothesis of 'multiple religious ends'. For him distinctive testimonies of different religious traditions undergirded by a concrete texture of myths, rituals and experiences as well as conditioned by different cultural–linguistic components. They reveal the distinctive ends which are deemed most desirable, or reckoned as ultimate, for the communities concerned. One should not devalue the other and impose one's vision of ultimate goal but recognize the overlapping nature of religious life including interior experiences and exterior behaviour. His view can be summarized as proposing a relative value equivalence of otherwise distinctive, and so uniquely different, religious ends or goals.

Interdependent pluralism

A third subset of pluralism paradigms exists alongside the standard and the radical sets adumbrated above. This is what I call the set of 'interdependent' paradigms, and there are again two variants, namely Complementarity Holistic and Dynamic Parallel pluralism. *Complementarity Holistic Pluralism* holds that religious differences may be discerned as complementary particular expressions which together comprise the universal 'whole'. The American scholar of religion, Paul Knitter, a Christian with close appreciative links to Buddhism,[40] exemplifies this category in that he proposes an idea of 'unitive pluralism'.[41] He argues that 'in the contemporary pluralistic world there cannot be just one religion, but neither can there be many that exist in "indifferent tolerance"'.[42] Knitter holds a relational view of truth wherein the differences and particularities of religions are reconciled, but not materially equivalent. The plurality of religions is not so much a matter of non-competing variant outworkings of a common ground or goal, but rather the mutual complementarity of different parts together comprising a complex whole. The world's religions together comprise the whole of what religion is as such. The divine reality encountered and varyingly expressed in and through different religions is not the One Reality behind religions, as it were, but the One Reality that is comprised by them all.

In similar fashion *Dynamic Parallel Pluralism* holds that religious differences are perceived as reflecting a parallelism of religious phenomena. This paradigmatic perspective may be gleaned from the phenomenological study of religion espoused by Ninian Smart, a pioneering mid-twentieth-century English scholar of religions, and others.[43] The affirmation of pluralism asserts authenticity of phenomena without commenting on matters of validity or veracity. What is observed as a result of analysis of presented data – the phenomena that together comprise any given religion – is the presence of dynamic parallels rather than substantive 'sameness'. Religious plurality may then be interpreted in terms of dynamic parallels of religious intuition and response, for example. This yields a point of commonality that yet preserves the integrity of difference. Religions are not variants of the same thing, but they may variably express parallel processes. The inference is that the reality of religion lies in the dynamic processes rather than the veracity or otherwise of commensurable substantives.

The question of commonness of goal or ground, let alone the notion of religions as parts that collectively comprise a whole, is not the focus. Rather, from the observation and concomitant analysis of religions can be discerned a number of dynamic parallels that are operative in and through the various narrative traditions of the religions of the world. For example, all major religions contain a narrative account of an inherent less-than-satisfactory state of affairs for human existence, howsoever arrived at in terms of specific narratives. In all cases, however, this state of affairs requires some transformative action to overcome and so enable the attainment of an ultimate outcome or destiny. The stories expressing this vary, as do the doctrines and teachings relating thereto. But the dynamic contained within the differing narratives redounds with parallel similarities. Religious plurality may be interpreted in terms of dynamic parallels of religious intuition and response. This is the point of commonality that yet preserves the integrity of difference. Religions are not variants of the same thing but they are variant expressions of parallel processes.

Ethical pluralism

Forming in effect a third subset of pluralist paradigms is another new slant on religious diversity arising out of global ethical concerns and the awareness of religions contribution to the future of humankind – for good or ill. Mutual understanding, peaceful coexistence and cooperation for common welfare among people of different faiths are not new ideas. However, they have been reinforced with new slogans and novel frameworks. The Global Ethic of the German Catholic scholar Hans Küng represents a serious theological exploration in dialogue with partners from other religious traditions; he has chosen to promote an idea which is appealing and more respected in the world scene today.[44] When Küng, in 1990, launched his new project on global responsibility and a world ethic, his concern was very clear. It is succinctly expressed:

No world peace without peace between the religions.
No peace between the religions without dialogue between the religions.

Küng has been joined by Knitter, among others, in the quest to promote inter-religious détente and dialogical relations centring on global ethical concerns.[45] In the process this promotes an affirmation of religious diversity on the basis of shared ethical responsibilities.

Religion and Extremism

Comprehensive integrated pluralism

Stanley Samartha was a theologian of southern India and pioneer of interfaith dialogue work at the ecumenical level through the World Council of Churches. He was neither comfortable with any of (standard) pluralism and inclusivism, nor of exclusivism (to be discussed shortly), yet in some sense one can relate him to each alternatively.[46] Samartha warned against a kind of relativism which can make persons non-committal, passive and indifferent and argues that there can be a positive act of relativizing if the starting point is a deep commitment to a particular faith and community, however imperfect it is. He was fond of the images of travel and pilgrimage, but not without commitment and openness: 'We are always *on the way*', he would say: 'Every arrival is a point of departure, and every journey looks for a new destination'. It is in the light of the lead given by Samartha that a way forward may be found in terms of what I call a *Comprehensive Integrated Pluralism*. This affirms religious diversity in a context of concrete religious commitment and firm religious identity. It is marked by a stance of critical openness to the other and to the greater truth and understanding that lies beyond our inevitably partial and particular expressions of them. Further, it rediscovers and carefully articulates a transcendental metanarrative, one which is inclusive of the otherness of the other, and which therefore is able to pursue and develop a new theology or ideology of the religious other.

Having been introduced to these different ways of seeing and understanding what we mean by way of affirming diversity, we now turn to other modes of responding to the reality of religious plurality. On the one hand, there are paradigms that seek to absorb or include the presence of diverse otherness within a single worldview frame. Paradigms of inclusion affirm diversity, but only to a point. On the other hand, there are perspectives that simply deny the validity, if not reality, of any other religion. In other words, one seeks to take account of religious diversity by looking to ways of relativizing variants and otherness as accounted for within one's own religious worldview, the other tends to dismiss all that is different as necessarily false or fatally deficient on the basis that there can only be one right and true religion, and so one valid religious worldview, which of course is 'mine'. The first, inclusivism, we will examine below; the second, exclusivism, we will explore in the next chapter.

Inclusivism: Paradigms of incorporation

In general terms I define religious inclusivism as the *effective identity* of any given particular religion with the notion of 'universal religion' as such, albeit with some allowance made for other religions. Inclusivism suggests the 'other' is included surreptitiously by being understood as already – 'anonymously' and indirectly – within the fold of 'true religion'. And this is identified, of course, as being the religion of the proponent – it is the only *fully* right one. However, as with the issue of what constitutes pluralism as such, so with inclusivism there is more than one version. I detect on the one hand what I call

Triumphal Inclusivism as being a dominantly Christian paradigm which nevertheless, in terms of its structural dynamic, can arguably apply to other religions and especially Islam. On the other hand, there are a number of distinct variants which I identify as *Gatekeeper*, *Imperialist* and *Mutual Co-inherence Inclusivism*.

Triumphal inclusivism

Within Christianity inclusivism has been embraced formally by the Roman Catholic Church since Vatican II, and it reflects most official contemporary Protestant Church positions. There are two classic examples of Christian inclusivism worth noting, and although the dynamics of each may find echo in other religions, from a Christian perspective they express a form of triumphalism. *Cosmic-Rational Inclusivism* in its Christian form is derived from the doctrine of the *logos* (a Greek term meaning varyingly 'word' or 'rationality'). The author of the fourth gospel (St John) made use of the term logos, to mean the 'Word' which was 'with God' and which was God-like or divine, identifying the logos with the *Christos* (Christ). In the second century of the Common Era, Justin Martyr, one of the earliest Christian apologists, also focused on the idea of Christ as this logos. He proposed that, as the energetic 'Word' (*logike dunamis*), the logos was the creator and organizer of the cosmos, and as the seminal reason (*logos spermatikos*) inherent to the creation, the Logos (as now a synonym for Christ) on this view inspired the Greek philosophers and is present in all humans, as indeed within all of the created realm. The second-century theologian Irenaeus explained that all divine manifestations take place through the Logos. Knowledge of God within creation is itself a response to the revelation brought about by the Logos, for creation itself is a divine manifestation. Thus, by virtue of the universal principle of creation, all that is created is brought into being by the Logos of God. Thus everything that exists is included within its cosmic purview. Although articulated within the orbit of Christian thought, in essence the underlying dynamic of this variant on inclusivism can find an echo, if not a clear parallel, in other religions.

Inclusivism of Implicit Fulfilment is a chief Christo-centric construct that seeks to relativize other religions in relation to itself. For example, Bartholomaus Ziegenbalg (1682–1719), the first Protestant missionary to India, perceived a sense of Supreme Being and what he called the 'broken lights' of a higher truth among the Hindus. G. U. Pope (1820-1907) was fascinated by the devotional fervour of the Shaiva community in southern India and saw in that a spirituality 'awaiting fulfilment'. J. N. Farquhar (1861-1929) wrote his famous *The Crown of Hinduism* in which he argued that Christ and Christianity fulfils all the aspirations of Hindus and brings to the highest point all the noble values of Hinduism. He highlighted Jesus's words – 'Not to destroy but to fulfil'. This approach of religious inclusivism was taken up and expounded by several theologians. F. D. Maurice (1805–72), for example, affirmed that the reign of God is a present reality and that Christ is the redeemer of humanity in all ages. He observed deep truths in Hinduism and regarded Islam's

Muhammad as a witness for God. Such observations, for him, provide a basis for further dialogue with both Hindus and Muslims.

In short, in Christian terms, this form of inclusivism, of whatever variant expression, holds the Christ figure to be the absolute fulfilment of human destiny per se. Christianity thus claims to be *the* absolute religion, but not the only religion with any value. Nevertheless, Christians should consider non-Christians as 'anonymous Christians' because of the ever-present divine grace touching each individual irrespective of their religious identity as such. At different stages many are on the way to salvation, yet preaching makes them realize the victory of grace and impels them to join the Church, which in effect is the social form, or context, of salvation. Again, arguably, the underlying dynamic of this form of triumphalist inclusivism can find echo in other religions.

Gatekeeper inclusivism

This variant allows for limited particular-universal connections in respect of other religions, but the validity of such connectivity is found only through one religion – 'mine' – as only it is the 'fully right' religion. It allows for partial validity (i.e. truth value) as well as partial efficacy (i.e. salvific value) in respect of other religions. A measure of generosity of heart can be extended inasmuch as the religious 'other' is perceived as not completely beyond the pale. That is to say, other religions may be said to enjoy a measure of veracity or a limited representation of the Universal Truth. However, even these religions must, in some sense, go through the 'gate' of the inclusive religion to obtain full religious or salvific validity. But the governing context is clear and unequivocal. The religion of the inclusivist is the only *fully* right way to salvation, the only final or ultimate *valid bearer* of religious truth. It constitutes the 'gatekeeper' wherein, at best, others may be admitted to the pen. There is a hint of pluralism inasmuch as some theological value is accorded to other religions. But there is no doubt as to how that is contextualized: others are viewed as variant and limited expressions of the universal or religious truth that is yet best expressed by *our* right one. The 'our', of course, is important: any religion could theoretically, if not actually, take this view. Each can view itself as possessing in full that which others lack or have but partially. Much of evangelical Christianity that is not hard-line fundamentalist–and so has an open or even a measure of 'universalist' understanding–fits in this category. Friendly openness may be extended to persons of other faiths in recognition that they are, indeed, people of faith and that their faith as such is valid, but it lacks the fullness of truth and salvation which only the Christian (evangelical) faith can provide. This viewpoint is also echoed in the official teaching of the Roman Catholic Church.

Imperialist inclusivism

This third variant also allows for partial truth validity and salvific efficacy in respect of other faiths (but only those deemed 'authentic' religions) in that these may be viewed as legitimate variant outworkings of the only *comprehensive* right one. That is to say, as a sort of advance over the notion that other religions, in some incognito fashion, express in part what the inclusive religion has in full, there is in this variant of inclusivism an allowance that certain other religions may, indeed, be living out, in an authentic way, that which is nevertheless to be found fully in the one comprehensively true or right religion. Other religions, at least under certain conditions, are already and 'anonymously' included within the worldview framework of the dominant religion in this schema. This is also a formal position of the Roman Catholic Church. Other 'valid' religions many enjoy a partial measure of being right relative to that which is the fully right religion, but not a full or complete 'rightness'. An illustration of this paradigm may be found in the view of Islam with respect to Judaism and Christianity being 'religions of the book'. Islam has, knows and lives fully that which has been given to these others, but which they now express in only a limited, if not corrupted, fashion. From the Christian perspective, Diogenes Allen expresses this paradigm when he asserts 'A Christian theology of other faiths reaches out toward other faiths, retaining the conviction that Christ is the Savior of the world, and bringing another faith or aspects of it into a vital relation to Christ'.[47] In the end the generic inclusivist stance is modified by an imperialist assertion of non-negotiable or superior perspective. Imperialist inclusivism highlights the basic assumption inherited from the exclusivist stance: the total identification of a universal value, such as religious truth or salvation, with the particulars of but one religion.

Mutual co-inherence inclusivism

The final variant, also a distinctly Christian one, derives from the work of the Indian scholar of religion, Raimundo Panikkar,[48] who claimed that Christianity and Hinduism meet only in Christ, for although the man 'Jesus' is certainly the 'Christ', 'Christ' is not only Jesus. Panikkar regarded the Hindu reality of the personal Lord (*Isvara*) as identified with Christ, the personal Lord. This form of inclusivism, which in its essential dynamic can arguably apply to other religions, is less a matter of a one-way including of the worldview of one religion within that of another. It holds rather that at certain critical points there is a measure of mutual including, especially where there is a careful deepening of doctrinal understanding, as with the issue of delineating what is meant by 'Christ' from the understanding of the person 'Jesus', for example.

A sub-variant is what may be termed 'participatory inclusivism' and it also has an Indian pedigree. It derives from the work of Indian theologians P. D. Devanandan (1901–62), the founder-director of the Christian Institute for the Study of Religion and Society, Bangalore, and his successor M. M. Thomas (1916–96). They bridged the work and perspectives of the early Indian Christian theologians who suggested points of contact and interpretive tools in certain Hindu religious categories such as avatar, and the more radical stand concerning the universal presence and action of God where the inclusivist motif is more readily discerned in a notion of the different religions equally, yet differingly, participating within the greater outworking of God's active presence in the world. The work of the 'Spirit' was seen to be effective within the modern religious and secular movements of India, particularly the reform and renaissance movements of the time. History itself was regarded as God's platform of interaction; Christ was regarded as the beginning of a new creation for which the church is called to witness through word and service. In particular, Thomas, interpreting salvation as humanization, was open to the inspiring thoughts and alternative models of community coming from other religions and even secular ideologies. He centred them on Christ, but had no fear of syncretism if it was Christ-centred.

The option of responding to religious diversity by way of some concept of 'inclusion' has been a feature of changes wrought within Christianity in the late modern and early postmodern periods. Whereas for centuries other religions were deemed, virtually automatically, as falsehoods, with their people floundering in darkness and untruth – for which the light and truth of Christianity would be their salvation – it has only been in the last hundred years or so that the main Christian Churches have varyingly modified this stance. In an age of dialogue and détente, the religious 'other' emerged as a dialogical partner, as a fellow-traveller. Inclusivism marked a major step for Christianity and it is echoed in different ways in other religions – including Hinduism, for example, with its motif that all religious paths lead eventually to the same mountain top of Truth. For the most part, Christians and Muslims who take a benign and relationally positive stance towards each other and towards other faith communities, tend more towards framing that stance within an inclusive ideology than a strictly pluralist one. But either way, religious otherness is given value. Diversity is affirmed.

Conclusion

Diversity is very much a normal feature of life. How it is responded to, is the key. This chapter has examined a range of positive responses. While the discussion has religious diversity as the point of focus, the paradigmatic patterns involved can also be equally applied to contexts of diverse ethnic, racial and also cultural–social mixes. Few societies today are fully homogenous. It is the measure of an open, liberal, tolerant and inclusive society that it can, indeed, accommodate these diversities. And how this accommodation occurs – the very nature of a society's constitution in respect of these diversities – will point the way to the success or otherwise, of such accommodation. One thing, however, is clear. In today's world it is the rise of policies and platforms that seek to reject diversity, whether in the form of resisting immigration, repelling asylum seekers, rejecting any further apparent 'dilution' of current, albeit relative, homogeneity, which is of real concern and challenge. And this appears sharpest when it comes to the promotion of the rejection of a religious other – especially that of the Muslim other. But equally, there are Muslim contexts that reject, or promote the rejection of, Christians – and certainly Jews. And the Jewish state, Israel, is confronted with the reality of many Muslim states that utterly reject its very existence. Their stated aim is to see the Jewish state, and even all Jews, eliminated from the Holy Land. The reality that confronts us today is that, along with these – and other – geopolitical contexts that seek to reject the presence of a particular, especially religious, diversity, there is evidence of increasing breakdown of liberal, tolerant and diversity-affirming values, policies and ideologies and a concomitant increase in exclusionary, rejecting attitudes. We will explore further, in the next chapter, the issue of diversity rejection as the main plank of religious extremism by way of examining the very particular ideological position of exclusivism that is itself a platform and key driver for this rejection, and a close examination of the allied phenomenon of 'fundamentalism' and its link to extremism.

CHAPTER 3
DIVERSITY RESISTED: EXCLUSION AND FUNDAMENTALISM

Mark Juergensmeyer has noted the irony that 'although religion has been used to justify violence, violence can also empower religion'.[1] He points out that 'the religious imagination, which always has had the propensity to absolutize' plays a significant role in the formation of extremist religious ideologies of power and dominance on account of its appeal 'to those who want to make dramatic statements and reclaim public space ... to remind the populace of the godly power that makes a religious ideology potent'.[2] Divine judgement is meted out according to the imagined notion of 'rightness' that inheres to an extreme religious ideology. Extremists create 'incidents of fear on heaven's behalf, as if its perpetrators could discern the mind of God'.[3] Investigation into the phenomenon of contemporary religiously driven terrorism shows the presence of a distinctive and rigid form of exclusivity inherent to religious fundamentalism.[4] Such exclusivity can certainly be understood as a variant of the paradigm of exclusivism, and exclusivism is itself an element of fundamentalist ideologies, whether religious or otherwise.

Despite some parallels and affinities across religions where fundamentalism is seen to apply, in reality the wider application of the term 'fundamentalism' beyond its originating Christian context is certainly not without problems and difficulties. It does not transfer well into other religious contexts, and it is imprecise enough even within the Christian camp. Nevertheless, the term has gained wide coinage and we have to live with it and utilize it as best we can. The usage of it has undoubtedly broadened: 'fundamentalism' as a referent for the stance of a 'closed mind' coupled with intransigent beliefs and, usually, a negative if not hostile stance towards the status quo, has migrated into political discourse and into the wider religious realm. In regard to the latter, 'fundamentalism' now broadly names a religio-political perspective found in most if not all major religions. And the resurgence in totalizing claims of fundamentalist ideologues – in Islam, certainly, but also in Christianity, as well as in Hinduism, Judaism and other religious communities – together with the utilization of global communication, transportation and related modern technologies, means that the issue of religious fundamentalism requires careful consideration and critical analysis. In a nutshell, 'fundamentalism' is today often defined in terms of what it is 'against' and is used as 'a pejorative description for anyone who is regarded as having a closed mind with regard to a particular issue'.[5]

A fundamentalist perspective is inherently absolutist: all other relevant phenomena are simply explained on its terms, or viewed in a relativizing, even negating, way with reference to it. Fundamentalism, as a mindset, is a mentality that expresses the modern quest for universality and coherence writ large: only one truth, one authority, one authentic narrative that accounts for all, one right way to be. Fundamentalism typically excludes nuanced and variant readings of whatever is its authoritative text or guiding source. This is sometimes understood as 'literalism', that is, reading the authoritative text, such as a scripture, as literally true in every respect – as not needing to be interpreted for a different, deeper, or other meaning than what the words simply say. For a fundamentalist the key issue is that the source authority is such that no intermediary interpretive framework is required – the text itself provides pellucid expression of truth, whether in terms of an abstract universal, or in respect of a pragmatic or programmatic articulation of the values and views espoused by the fundamentalist as 'The Truth'. Fundamentalism may do little more than express an exclusive religious identity and worldview, and to that extent amounts to little more than a passive belief. On the other hand, it may also tend towards a more active, assertive, and even an extreme perspective which, under certain circumstances, leads to violence and terrorism. By this point, the initial passive belief is both assertively active and programmatically impositional.

This chapter examines the patterns and paradigms of exclusivism and engages a critical examination of fundamentalism. Each supports and promotes the other and both enact forms of diversity rejection. Hence this chapter moves from one to the other. Together, they provide a key to understanding how the ideological rejection of diversity leads to extremism, and so to acts of violence and terrorism. Exclusivism, as an ideological response to the fact of diversity, is conceptually intertwined with fundamentalism. And fundamentalism refers to and names a worldview perspective and type of religious phenomenon that can be found across many different religions. As fundamentalism develops in terms of ideological process, which will be explained below, it demonstrates a shift in mentality from the relative harmlessness of an otherwise quaint, decidedly conservative, belief system to the reality of an extreme perspective of religiously motivated and fanatically followed engagement in aggressively impositional, even terrorist, activity. Extreme ideas, values and activities are not necessarily those of the margins or fringe groups of a religion. But at the same time, most of what we see as extremism is, indeed, something that lies at the margins, or 'fringe', relative to the wider tradition. What we need to acknowledge is that what might count as 'fringe' in one period of time may, in fact, be regarded as the 'norm' in another. Either way, the key component of extremism is clearly some form of exclusivism. So what do we mean by this term?

Exclusivism: Patterns of diversity rejection

Exclusivism has been posited as the default position inimical to any form of détente or dialogue with other faiths or even to alternatives within the one faith. Furthermore, some critics charge that, in the end, a pluralist must necessarily be an exclusivist of some sort, and that inclusivism, when pressed, also tends to collapse into some form of exclusivism. Be that as it may, the critical issue today is not so much to do with pluralism, nor even problems raised by inclusivism. Rather it has to do with questions posed by the persistence – even growth – of religious exclusivism. As we will see, this is closely linked to certain forms of fundamentalism and also to religious extremism. The rise of exclusionary religious extremism of varying sorts can be understood as a manifestation of the paradigm – or patterns – of exclusivism. What, then, is the paradigm? Exclusivism, I suggest, amounts to the *material identification* of a particular religion (or form of that religion) with the essence and substance of true universal religion as such, thereby excluding all other possibilities to that claim.[6] For the exclusivist the mere coexistence of religions is not possible – the natural tendency to an exclusive self-assertion predominates. From this viewpoint, the exclusivist's religion is the '*only* right one'. Religious exclusivism involves the identification of a particular religion (or form of that religion) as being, in fact, the essence and substance of true universal religion as such. From a religious viewpoint, truth and salvation are universal values. The exclusivist holds that this universality is materially identified with just one religion, namely that of the exclusivist. By its very nature, exclusivism is hostile to inter-religious dialogue and interfaith engagement more widely. It impinges on such activities, most often contributing towards efforts that undermine them.

> The exclusivist affirms identity in a complex world of plurality by a return to the firm foundations of his or her own tradition and an emphasis on the distinctive identity provided by that tradition … Exclusivism is more than simply a conviction about the transformative power of the particular vision one has; it is a conviction about its finality and its absolute priority over competing views.[7]

For the strict exclusivist, the mere coexistence of religions, or even of radically different variants within their own religion, is not allowable – the natural tendency to an exclusive self-assertion predominates.

Certainly, before the terms exclusivism, inclusivism, and pluralism had appeared, the viewpoints – or ideology – they name certainly existed, to greater or lesser degrees. More recently a fourth term – particularism – has been added as denoting yet another paradigm option in respect of understanding the context of, and possible responses to, diversity.[8] In my view particularism is not so much a genuine alternative to the initial three terms and what they refer to, but rather a variant of exclusivism and so effectively subsumed within the exclusivist categories to be discussed below. A close examination of the ideology of exclusivism reveals a number of sub-possibilities that give a more nuanced understanding to the perspective named, as is the case with both inclusivism and pluralism. Phenomena pertaining to religious exclusivism increasingly confront peoples of faith and goodwill who wish only for peaceful coexistence in equality and freedom with their religious neighbour. There is more than one variety of religious exclusivism and here I touch on salvific-eschatological exclusivism, which is particularly pertinent to Christianity, and three general variants: open, closed and extreme. Further, inasmuch as exclusivism indicates a positing of religious identity over and against any 'other', then it will be argued that the various exclusivisms themselves reflect a continuum of ideological and theological stance that is taken towards the religious 'other' per se. This ranges through antithetical acknowledgement, manifest ignorance and the intentional invalidation of variety. It is the specific issue of the invalidation of otherness which, I contend, constitutes the severe problem of religious exclusivism in extremis.

Christianity has classically held an exclusivist line with respect to salvation and eternal destiny – this can be denoted as *salvific-eschatological exclusivism*. It is a militant and triumphant expression of religion and it adamantly holds to the view that there is but one way to God, one way to access this salvation and eternal destiny. Specifically, it is based on the claim that Jesus is the only way to God or heaven, and the only name for salvation. Since the epoch of the early Church Fathers and up to the Council of Florence (1442), the view that no one outside the Church could possibly be saved was developed and refined.[9] Christian exclusivism regards all but its own way as invalid or void. From the Catholic dogma of *extra ecclesiam nulla salus*[10] to various conservative Protestant declarations of condemnation of any but their own viewpoint, the 'controlling assumption is that outside the church, or outside Christianity, there is no salvation'.[11] Although now a clearly dated theological view, exclusivism is nonetheless widespread, at least at the level of much popular conservative and fundamentalist forms of Christianity.

We turn now to the three general categories of contemporary exclusivism that I have identified. Although my discussion focuses on their appearance within the orbit of Christianity, arguably the categories I adumbrate apply also to other religions, including Judaism and Islam.

Open exclusivism

While maintaining cognitive and salvific superiority, open exclusivism may at least be amenably disposed towards a religious 'other', if only to allow for – even encourage – the capitulation (by way of conversion, for example) of the other. Some early twentieth-century Christian 'open' exclusivists include Visser t'Hooft, a leading ecumenical figure, who argued against what he viewed as 'incipient pluralism' wherein syncretism and the notion of a single world-faith were viewed as inexorable outcomes of taking a non-exclusivist line. Yet he affirmed the value of cultural plurality.[12] Similarly, Hendrikus Kraemer, for many years a Christian missionary in Islamic Indonesia, popularized and promoted the view that, at the level of human institution, Christianity was no different from other religions in being yet another religion. However, with respect to its basis in revelation and the uniqueness of its truth-claims, Christianity is essentially *other than* the religions. 'Religion' thus names the human seeking for the divine; Christianity, by contrast, is the sole authentic arena of the divine encountering the human. Christianity stands apart, holding a position of exclusive privilege: 'Christianity understands itself not as one of several religions, but as the adequate and definitive revelation of God in history'.[13] Kraemer upheld the validity of cultural plurality, just like Visser t'Hooft. Nevertheless, the open exclusivism espoused by such early ecumenical Christian leaders asserted a triumphant Christocentric salvific proclamation of essential Christian identity. Openness has limits, at least in so far as what openness might mean for the self-identity of that which is taking a stance of openness. Open exclusivism implies openness to some form of relationship with another without expectation of, or openness to, consequential or reciprocal change of self-identity with respect to that relationship.

Closed exclusivism

In contrast to open exclusivism, closed exclusivism simply dismisses the 'other' out of hand. Relationship to the 'other', especially any religious other, is effectively ruled out. The 'other' may be acknowledged as having her or his rightful place, but that place is inherently inferior to that of the closed exclusivist who, inter alia, prefers to remain wholly apart from the other. An 'open' exclusivism may yet entertain a 'dialogue' of sorts – perhaps a conversational interaction – if only with a view to understanding the perspective of the other in order, then, better to refute it and so proclaim the 'only right one' religion. By comparison, a 'closed' exclusivism will spurn interaction with another religious viewpoint altogether: imperialist assertion is the only mode of communication admissible. The contrast between the 'open' and 'closed' forms of exclusivism is given clear instantiation by two denominations of protestant Christianity, the Open Brethren and the Exclusive Brethren. The former function as an ultraconservative Christian community, the latter live a sectarian existence, effectively withdrawn from the wider world. The Exclusive Brethren, whose members live and work within wider society, is nonetheless a closed community with a separate schooling system, and members associate only with each other for all social, recreational and religious activities. They see themselves not just as superior to other forms of Christianity but, indeed, as the only true form which must be protected from contamination with lesser and corrupt forms of the faith as well as all who are outside that faith.

Extreme exclusivism

This third variant marks a shift from the 'closed' form, which can be understood more simply as the exercise of the right of a community to withdraw into itself, to an expression of hard-line rejectionist exclusivity. This asserts an exclusive identity to the extent that the fact and presence of an 'other' is actively resisted, even to the point of taking steps to eliminate that other. If examples of such extreme forms of exclusivism can be adduced from within the history of Christianity, then it is certainly the case that today the more obvious instantiations are to be found at the extremities of most major religions, with Islam currently to the fore. The distinguishing feature denoting extreme exclusivism is the negative valorizing of the 'other' – howsoever defined – with concomitant harsh sanctions and limitations imposed upon the other. It is this level of exclusive religion which, in its hostility to 'otherness' per se, inherently invalidates variety and alterity. It is this level, or version, of religious exclusivism which lies at the heart of so much religious strife – not to mention terrorism and insurgency – and thus poses an acute challenge to those who would advocate religious freedoms, toleration and peaceful coexistence. It is this exclusivism that inheres to the extreme wings of religious fundamentalism, to which we now turn.

Religion and Extremism

Religion and fundamentalism

Today the term 'fundamentalism', which is a shorthand denotation of a complex religious perspective, tends to evoke a negative reaction of some sort – none of us regard it with indifference. And what about the apparent link to terrorism – how are we to understand that? J. Harold Ellens speaks of Judaism, Christianity and Islam, in respect of their action-oriented fundamentalisms, in terms of 'the quest for a final solution … to the underlying cosmic conflict between God and devil, between all things good and all things evil'.[14] What an analysis of fundamentalism shows is that a religiously extreme perspective can be simply a passive viewpoint, an assertive identity orientation, or a fanatically imposed programme of behaviours and actions. In some situations it is very clear that the driver of the action is the extremist religious ideology. In others, it is more complex: religious ideology may be one of many factors involved. There is certainly a propensity for religion to be instrumentalized in the cause of what is otherwise yet another political power play – by a warlord, despot, dictatorial monarch and social manipulator seeking to shape society according to a political vision and ideology that is not of itself religious but which will readily make use of religious sensibilities in the achievement of its aims and objectives. For example, LeRoy Aden, in considering various contexts of religion-related violence, notes the apparent 'triadic link between religion, self-righteousness, and violence' for which, ironically and disturbingly, he avers, it would seem that 'instead of putting a rein on, or an end to, self-righteousness', religion is used to provide support and justification for it with the resultant 'aggressive acts in the name of God … with the blessing of their own self-proclaimed righteousness'.[15]

Such instrumentalization of religion, including, ironically, of religious extremism – as in accusing opponents of being religious extremists or terrorists – appears to be the case with the phenomenal rise and relative success of the Islamic State, or Caliphate, on the one hand, and the re-emergence of dictatorial presidential leaders in many otherwise modern democracies today on the other. Indeed, the 'process of creating satanic enemies is part of the construction of an image of cosmic war … aimed at reducing the power of one's opponents and discrediting them'.[16] Thus delegitimizing the 'other' is part and parcel of the rhetoric of religious – and political – extremism. As we will see, it can be located as a factor within the evolving process wherein a religious fundamentalism becomes a religious extremism. Indeed, Juergensmeyer signals something of this when he notes the incremental process 'in which acts of terrorism appear only in the later stages of a pattern that begins with a feeling of helplessness' and which he identifies as the 'world gone awry' followed by a 'foreclosure of ordinary options', the juxtaposition of 'Satanization and cosmic war' and the exercise of 'symbolic acts of power'.[17] This is one way of naming the process that underlies the ideological development of religious extremism. I offer another. A close study of religious fundamentalism, which is premised upon, and expresses, an underlying absolutism, reveals a more nuanced pattern that may result in religious extremism and acts of religiously motivated and justified terrorism. But before beginning this analysis, we need to remind ourselves of the origin, and limited nature, of the very term 'fundamentalism'.

The origin and nature of 'fundamentalism'

The term fundamentalism, in its originating Christian context, was coined in America in the early twentieth century. A series of booklets, issued between 1910 and 1915, called *The Fundamentals*, were published to promote a defining and non-negotiable set of traditional, or fundamental, Christian doctrines. The substance of the booklets was developed from a position statement of an 1885 conservative Christian Bible conference held at Niagara. The key points of fundamental Christian belief as articulated by that statement included 'the verbal [or literal] inerrancy of Scripture, the divinity of Jesus, the virgin birth, the substitutionary theory of the atonement, and the physical, bodily return of Jesus'.[18] These were taken up and amplified into the booklets. Although it was not until July 1920 when the editor of the *American Baptist* magazine coined the term, the proposition that Christianity rests on this set of fundamental doctrines led to the widespread use of the term 'fundamentalism'. And the reason for it was because of a perception at the time that the term 'conservative' was too derogatory. In an age where theological liberalism had been in the ascendancy, the magazine's editor had sought a fresh term wherein to denote a new countering viewpoint.[19] A palpable sense of needing to fight for the fundamentals of the faith had emerged, and in this context the badge of 'fundamentalism' was proudly worn. Thus, as a term of Christian discourse for nearly a century, 'fundamentalism' has referred to a set of specific dogmatic beliefs on the one hand, and more widely applied to a broadly ultraconservative Christian worldview on the other. Fundamentalists kept conservatives on their toes and provided liberals with an easy target. J. Harold Ellens speaks of Christian fundamentalism today as 'a uniquely American heresy' that, thanks to the efforts of certain missionaries, 'has been exported worldwide'.[20]

Christian fundamentalism is a 'strange kind of orthodoxy', to use Ellen's phrase, that holds to the Bible as being verbally – that is, directly – inspired by God. It is thus regarded as 'totally inerrant in every word and detail of content', and so read as literally true. As a direct outcome, Christian fundamentalists often hold to an apocalyptic worldview that regards the idea of a cosmic conflict between God and the Devil as factual, and believe that this conflict 'rages everywhere and at all times'.[21] Contemporary social and political events are thus construed as mirroring or even indirectly expressing this conflict. The Christian version of this fundamentalism is echoed in comparable Islamic versions, as a perusal of the rhetoric and propaganda of ISIS (the Islamic State) and other Islamist ideologues readily shows.[22] But the Christian version also carries some other unique elements. These include the duality of 'the righteous and the unrighteous' – applied both to the human realm and also to the realm of angels or transcendental spiritual beings – with the application of both 'temporal blessing and eternal destiny' according to how well and faithful, or not, there has been conformity to the law and will of God. Furthermore, Christian fundamentalism applies a particular interpretation of the Christ event in respect of a 'mechanism of escape from the eternal judgement of God', namely, 'confession of sin and correction of behavior (ameliorated by the merits of the sacrifice of Jesus on the cross thus assuaging the demands of divine justice)'.[23] But the fifth element, namely that 'ultimately God will win the cosmic conflict ... and terminate history in a cataclysm that will damn the unrighteous to eternal hellfire and embrace the righteous into a blissful heaven' will find a direct parallel within comparable expressions of Islamic forms of fundamentalism.[24]

As a subject of critical academic scrutiny in respect of its Christian context, fundamentalism has been the focus of a number of notable books and studies, especially in the closing decades of the twentieth century.[25] This has also broadened out into studies of it on a wide-ranging front, inclusive of both religious and political variants.[26] One very significant event was the five-year 'Fundamentalism Project' which commenced in 1987. It has led to the publication of several substantial volumes of research output.[27] There have also been a large number of studies in recent years where the focus has been on Islamic fundamentalism.[28]

The result of such studies has been, among other things, to identify a number of generic elements or dimensions of fundamentalism per se. For example, Martin E. Marty, the director of the Fundamentalism Project, observed that 'fundamentalisms look backward and set out to "freeze" some moment, some event, some text or texts from the past as the perfect place in time or space from which to measure' life in the present.[29] An imagined 'golden age', believed to have pertained to the religion's foundation, is held up as the model and reference point for contemporary reality. In response to the possible critique that religion, and in particular fundamentalist religion, is but an epiphenomenon riding on what are really political ideas and actions, or that fundamentalism is really just a passing fad, such studies have only served to highlight what subsequent history and recent events underscore: that religious fundamentalism is a deeply rooted phenomenon that can give rise to, rather than relies upon, political acts. One important conclusion that arose from the Fundamentalism Project was the recognition that fundamentalists

> fear loss and change through whatever serves to relativize the world and their worlds. There is constant fear of pluralism, or the stranger who brings other ways which may be alluring or threatening ... Pluralism confuses; it presents not only the threatening but also the attractive neighbour at hand, and that could lead to loss of identity in a group.[30]

Far from being archaic and fossilized, fundamentalist movements 'are lively, intense, creative' and they set out to make a difference – indeed, to change the world.[31] Religious fundamentalism can imply a narrow, strict and limited metaphysics and set of doctrines, which to a greater or lesser degree hardly impinge on the wider life of a society; it can mean a worldview perspective that engenders, if not demands, the advocacy of a sociopolitical ordering and action to achieve an intended outcome. There is nothing startlingly new about that, of course. But the key difference between religion-driven political actions today, in contrast with any previous point in history, is the pervasive context of globalization. Instead of localized, even regional, levels of action, the technology and mentality of a globalized world now allow for a degree of internationalization of the ideologies and activities of fundamentalist movements as never before.

The phenomenon of fundamentalism: Phase, feature and factors

As a framework phenomenon that applies to more than just religion, fundamentalism comprises a series of key factors. Others may be adduced, but the twenty that I have identified, and the way they are interconnected in terms of denoting features and phases, need to be carefully understood.[32] The factors I have identified are analysed in terms of a progression of ten features, or sets, of paired factors. These are further subgrouped into three phases so as to distinguish between what may be termed passive, assertive and impositional forms of fundamentalism (see Table 1).

I suggest that all forms and expressions of religious fundamentalism begin with, or at least include, the features that denote a 'passive' phase. Much conservative religiosity would identify with this phase and would not be overly troubled by that. Indeed, variant forms of reactionary conservatism across both Christianity and Islam, as well as other religions, would easily classify as expressive of passive fundamentalism. However, some religious groups or movements go beyond this such that we may identify them as belonging to an 'assertive' phase that tends to display distinct hard-line attributes of belief and behaviour. Most sectarian and similar movements tend to fit within this phase. But there are some that, incorporating all the marks of an assertive hard-line fundamentalism, then go further to manifest what can perhaps be best described as variant forms of 'impositional' fundamentalism. This is manifest in harsh exclusionary rhetoric and behavioural tendencies. It is here that we discover the propensity for fundamentalism to yield to extremism and terrorism. However, it needs to be stressed that what I am proposing here is a theoretical construct for which I give examples at different points, and that show ideological movement in respect of at least one case. I do not suggest this construct implies that all stages, or phases, are passed through, nor necessarily in the way I lay them out in terms of the features and factors, by a religious group or movement on the way to becoming radicalized and so extremist. Nevertheless, I suggest it is likely that any religious extremism will manifest most, if not all, of the factors and features I have identified, for what I attempt to identify is the inherent logic of the fundamentalist ideology whereby a religion or religious group becomes extreme to the point of violence and terrorism.

A passive – or 'normative' (in the sense of representing what prima facie fundamentalism is usually taken to mean) – fundamentalist group 'minds its own business' so far as the

Table 1 Fundamentalism: Phases and features

Phase I: *Passive Fundamentalism*

Features: Principal Presuppositions – Authority Derivation – Implicit Verification

Phase II: *Assertive Fundamentalism*

Features: Epistemological Construction – Identity Structure – Contextual Scope – Condemnatory Stance

Phase III: *Impositional Fundamentalism*

Features: Value Application – Explicit Justification – Enacted Extremism rest of society is concerned, an assertive hard-line group perhaps somewhat less so. But an impositional and exclusionary group certainly does not. An impositional fundamentalism wants to see things change to fit its view of how things should be, and will take steps to make its views known and, if need be, to actively bring about change – by covert or overt interventions, including fomenting revolution or enacting terrorism. Hence the need to construct a paradigm that attempts to show a distinct progression whereby the sequential and correlative links between the ideology of religious fundamentalism and the propensity for extreme, even terrorist, action is made clear. It is this underlying dynamic of ideological development which the following paradigm attempts to map in some detail.

Phase I: Passive Fundamentalism

The phase of 'normal' passive fundamentalism shows evidence, I suggest, of six basic defining factors which may be grouped in paired sets in respect of three features: principal presuppositions, authority derivation, implicit verification. Each feature contains two factors, as seen in Table 2.

These three features denote the root essence of fundamentalism per se, whether of a religious or non-religious sort. It is not just religions that can throw up fundamentalism. Virtually all aspects of human activity that involve an ideological perspective are susceptible – from economics to environmentalism, politics to pacifism, ethics and morality – as the wide-ranging study of fundamentalism noted above has demonstrated. All display principal presuppositions; all derive support and endorsement from an authoritative source, be it a text such as a manifesto or other source of the guiding ideology; all gain from that the verification of their perspective and views. So how does this work for religion?

Feature 1 – Principal presuppositions

- Factors (i) *Perspectival Absolutism* and (ii) *Immediate Inerrancy*

The fundamentalist perspective is inherently absolutist. Fundamentalism is a mindset, first and foremost: only one truth, one authority, one right way to be. The fundamentalist perspective deems itself privileged, for it presumes superiority of knowledge and truth. Indeed, this is inherent to holding an absolutist perspective as such. Allied to absolutism is the view that the grounding text – be it political

Table 2 Phase I: Passive fundamentalism

Feature 1: Principal Presuppositions
 Factors: Perspectival Absolutism – Immediate Inerrancy
Feature 2: Authority Derivation
 Factors: Apodicity Assumption – Narrow Narrative Indwelling
Feature 3: Implicit Verification
 Factors: Narrative Correlation – Rhetorical Corroboration

manifesto or holy writ – is to be read as conveying an immediate truth or value, without error – that is, 'inerrant'. However, the assertion of the immediate inerrancy of the text – reading the text as being immediately applicable and providing direct access to ultimate or divine truth – in fact involves an implicit assertion that there is only one normative interpretive reading that is allowable, namely that which is undertaken through the fundamentalist's lens. From the fundamentalist perspective, alternative and variant interpretations are deemed inherently false or heretical, and so are rejected.

Feature 2 – Authority derivation

- Factors (iii) *Apodicity Assumption* and (iv) *Narrow Narrative Indwelling*

Building directly upon the preceding set, the third and fourth factors constitute the basis of authority claimed by a fundamentalism. This involves the assumption that the authority source – most usually textual – is unambiguous; the meaning can be 'read off' directly. This is most often understood as 'literalism', although, in reality, it reads the text as 'factual'. The typical meaning or usage of 'literalism' is to understand the holy text to be a compendium of divinely revealed facts. For, as noted above, the key assumption is that the authority of the text is such that no interpretive framework is required; the text at hand is clear in its composition; the message conveyed by the text is apodictic – that is, it provides an adequately clear expression of truth.

Allied to the assumption of apodicity is the factor of narrow narrative indwelling. Arguably all religious people 'indwell', to a greater or lesser degree, their respective religious narrative. The life references, points of meaning and frameworks of understanding which inform a religious individual's existence are more often than not traceable to the paradigms, models and values that are given within the religious narrative. And the narrative is to be found within the scriptural record as well as accompanying histories, stories and other significant accounts and sources from which springs any particular religion. Where the narrative base is broad, the religious life that indwells it likewise reflects breadth. But where the base is narrow, the resultant indwelt religious life is correspondingly confined. So my thesis is that, in the case of fundamentalism, a distinguishing factor has to do with the narrowness of narrative indwelling. It is, indeed, this very narrowness which often marks a fundamentalist out from the wider religious tradition and community.

Feature 3 – Implicit verification

- Factors (v) *Narrative Correlation* and (vi) *Rhetorical Corroboration*

The evolving fundamentalist perspective begins now to move from a variant conservative expression of a religious worldview to a more intentional advocacy of a religious viewpoint as being, par excellence, the expression of authenticity and truth applicable for, or to, all. The fundamentalist's verification of their position marks the closure of the passive, normative phase, and a point of transition to the assertive hard-line phase. A deepening of the correlation between the religious narrative espoused, and the lived reality of the religious community concerned, is the first of the pair of factors here. It is, of course, quite normal for a religion to offer some degree of correlation between its narrative and the 'real world' in which the followers of the religion live – otherwise religion would reduce to a simple and obvious fairy tale. However, a distinction can be made between the broader traditions of a religion whose narrative correlation will be relatively loose, flexible or at least provisional, and the fundamentalist whose degree of correlation will be that much greater and intense.

This factor sharpens – and is prefaced by – the factors of absolutism and inerrancy. For a fundamentalist the correlation will be such as to yield an unambiguous outcome – America *is* the Great Satan, ontologically, for example – whereas, for a non-fundamentalist critical of the West, America may be deemed or judged corrupt or inherently evil, or whatever, in a more general way. The difference is one of the degrees of correlation between the religious narrative and the external realities of the world in which the fundamentalist lives. Allied to narrative correlation is the factor of rhetorical corroboration. Here the discourse of fundamentalism can be more readily tested, perhaps. For in the articulation of narrative correlation there is likely to be found a corresponding intensification of a corroborating rhetoric that situates, endorses and justifies the fundamentalist perspective with respect to the judgements and assessments made about the external world. Rhetoric will be sharp and self-affirming; judgements will be clear and reflective of both the correlation factor as well as the corroboration factor. Thus the perspective of the fundamentalist derives implicit verification and the scene is set for the next phase.

Phase II: Assertive (hard-line) fundamentalism

This phase deepens and strengthens the ideological structure of fundamentalism and its application, both real (in terms of fundamentalist groups) and potential (in respect of the wider society in which any particular fundamentalism is situated). It involves the features of construct of knowledge, identity structure, the hardening of what may be called 'contextual scope' and evidence of a deepening condemnatory stance taken in respect of any opposition or competition, however that might be conceived. (See Table 3).
The details of this phase are as follows.

Feature 4 – Epistemological construction

- Factors (vii) *Hard Factualism* and (viii) *Applied Necessity*

Fundamentalism hardens, and becomes more self-assertive, as it tightens its own grip on what is knowable, and how what is knowable is known. In essence the range of what is admitted as genuine knowledge is truncated: true knowledge is reduced to facts that are held to be true, for the most part – all else belongs to the realm of falsehood. Some hard-line fundamentalists, for example, reject scientific hypotheses and theories which,

Table 3 Phase II: Assertive (hard-line) fundamentalism

Feature 4: Epistemological Construction
Factors: Hard Factualism – Applied Necessity
Feature 5: Identity Structure
Factors: Communitarian Intent – Individual Constraint
Feature 6: Contextual Scope
Factors: Ideological Exclusivism – Polity Inclusion
Feature 7: Condemnatory Stance
Factors: Judgmental Values – Pietistic Tyranny

in their view, challenge or deny the 'facts' as they know them. Furthermore, however, the focus on facts – allied to the reading of scripture as a compendium of God-given 'facts' to be relied upon implicitly – brings with it the dimension of the 'necessary-ness' of the fundamentalist's construction of knowledge: alternative approaches to knowledge, to ascertaining truth and falsity, as well as to meaning and value, are necessarily ruled out. The fundamentalist's own perception of knowledge is that of an applied necessity of perspective in respect of the focus on purportedly hard facts.

Feature 5 – Identity structure

- Factors (ix) *Communitarian Intent* and (x) *Individual Constraint*

The fundamentalist mindset is not simply a matter of opinion and perspective as held by an individual, or by a collective of individuals. Rather it tends to embrace a particular dynamic. A 'communitarian intent', or set of normative community values and expectations, is juxtaposed with some form of 'constraint' placed upon the individual who is a member of that community. The identity of a fundamentalist individual is intrinsically bound up with that of the fundamentalist community. Indeed, the stronger the fundamentalism, the tighter this relation. The factor of communitarian intent denotes the way in which fundamentalist movements place value, to a greater or lesser degree, upon membership of the community. The factor of 'individual constraint' is the necessary corollary, and the two go together to form the structure of fundamentalist identity, irrespective of the specific religion.

Feature 6 – Contextual scope

- Factors (xi) *Ideological Exclusivism* and (xii) *Polity Inclusivism*

Ideological exclusivism refers to the reality that, for hard-line fundamentalism, no competing or variant ideological view is granted credibility. A fundamentalist perspective will exclude, virtually automatically, anything that relative to it appears 'liberal', anything that admits limitation, provisionality, otherness, openness or promotes change or novelty. But alongside this exclusivity there may be discerned, as a twelfth factor to fundamentalism, a form of inclusion, namely polity inclusion. This is the propensity to include, in respect of considerations of the policies and praxis, or social organization of a fundamentalist movement, all others that fall within its frame of reference and worldview. This may still appear innocuous, especially if the fundamentalists concerned are a minor or marginalized group relative to the wider society in which they exist, or where such an inclusivist stance finds a more benign setting within a normative or orthodox religious tradition. Excluding all other ideological variants and perspectives necessarily implies the wholesale inclusion of a society in terms of the outworking of polity considerations. It is at this juncture that the fundamentalist – for whom polity inclusiveness is a primary element – is poised to become activist, to act on this inclusivism in terms of polity, whether covertly (as in the Church of Jesus Christ of Latter Day Saints vicariously baptising the dead, for example) or overtly (as in the Taliban's insistence that everyone in Afghanistan live according to their application of Islam, and variations on this theme found currently in parts of Pakistan, Nigeria, the Islamic State and elsewhere). And in reference to war and violence within the biblical corpus, for instance, Mark Elliot examines the divine sanction to the Hebrews to cleanse the promised land of inhabitants in order to possess it (Deut. 7:1–4). He suggests that this may 'be read as contextual self-justification, or revelatory absolute sanction', in which case it has the potential to be universally applied.[33]

Feature 7 – Condemnatory stance

- Factors (xiii) *Judgemental Values* and (xiv) *Pietistic Tyranny*

Hard-line fundamentalism is distinguished by strident assertions of a condemnatory or judgemental sort such that their expression amounts to an instance of 'pietistic tyranny'. This is the expression of judgemental values that a hard-line assertive fundamentalism displays towards any who would dissent from within, or oppose from without. Inherent in this is often a deprecating attitude towards others, whether in regard to virtually any other (the world at large), or focused on specific others (particular groups or categories of people, such as Jews, blacks or gays). Such judgementalism can be found in the generalized sense of the Exclusive Brethren's dismissal of all outside its fold as 'worldlies', for example, or in the sweeping condemnation of Western society found within some expressions of contemporary Islamic rhetoric. It can also be found in a more targeted sense, as in variant forms of both political and religious fundamentalism that dehumanize opponents. Or in contemporary instances of Islamic antisemitic rhetoric with its deprecation of Israel. It is in the inward application of judgemental values – that is, applying such values for the purpose of control and censure within the fundamentalist's own community – that the factor of pietistic tyranny is clearly discerned. This is where fundamentalism shows itself to be truly hard-line and self-reflectively assertive. The faith-values it espouses – its 'piety' – then becomes, in effect, a tool of tyranny: newly won converts must cut themselves off from their family of origin (as with the Rev. Moon's Unification Church, for example); or members of the community must have no social intercourse with anyone not in fellowship with them (as with the Exclusive Brethren). The advocacy by a particular religious community that its members should have no truck with those of another community of the same faith-family, for instance, may give evidence of a pietistic tyranny in action. This is perhaps the case currently in respect of the Sunni and Shi'a divide in Iraq, as elsewhere in the Muslim world.

We have seen that all forms and expressions of religious fundamentalism begin with, or at least include, the sets of factors which denote the passive phase and that some religious groups or movements go beyond passive fundamentalism such that we may identify them as belonging to an assertive, or hard-line, phase. We look now at the third phase, that of impositional, or exclusivist, fundamentalism.

Phase III: Impositional fundamentalism

Once we come to the third and final phase we discover that what began, as it were, as something 'merely' fundamentalist is now transformed, or has evolved, into something of a distinctly radicalized or activist nature such that extreme actions, including violent behaviours and even terrorism, may be contemplated, advocated and engaged. The three features of this phase are identified as value application, explicit justification and enacted extremism. (See Table 4).

The details of this final and critical phase are as follows.

Feature 8 – Value application

- Factors: (xv) *Otherness Negated* and (xvi) *Self-Superiority Asserted*

At this juncture in the development of a fundamentalist's outlook, the sense of self-assertion and confidence is such that the values of fundamentalism are actively and intentionally applied impositionally. And these values are primarily two: the negation of otherness, or alterity as such, and the corresponding assertion of self-superiority over all opponents, real and putative. The negation of otherness is perhaps critical, for the scene set by the sixth set of factors – the contextualizing effect of exclusivism and inclusivism – together with that of the feature of condemnatory stance now emerge into a devaluing and dismissal of the 'otherness' as such, whether in terms of rival community or of competing alterities, ideological or otherwise. Indeed such alterities may be – and in fact often are – demonized. The religiously 'other' on this view is often cast as 'satanic', or at least seriously and significantly

Table 4 Phase III: Impositional fundamentalism

Feature 8: Value Application
   Factors: Otherness Negated – Self-Superiority Asserted
Feature 9: Explicit Justification
   Factors: Sanctioned Imposition – Legitimated Violence
Feature 10: Enacted Extremism
   Factors: Manifest Contempt – Terrorist Events

labelled as a hostile opponent, and so hostilely regarded. In the process of negating the other, the self is asserted as inherently superior. My God is greater than your God. My truth reigns over your ignorance. The authenticity of my faith contrasts with the feeble delusion you entertain. My laws express the divine reality directly which is infinitely superior to the laws which derive merely from human ideas. The salvation offered by my faith is the real thing by contrast to the lost way that you proclaim. And so we might go on. However expressed or referenced, it will be clear enough that the fundamentalist is applying negative value to 'otherness' as such, together with a corresponding assertion of self-superiority. The scene is now well set for the next feature – the rendering of an explicit justification not just for a viewpoint but also for actions premised on that viewpoint.

Feature 9 – Explicit justification

- Factors: (xvii) *Sanctioned Imposition* and (xviii) *Legitimated Violence*

It should be clear that, once the preceding sets of factors are in operation, it is but a short step to the penultimate pair that signals the expression of fundamentalism in some form of direct sociopolitical action. The notion that the very imposition of the fundamentalist's views and polity as being, in fact, sanctioned by a higher or greater authority, such as God, gives powerful motivating support to extremist behaviours. This factor undergirds the imposed requirement to be, live and do in accord with the fundamentalist's ideological dictates. And the higher sanctioning of the imposition of the fundamentalist's programme leads naturally to the next factor of this analysis: violence is now legitimated; a platform of justification is established, at least in the mind of the impositional activist fundamentalist. Sanctioned imposition and legitimated violence are the two sides of the chief coin of justification in the currency of extremism. We are now brought to the final feature of the sequential paradigm of fundamentalism – enacted extremism.

Feature 10 – Enacted extremism

- Factors: (xix) *Manifest Contempt* and (xx) *Terrorist Events*

There are two interrelated factors that comprise this final feature. On the one hand there may be a manifestation of contempt as an expression of negative judgements, or the negation of the 'other' instantiated in various contemptible behaviours – intimidation, coercion, violent and destructive actions directed at non-human symbolic targets (works of art, places of worship), and so on. The aim is to assert superiority, impose an ideology or enforce submission, but not necessarily inculcate terror as such, at least not on too grand a scale. On the other hand there is an extremism that apparently knows no bounds: the terrorizing and subjugation of a targeted populace is itself both means and end. For example, as we have seen in Afghanistan not so long ago, not only was it the case that all Muslims ought to submit naturally to Shari'a, but according to the fundamentalist ideals of the Taliban, all of society should be made to submit, like it or not, for impositional submission is an inherent element of its extreme application of an otherwise comparatively passive Islamic ideal (viz., the peaceful submission to God by way of living according to

God's law). Submission to the dictates of the fundamentalist is at this juncture a matter of necessary imposition, as Afghani women found to their cost. And the alternative to even an involuntary submission is outright destruction: hence, from the Taliban's extremist perspective, the Buddha 'idols' had to be destroyed. How else does the extremist ensure that the imposition that has been sanctioned can, in fact, be effected?

Terrorism, as a descriptor for extreme and violent behaviours, is by no means the sole province of fundamentalism. But it can be, and is, the end result of a fundamentalist ideological trajectory. This is the issue that we are faced with today, in both localized and globalized modalities. An absolutist perspective does not necessarily result in terrorist events: not all fundamentalists are terrorists. Yet, given a progressive ideological development as hypothesized in this paradigm analysis, it is arguably the case that religious fundamentalism may – as indeed we know that it does – produce terrorists. Fundamentalism is not simply a religious or even political option in terms of belief perspective. It is a package-deal phenomenon denoted by a sequence of factors whose cumulative impact once – or if – the final factor is reached, can be devastating. The Taliban, to return to this example of Islamic fundamentalist extremism, took an absolutist, inerrant and exclusivist line with respect to their religious identity and behaviour, which was extended to include all who were within their purview – namely, the inhabitants of Afghanistan. Actions taken to bring about their aims were deemed sanctioned by the highest authority – Allah (God) – and their extreme measures were in consequence deemed legitimated; their contempt of all who were different, or outside their 'world', was manifest and terrorizing activity was the modality of coercion and control. Thus no opposition was brooked; all had to submit and obey or face the consequences.

Conclusion

The fundamentalist paradigm of religious extremism is now complete. What began with 'normative' absolutism, that form of religious believing and concept that holds rigidly to a set of assumptions, presuppositions and ideas as absolute truth, then may evolve or emerge through a process of hardening assertion to becoming, in extremis, an impositional form of religious ideology that is expressed in terms of terrorizing behaviours and acts of violence. Many examples across different religions, both historically and contemporaneously, could be adduced to make the point. And the one key consequence of the absolutism expressed within this paradigm is the reality and impact of exclusivism. As we saw above, exclusivism is one of the key forms of response to diversity, both religious and other forms. It is the response of rejection and negation. It may be simply, in the context of a passive or normative fundamentalism, an item of expressed belief: a smug satisfaction that my belief is right, and yours is rejected as wrong. It may take on a more sinister tone when articulated in the context of an assertive fundamentalism as in a Christian pastor denouncing Islam as a false religion. It may emerge as an act of hate when, in the context of an impositional fundamentalism, the pastor organizes a Qur'an-burning event. What the fundamentalism paradigm has attempted to show is that there is a continuum of beliefs, values, attitudes and dispositions that range through passive, assertive and impositional modes of expression and enactment. It is not necessarily the case that an individual or group subscribing to a passive fundamentalist form of their faith will become an extremist or terrorist as such. But arguably, from the perspective of a religious ideology that drives extremism, most if not all such religious ideologues manifest an assertive and impositional form of fundamentalism, the content of which reflects their specific religious identity and orientation within which the extremism is grounded.

As we shall see through an examination of extremism in Judaism, Christianity and Islam, the dynamics of extremist ideologies and actions in all cases reflect closely the structure of the fundamentalist paradigm, for they all express a form of religious absolutism which, in turn, results in an exclusionary stance with respect to any 'other' deemed to be unacceptable or in some sense invalid. Thus Christianity, for centuries, had normativized an extreme ideological perspective with respect to Jews: they were the 'Christ killers'. And, similarly, Muslims have also for a long time been hostage to an extreme judgement against both Jews and Christians to the effect that their scriptures have been deliberately corrupted, hence only the Qur'an is the true word of God.

CHAPTER 4
TEXTS OF TERROR: SCRIPTURAL MOTIFS FOR EXTREMISM

It was the feminist biblical scholar Phyllis Trible, whose expository study of gender-oriented violence embedded within certain biblical narratives first coined, as far as I know, the arresting term 'texts of terror' to denote certain stories and passages of holy scripture.[1] I use this phrase here with a wider reference in mind – to point to the uncomfortable reality that the holy scriptures of the three religions contain not only stories of profound violence but also injunctions, commandments, allusions and examples – in short, an array of motifs – that result in providing a fund of scriptural resource for a range of terrifying and terrorizing behaviours. In short, the texts of terror in the Jewish and Christian bibles, and in Islam's Qur'an, range far wider than those addressed by Trible, and it is these that take our attention here. They provide ideological justification for extreme attitudes, values and actions. Furthermore, studies such as Trible's show up a key issue that we need to note. While these texts of terror undeniably exist, the extent to which they influence religious faith, beliefs and behaviours is a matter of how scriptural texts are read and the presuppositions about the nature of these texts as held by the reader(s). As we have seen, it is very much the fundamentalist forms of religion which are inclined to take the respective scriptural text at literal or face value on the assumption that that is how holy writ is meant to be taken. It is here where we see the import and impact of the analysis of fundamentalism and what is broadly in common to all three religions: a long-standing tradition of apparently 'literal' or 'factual' reading of the scriptures. In fact, they bring to bear a very specific hermeneutical lens.

However, each religion has indeed ever engaged other modes of 'reading' – that is, modes of interpretation – in order to get around some obvious problems associated with a purely 'literal' reading. The fundamentalist's lens is by no means the only one. A long-standing pattern in each of the three faiths is that of presuming there is a 'spiritual' meaning hidden within an otherwise 'literal' reading of the holy texts, especially given poetic and opaque passages. A spiritual reading has often been taken as the superior, even proper, mode of reading and so interpreting the holy text that is being read. This has led to a variety of more nuanced ways of reading and understanding religious texts, ways which tend to seek out symbolism or highlight metaphorical language and that wishes, in particular, to distinguish between the originating context of a text and its subsequent meaning and application in other contexts. In some cases this has resulted in regarding certain texts as effectively 'locked' within their context and so not to be taken 'literally' today. They provide meaning and understanding for events, beliefs and values as applicable in their original context. Often these problematic texts have been regarded as varyingly either superseded by other and later textual references, or otherwise constrained in their applicability by virtue of subsequent developments in wider relevant religious self-understanding or especially in respect of different and changed contexts into which the texts are read. So, for example, abrogation – whereby later Quranic recitations trump earlier ones where there is conflict or inconsistency – has long been employed within Islam. Hebrew texts which Christianity had incorporated into its own scriptural canon, have for centuries tended to be read through the lens of its own unique New Testament corpus and the worldview accompanying it. Rabbinic Judaism, which also emerged out of the same ancient Hebrew religious context as did Christianity, evolved a pacifist, even quiescent, reading of its biblical record which, until very recent times, successfully corralled problematic texts and their potential extreme and violent implications.

However, Jewish extremists today, for example, are reading such texts in a way that makes them freshly alive and empowering, thus enabling these texts to provide support for their particular brand of ideology and accompanying behaviours. And while it is true that there are Jews – such as the Orthodox – who likewise read their Bible from a perspective of naïve literalism, passive Jewish fundamentalism, which has enjoyed a long pedigree, has only relatively recently emerged into full-blown impositional extremism capable of sustaining an ideology of violent intervention. Similarly, forms of Christian fundamentalism that are likewise grounded in a fairly widely held conservative and naïve reading of scripture, with its tendency to take the Bible at face value, has had a history of ebb and flow with respect to what we would today call 'extremism', with contemporary expressions of it increasingly complex and murky, and disturbingly growing in prevalence. The purview of Christian extremism seems to be expanding. But for Islam, for which the naïve reading of the Qur'an is part and parcel of its normative tradition – both Sunni and Shi'a – the notion of there being a fundamentalist variant makes little sense. Islam, almost by definition, is passively fundamentalist. Nevertheless, like Christianity, it has produced epochs and occasions of relative 'extremism of the centre' but now clearly manifests more examples of intense exclusivist and impositional fundamentalism. For all three faiths a belief in the Absolute, taken to an extreme, can and does degenerate into an ideology of absolutism.

Furthermore, all these religions are grounded upon a belief in a divine reality (G-d; God, Allah) that has self-communicated by way of revelation – in which there are commands, laws, rules, injunctions as well as exemplary stories of varying kinds – mediated via a diverse literary heritage, including that of oral literature. The term 'bible' is from a Greek word that refers to a collection of books. Both the Jewish (Hebrew) and the Christian bibles are a compilation of many 'books' ranging over a wide variety of literary genres, including poetry, letter (epistle), history, prehistorical or mythic narrative (for some, still read as factual history), quasi-biographical and so forth. In Islam the literary range is leaner. This is because, while still a compilation, the revelatory text is composed of recorded utterances or 'recitations'. Accordingly, it is primarily poetic in terms of genre. The term Qur'an simply denotes a collection of recitations (Arabic: *iq'ra*) – which in this case was given by, or through, one individual over a course of some twenty years. As a collection of poetic utterances, it is the 'Holy' Qur'an in that the utterances are believed to have divine origination. Strictly speaking, Muhammad was but the mouthpiece of Allah, or God, who is the source of the orally recited, and only later textually recorded, utterances. These were initially committed to memory and so were able to be repeated or recalled. The act of oral recitation is still the primary mode of liturgical 'reading' of the Qur'an. It was only after the death of Muhammad, and then of those who had heard the utterances when first given and so were the primary sources of remembrance, that these poetic stanzas – a primary form of oral literature – were committed to a written form, initially still as a prompt to memory, as memory is the primary repository of oral literature.

The Qur'an, as written literature, preserves the original recitations and allows them to be transmitted through time and space. Thus future generations who had never heard them in their original oral form are able to receive them. Nevertheless, the evolution of the written Qur'an, as with the Jewish and Christian bibles, is something that developed and emerged over time. And while, by its very nature, the literary range is narrower than that of the Jewish and Christian bibles, it nevertheless shares with them the fact of a process of coming into being as written text subsequent to origins in literature. The task of this chapter is to dip into the scriptural tradition that threads through Judaism, Christianity and Islam in order to highlight key texts and motifs that lend support for the extremisms that arise within these faith communities.

Extremism and the Hebrew Bible

Lying behind much contemporary, as well as historical, expressions of extremism and acts of violence committed by Jews, and also Christians, is a clutch of texts, models and supportive paradigms that are found within the Hebrew biblical corpus. Some of this is echoed within the Qur'an and forms of Islamic extremism. We will return to the case of Islam, as well as the specifically Christian New Testament, shortly. In the meantime, the task at hand is to explore something of the main contours and contribution to extremism as found in the Hebrew Bible, which we note at this juncture is also a major portion of the Christian Bible (namely, the Old Testament). For the most part, the texts and examples that apply are those that advocate some form of extreme behaviour, or violent – even deadly – action, either on the basis of a purported direct command from God or in the belief that in so acting or behaving, the will of God is being carried out. God is perceived as being honoured and pleased by the action and its outcome. Throughout their respective histories, down to and including today, there have been Jews as well as Christians who profess a direct, literal and so naïve belief in the Bible as directly given divine text, absolute for all time, containing apodictic truth and instruction that leads necessarily to direct obedient action. For the most part such absolutism, whether understood as manifesting fundamentalism or some other variant of an otherwise highly proscribed religious worldview, regards biblical narrative as largely comprising reliable historical reportage.

However, within the world of biblical scholarship – both Jewish and Christian – it has been long regarded, within the modern era of critical scholarly endeavour at least and corroborated by many years of archaeological investigations, that such narratives are not a report of any factual historical reality as such. Indeed, as John Collins notes, such 'biblical texts are not historically reliable accounts of early Israelite history but ideological fictions from a much later time', although 'this scarcely relieves the moral problem posed by the biblical texts, which portray Israel as an aggressive, invading force impelled by divine commands'.[2] They may be fictive constructs, composed often in another time and location, but they were nevertheless written to convey meaning, insight and perspective – even some form of timeless truth. And such truth and meaning requires interpretive discernment. This is the task of exegesis and theological scholarship whose aim is to enable deeper reflection in order to both comprehend the context of the manifest extremism within the texts and also to discern ways of ameliorating, if not outright vitiating, their ideological impact – or not – as the case might be.

With respect to passages that dwell upon themes of violence or other forms of extreme behaviours and judgements, biblical narratives have been vitally significant for their contribution to the formation of ideological themes and for modelling values and behaviours believed to be in fulfilment of the divine will. That such narratives and their respective models of behaviour and sanctioning ideologies are believed to be unquestioningly true and valid is a factor that cannot be glossed over or ignored. The repeated telling of select narratives reinforces group identity and moral perspective; they are the source of continual inspiration, guidance and action. And within both Judaism and Christianity there are today many individuals and groups, both those more obviously ultra-right and fundamentalist, and those that sit within a wide spectrum of conservative orthodoxy, who regard themselves as the inheritors and, indeed, the only true bearers of this sacred legacy. For example, as we will see in the chapter on Jewish extremism, contemporary Zionism which arose initially as a secular political movement came to adopt the Hebrew Bible as its core reference, in the process recasting it as a religio-political and jingoistic national text in distinction to being a purely religious text. So read, the biblical texts – as the books of the Prophets, for example – are a corrective to and critique of the cultural and social norms of the day such that ancient actions recorded therein are taken as excusatory exemplars of extreme behaviours today. Similar readings of these texts in the context of highly conservative and right-wing Christian extremism in today's United States of America is doing much the same thing: God bless America.

One undeniably violent biblical motif found within the Hebrew scriptures (*Tanakh*) is that of sacrifice. Indeed, there are a number of examples 'that confront us with scenes of human sacrifice, many of them perceived by the narrator of the story to have been overtly commanded by God'.[3] On the one hand there are instances of ritual human sacrifices, on the other there are accounts of various killings and 'monstrous massacres'[4] to do with war. Some examples of the first include Abraham's preparation and preparedness to sacrifice Isaac (Gen. 22.10–13), the demands for the death of all 'firstborn' as found scattered throughout the book of Exodus and echoed in respect of the narrative of the baby Jesus within the Christian New Testament, and Jephthah's vow leading to killing his daughter (Judg. 11.30–31, 34–39). As for the killings and massacres in times of warfare, there is the example of Joshua's destruction of Jericho (Josh. 6.1–16, 20–21; 7.1, 24–26a); the Moabite king's killing – by way of a sacrificial burnt offering – of his eldest son, in order to win a war (2 Kgs 3.26–27); the assassination of King Eglon by Ehud (Judg. 3.16–25); the murder of Sisera by two women, Deborah and Jael (Judg. 4.6–7, 9b–10, 13–15a, 17a, 21–22); the account of Samson and the Philistines when revenge was meted out by way of burning alive the opposition (Judg. 15.4–8a); the narrative of David and Goliath (1 Sam. 17.12–18:2); the abuse of the corpses of Saul and his sons (1 Sam. 31.1–9a, 10–13) and the death of Jezebel (2 Kgs 9.30–35). Elsewhere God (Yahweh) makes himself known through terrifying actions (Ezek. 38.14–15a, 16, 19–23) and military preparations are called for by way of beating ploughshares into swords and pruning hooks into spears (Joel 3.9–10). This last is often overlooked in favour of the pacifist counter-text that advocates just the opposite (Isa. 2.4; Mic. 4.3).[5] And when Israel calls upon God in the fight against the Cushites, the Almighty comes to the aid of Israel and the Cushites are eliminated (2 Chron. 14.9–15). It is clear that these – and many other – biblical references provide a fund of support and potential inspiration to extremist and violent ideologies that wish to root themselves within the Bible. Even the earliest biblical narratives provide a model of Cain not so much as murderer as 'sacred executioner'.[6]

Another category of violence within the biblical corpus is one that, while suggestive of certain extreme views, is focused on interpersonal, and often sexual or gendered, contexts and situations. A case in point is the narrative concerning the rape of Dinah, found in Genesis Chapter 34.[7] Horowitz notes that Genesis, especially Chapter 34, rather like the book of Esther, is 'littered with fratricide, incest, treachery and rape'.[8] The narrative is not simply about the violation of a young woman but more particularly about the justifying of revenge which goes far beyond the *lex talionis* restriction to that of like for like. On the one hand the story has been used as a warning to young women – don't go off on your own to strange places; let this be a lesson to you! Here the responsibility for the entire event – rapine and slaughter – is laid upon the female victim in the story. But that is not the only interpretive reception. On the other hand, the story lends licence to justifying duplicitous acts in the 'right' cause: that of meting out vengeance for a dishonouring wrong committed. The family of the young Canaanite man who succumbed to his lust for Dinah seeks to make amends, even to turn a misfortune into mutual fortune, but this openness leads them to the vulnerable position that facilitates their being slaughtered at the hands of the avenging Hebrews. Deceit and dissimulation are the venerated means to the justifiable end of revenge for the sake of purity and honour. Yet again later Rabbinic traditions re-presented the narrative as a morality tale and warning – not just in respect of promoting an ideal of female restriction but also as a reminder of the potential for excessive response and, indeed, the folly of 'giving way to revenge'. And as one genteel Christian commentator, Mary Cornwallis, averred in 1817: while it is 'natural that ... brothers should keenly feel the injury and the disgrace brought upon the family ... intemperate rage generally leads to unlawful revenge'.[9] Nevertheless, it has been noted that against opposition 'to the lesson about keeping women safely at home, which united

Christian and Jewish exegetes, sympathy (and even praise) for the subsequent massacre perpetrated by Dinah's brothers was to be found only in Jewish sources'.[10]

Phyllis Trible has commented that such ancient 'tales of terror speak all too frighteningly of the present'.[11] The focus of Trible's investigation had to do with violence towards and abuse of females by males – including the case of Hagar (Gen. 16.1–16; 21.9–21) who as Abraham's concubine was 'used, abused, and rejected'; of Tamar (2 Sam. 13.1–22) the princess who was 'raped and discarded'; of an unnamed concubine recorded in Judges 19.1–30 who was 'raped, murdered, and dismembered'; and finally of 'the daughter of Jephthah (Judg. 11.29–40), a virgin slain and sacrificed'.[12] Nevertheless, her observation has wider applicability and continued relevance. The purview of biblical extremism is broad, as are the ideologies that have sprung from it. To be sure, the Hebrew Bible / Old Testament 'provides a rich source of anti-violent themes, humanist ideals, and descriptions of idyllic peace and justice'.[13] But also, in common with other texts from the religions of the Ancient Near East, it is 'a remarkably militant text that includes an extraordinary range of aggressive themes and models, often confusing and contradictory'.[14] The image – and so the reality – of God seems saturated with violence. The treatment meted out to any portion of humanity deemed unworthy, together with rules setting out means of social control and even, at points, the specific demands of worship and obedience appear to bear this out. And in terms of the narratives of the Israelites, the preponderance of war, genocide and many internal conflicts together with apocalyptic prophecies constitute further indicators of a thread of violent extremism that, even in being assessed as extreme, is by no means marginal. Rather, such extremism is suggestive of a form of religiosity that, at times at least, may even be quite central and 'normalized'. Aran and Hassner, for example, note that as the image of the divine provides 'a model for human emulation (*imitatio dei*)', the inherent violence of the ancient Hebrew image of God has particular significance:

> The Hebrew God is a Lord of Hosts, vengeful and militant. He ruthlessly kills individuals, annihilates groups, and punishes humanity with plagues, brutal wars, and natural disasters. He also commands killing on a chauvinist basis: His chosen people are instructed to implement his fury against inferior peoples that are accursed from the moment of their inception, like the Ishmaelites, Moabites, Ammonites, and Edomites.[15]

On the basis of an *imitatio dei*, the perception of God as wrathful and prone to violence in order to achieve divine ends has huge import for both Christian and Jewish Bible-based extremism, as we will see below. Indeed, this God 'commands others to do violence on his behalf ... (and) ... his exemplar permits, or even requires, mimetic violence' and furthermore, this violence 'committed in the name of God and in emulation of God can absolve the perpetrator of agency and responsibility'.[16]

It is not only commands and prescriptions that lend a sense of violent extremism as 'normal' within the Bible. There are also many narratives of destruction and death that figure in the course of the history of the people of Israel – the so-called 'Chosen

People of God'. Thus, for example, the Exodus from Egypt commences with an Egyptian genocide targeting the Israelites then features the retaliatory killing of a violent Egyptian by Moses. This destructive act is a turning point and it culminates in the ten plagues that include a genocide against the Egyptians. The narrative ends in the drowning of the Pharaoh's army in the Red Sea – and the Children of Israel rejoice. The conquest of Canaan, the destruction of Jericho, the defeat and enslavement of 'foreign' peoples such as the Gibeonites and the Amorites, and much else besides, is accompanied by direct intervention from God. A series of campaigns conducted against rival or neighbouring peoples – the Aramites, Moabites, Midianites, Amalekites, Ammonites and the Philistines in particular – only serves to underscore and extend the reign of Hebrew terror in the name of God (to borrow Juergensmeyer's phrase).

On the one hand there was, as depicted in the scriptures, warring struggle against other peoples – the diversity of the day – which took place 'in the context of an existential struggle ... confined to a particular time and space', and thereby manifesting sheer hostility towards such peoples.[17] Depending on how they are read, such texts can be taken as inviting the contemporary reliving and re-implementation of a 'ruthless enmity in every passing generation, as epitomized in the commandment to "Remember what Amalek did unto thee" (Deut. 25.17)'.[18] But on the other hand, as well as the context of territorial struggle, there was also a religious struggle taking place to assert the supremacy of 'their' God over all other gods, lest the attraction of foreign gods lead the people of Israel astray and into idolatry. So, for example, the biblical text records the Prophet Elijah bringing about, by divine aid, the slaughter of some 400 priests of the god Ba'al. Violence, destruction and death is, however, a two-way street as recorded within the Hebrew Bible. The litany of violence conducted by the Hebrew peoples of the ancient period seems as long and severe as their own sufferings endured at the hands of others. It has been wryly noted that even while in exile, 'Jews suffer and commit violence, as described in the Book of Esther'.[19] But perhaps the most pernicious motif of extremism in the Hebrew biblical corpus is the line of injunction promoting an ethno-religious purity by way of commanding the elimination of that which threatens this purity. It lies at the ideological root of Jewish separatism and accompanying ideologies of Jewish exclusivism. It is known as the 'ban' (Hebrew: *herem*).

The Ban: Ethno-religious purity extremism

The eliminative 'ban' (*herem*) associated with the Ancient Hebrew concept of God and divine injunctions to violence was 'the practice whereby the defeated enemy was devoted to destruction'.[20] The action of eradicating a vanquished opponent was by no means unique to Israel, although neither was it widely attested – though it was certainly known and practiced in the wider Middle East context. Victims destined for elimination were 'offered' to the god of whoever was the victor, with the slaughter having 'a sacrificial character'.[21] Biblical references include the destruction of the Amalekites (1 Sam. 15.3); the vow to utterly rout and eliminate the Canaanites (Num. 21.1–3); and the vow of Jephthah to destroy the Ammonites (Judg. 11.31). And there are examples where it would appear that God commanded or requested such eliminative 'offerings' with the implication – which then becomes a source of later emergence of extremist ideologies – that the destruction of the damned 'other' is indeed pleasing to God. God wants the eradication and will reward the eradicator accordingly.

Most biblical passages that refer to the ban are in the book of Deuteronomy. By and large the text of Deuteronomy 'seeks to rationalize the practice by justifying it'.[22] The sacrificial dimension of such acts of destructive elimination is endorsed. Not only is a rival removed but also 'ethnic cleansing is the way to ensure cultic purity';[23] group identity as a specific people with a specific god is ensured. Yet, paradoxically, Deuteronomy 'repeatedly tells the Israelites to be compassionate to slaves and aliens'.[24] It would seem that both eliminating a putatively threatening opposition and being magnanimous towards the weak are not incommensurate values within the biblical context. And, indeed, over time the instances and models of Ancient Hebrew ritualized cultic practices of human – including child – sacrifice (cf. Abraham's willingness to sacrifice his son) gradually fade out and are challenged and replaced by the rising prophetic tradition that places stress on ethical relations rather than cultic practices. Nevertheless, the models of the ban remain embedded in scripture and so available for incorporation into a putative Bible-based extremism. That said, there is another dimension that needs to be noted, namely that in terms of academic investigation and analysis of texts and their reception there is wide consensus that such 'texts are not naïve reflections of primitive practice, but programmatic ideological statements from the late seventh century BCE or later'.[25] Nevertheless, the problem remains that the biblical texts do narrate a divine commendation of the destruction of the negated 'other' as, in effect, 'a model of the ways in which Israel should relate to its neighbors'.[26] Indeed, as Collins remarks, 'the moral problem posed by the biblical texts, which portray Israel as an aggressive, invading force impelled by divine commands' remains.[27] But there is one other model that has proved deeply appealing to both Jewish and Christian extremists, that of the priest Phineas and his act of sheer zealotry, to which we now turn.

Zealotry: The model of the priest Phineas

In the biblical book of Numbers, Chapter 25, there is an account of an impulsive murderous act carried out by a temple priest named Phineas (also: Phinehas). The grandson of the famed Hebrew priest Aaron, he killed an Israelite man and a Midianite woman while they were having intercourse in the Tabernacle precincts, by running them through with a spear. However, while this is a bare outline of the event, there is a wider context in which it is set and which is important to understand. At the time, on the way to Canaan following the exodus from Egypt, the Israelites had made camp in the Moab desert prior to crossing the Jordan River. During this pause the Israelites had begun to resile from belief in and fidelity to their God, instead turning their devotional attention to a pagan deity. Such development is idolatrous in the context of an exclusive religious identity, for the source of idolatry is in 'imitating the cult of foreign peoples' and, as such, is 'regarded as a capital offense' that in turn means 'the people are threatened with annihilation'.[28] The obvious implication is that, in order to remain religiously, if not also ethnically 'pure', the seductively attractive other is required to be annihilated. The threat of succumbing to idolatry, or the distraction of it, needs to be removed. So far, this seems another instance of the ban.

At the same time as they were sliding into idolatrous behaviours, Israelite men engaged in illicit sexual relations by turning from their own women and taking up with Midianite women. Thus, the anger of God was kindled against the Israelites for they enacted a twofold affront to the covenantal relationship that lay at the heart of Hebrew life and identity. Indeed, according to the wider narrative, God commanded Moses to hang the sinning Israelites. But Moses did not wish to precipitate direct confrontation with a people growing more fractious and so obviously losing their way in terms of religious fidelity and moral sensibility. To make matters worse, a prominent Israelite directly challenged the then tradition of obedience to the way of God, and to the covenantal faithfulness, that had led the people thus far. He brought his Moabite woman into the camp and engaged in sex with her in close proximity to the Tabernacle – the sacred tent that contained the Ark of the Covenant which the people had carried with them on their Exodus journey. This was a very public act of blasphemy, an affront to both the sacred law and the authoritative leadership of the people of Israel. The divine response to this was to punish the Israelite people as a whole with a deadly plague. Thousands are reported to have died. But the leaders – that is, Moses and the judges – neither intervened to prevent the original scandal nor did they act to punish the offender. Instead, Phineas took the initiative to bring about a resolution that assuaged the affront and relieved the plague. For, in acting out of true belief and in honour for the integrity of divine law and person, the impulsive killing of the couple is recorded as having appeased, and pleased, God. Indeed, this zealous act was rewarded by being denoted the divine 'covenant of peace' and it guaranteed high priesthood both for Phineas himself and his descendants. Thus the biblical narrative records Phineas as being commended by God for having prevented Israel's fall to idolatrous practices brought in by Midianite women, as well as putting a halt to the desecration of God's sanctuary.

The action of Phineas, and the apparent divine post facto sanction, amounts to a very specific biblical paradigm of violent extremism, a paradigm that has resonated and supported violent extremists within both Judaism and Christianity, as we will see below. Furthermore, as it is a relatively detailed presentation, it enables 'the subtleties and ironies of the status of violence in Jewish tradition' to be seen.[29] This biblical precedent highlights the meaning of zealotry as 'religious violence aimed against those who are perceived to be opposing the divine will, particularly by violating the boundaries of the collectivity and thus threatening its identity'.[30] Phineas's act of zealotry has ever since posed a model and ideal of what it means to be religiously virtuous within a context of personal monotheism – belief in one God with whom there is a moral relationship: 'Bible believers can hardly stay indifferent to the grandness of Phinehas; the faithful cannot simply relegate to the margins the obligatory potency of the incident in Numbers 25'.[31] Yet, of course, even this text can be read in many different ways – including a counter-reading that, rather like the account of the rape of Dinah and consequent revenge meted out, makes of it a cautionary morality tale: you should neither provoke nor succumb to being provoked. As ever, interpretation of text and context is the key, and extremists will bring to the text their particular reading. We will return to the impact of this biblical paradigm when examining both Jewish and Christian extremism. But for the moment we need to take some account of the motifs of and for extremism that may be found in Christian and Muslim scriptures.

Extremism in the New Testament and the Qur'an

Keith Ward identifies two general attitudes to ancient biblical texts that have to do with value judgements or behavioural instruction, namely that either they may be regarded as 'examples of primitive moral attitudes, projected onto an imagined past, which were very rarely if ever put into practice, and are now totally obsolete' or else 'that God really did give such a command, but only to people who were morally primitive and in the unique circumstance of the conquest of Canaan' and in which case they belong to that epoch and so have no direct applicability today.[32] However, he also notes a third option, namely that such texts express 'some perceptions of the divine will' and in consequence, with respect to devotees, 'a will for total devotion to God'.[33] Moreover, there is much biblical evidence suggesting that the will of God is concerned more with justice, respect and concern for others, including even one's enemies. This evidence reflects perspectives and values that the later prophetic tradition within the Hebrew scriptures tends to emphasize and promote. It is a counter to the texts favoured by extremists.

Thus far I have focused on Hebrew scriptural examples. For the most part, they can apply also to Christianity. To be sure, texts of terror are not perhaps as obvious in the Christians' New Testament as they are in the Hebrew Bible – which, together with additional (Apocrypha) material, is incorporated into the full Christian Bible. Hence Christian extremism draws its biblical motifs largely from the same source as do Jewish extremists. But violence is not unknown within the New Testament (NT). There are some NT texts that lend themselves to extremist interpretations and in recent times these have begun to be examined and critiqued. One attempt at redressing the often-found bias towards the Hebrew scriptures as being the source of all violence – thereby often presuming to exempt the later Christian texts – explores elements of extremism in regard, for example, to 'the Apostle Paul's violent desires' or 'the Gospel of Matthew's depiction of tortured slaves' and 'the fiery and forceful Son of God sitting in judgment in Revelation'.[34] One sequence of studies focuses on a set of 'specific textual complexes' that 'consider a broad range of violent depictions and exhortations, including pronouncements that God condemns nonbelievers to a fiery hell, accounts of Jesus engaged in battle with demons, and Paul's desire to castrate his Galatian opponents'.[35] The relationship of text and reality, and of narrative and history, are questioned 'in the face of the embedded memories of Christian innocence and Jewish culpability forged on the multiple New Testament depictions of Jesus and his followers as victims of violence, and other Jews as agents of that violence'.[36] Such studies raise the issue of the formation of hostile depictions of the 'other' in the narrative construction of identities of distinction and difference, and the relation of these to the formation of religious identity qua 'narrative belonging', an element within the fundamentalist paradigm that is by no means reserved for that paradigm, since arguably all religious identity – and so ideology – is a function of such belonging.

J. Harold Ellens has explored the motif of the 'violent Jesus' that can be derived from the gospel narratives as, for instance, with the cleansing of the Temple episode and the comment about dividing families: 'Do not think that I have come to bring peace on earth; I have come not to bring peace, but a sword' (Mt. 10.34). Ellens avers that in the attempt 'to understand the nature of religious dynamics in human life, too little attention has been given to the manner in which the narratives of our sacred scriptures and the metaphors they generate shape our unconscious motives and goals'.[37] And Perry Schmidt-Leukel notes that 'the dominant line in both the Hebrew Bible and the New Testament consists of texts and verses that display exclusivist claims in relation to the religious other'.[38] Whereas it is the Hebrew scriptures that have produced the most dramatic stories and clear-cut models for later religious extremists – both Jewish and Christian – to utilize, there are but a very few that similarly register in the New Testament. But in both scriptures the underlying subtle and not-so-subtle messages of exclusivity – of positing one religious identity as wholly right, and all others as deficient, even false and to be accordingly disparaged, deprecated and denied – have played a major role in shaping not only normative orthodox identities and beliefs, but also granting substance to the claims of extremist positions. What this serves to highlight is that, as I have argued above, religious extremism is an extremism of a specific religion. Such extremism draws its ideology from the fund of existing beliefs, suppositions and value orientations of the religion in relation to which it is extreme. And while Jewish religious extremists draw from tropes found in the Hebrew Bible, Christian extremism draws both on those same tropes plus a fund of suggestive ideas and motifs that are given in the New Testament. The NT is compiled of writings that were themselves produced over a period of about a century following the death of Jesus. Within this corpus there are indications concerning early Christian attitudes towards, and beliefs about, those who believe differently or who have a wholly different religious identity – in other words, religious 'others'. Extremism as a rule involves a very particular element of 'othering' that which is problematically, if not also in some sense threateningly, different. There are NT texts that point to an embracing inclusion of others, and texts that indicate the rejection of otherness on the grounds of a stark exclusionary position. In this latter regard, examples can be seen

> in the Gospel of John where Jesus appears as the only way to 'the father' (John 14:6–7) and where 'the Jews', because of their rejection of Jesus, are collectively blamed as those who don't know God (John 7:28; 15:21; 16:3) and are sons of the devil (John 8:44), or in Matthew … with the collective blaming of the Jewish people for the murder of their Messiah: 'His blood will be on us and our children!' (Matt. 27:25)[39]

Christian 'othering' of Jews was the first, and so the archetypical, expression of an exclusionary rejection. Coupled with exclusive claims concerning salvation, and even the access to relationship with God (cf. Acts 4.12), this 'othering' laid the basis for contemporary Christian extremism, as we will see below. Christian extremism in respect of Jews is antisemitism and lead to the horror of the Holocaust in the mid-twentieth century. However, heretical Christians were, for centuries, subject to extreme measures of rejection and even violent death. And reference for this action is found in a text such as the Second letter of Peter where, in respect of such Christians deemed to be a threatening 'other' to the life of pure faith, they are regarded as being like 'irrational animals ... to be caught and killed' (2 Pet. 2.12). And so a warrant is given – and not the only one – to the legacy of a dominant Christianity damning those who are different.[40]

Within Islam the sanctioning of violence is principally with regard to the defence of 'the faith and the community (Ummah), and not for the terrorising of innocents'.[41] This is not unlike the strictures of Just War theory and practice that have applied, at least in principle, to modern secular states with a Judeo-Christian heritage. For Muslims, however the Qur'an gives a clear injunction: 'Fight in the cause of God those who fight you. But do not transgress limits; for God loveth not transgressors' (Sura 2:190).[42] Nevertheless, as with Jewish and Christian scriptural texts, the Qur'an contains mixed, even contradictory, messages. Whereas verses coming from the early Meccan period of Muhammad's prophetic utterances took a line of tolerant persuasion with respect to religious 'others', especially Jews and Christians, such verses are traditionally deemed to have been repealed or supplanted by verses of derogation and compulsion such that the religious 'other' is viewed with caution if not outright hostility as a result. The seedbed for jihadist extremism towards non-Muslim 'others' was thus laid as the normative tradition of Quranic commentary consolidated. Thus, for instance, as a result of changes to Muhammad's attitude towards Jews and Christians consequent upon his move from Mecca to Medina, and the developments that occurred there, including further revelatory utterances, the Qur'an emerged as combining 'a contradictory mixture of the peaceable and the bellicose'.[43] Furthermore, according to contemporary strict Muslim viewpoints, on account of 'the rule of abrogation (*naskh*), it is the harsher and more violent Medinan passages that apply today because they are later, while the earlier conciliatory passages dating from Muhammad's days in Mecca are not applicable'.[44]

To be sure, the Qur'an contains peaceable, conciliatory and balanced or otherwise 'open to the other' verses such as: 'Those who believe (in the Qur'an), and those who follow Jewish (scriptures), and the Christians and the Sabians – any who believe in God and the Last Day, and work righteousness, shall have their reward with their Lord: on them shall be no fear, nor shall they grieve' (Sura 2.62), and with respect to Muslims being subject to attempts by 'a number of the People of the Book' to renounce Islam, the scriptural advice is: 'But forgive and overlook, 'till God accomplish His purpose; for God hath power over all things' (Sura 2.109). Sura 2, *al-Baqara*, is an early Medinan revelation that gives a comprehensive summation of the overall teaching of the Qur'an. It is thus a primary Quranic source for understanding Islam as such, and arguably a point of hermeneutical reference that counters a crude or strict application of the doctrine of abrogation – but that is a matter for Muslim exegetes to determine. Of interest here is that throughout this Sura there are verses that assert the superiority of the way of Islam over that of both Jews and Christians and, indeed, assert the propriety of defensive fighting for the faith – although within limits, as for example the clear command of Sura 2.190 (given above). Yet this is immediately followed by a verse, also decisive, thorough and with justification given that seems to urge no limits: 'And slay them wherever ye catch them, and turn them out from where they have turned you out; for tumult and oppression are worse than slaughter; But fight them not at the Sacred Mosque, unless they (first) fight you there; but if they fight you, slay them, such is the reward of those who suppress faith' (Sura 2.191; cf. Sura 8.39).[45]

As with examples from the Hebrew biblical corpus, if such texts are taken as universal injunctions they become contemporary texts of terror. It is not hard to see how a hard-line assertive Islamic view would apply such a text today – effectively literally – to the context of tensions with Israel, for example, and in particular with respect to Jerusalem. Traditionally, for Islam, Jerusalem is the third holiest city after Mecca and Medina. Other Quranic passages which tend to favour militancy, and so, when taken in isolation from the wider tradition of both the Qur'an itself (which references mercy and peace far more often) and of Quranic commentary and accompanying consensus of interpretative options, become fodder for hard-line and extreme Islamic ideologies, include verses that speak of non-Muslims, including Jews, Christians and Pagans, as the enemies of Muslims (e.g. Sura 5.54 & 85). Yet the Qur'an considers Jews and Pagans as worse than Christians, for 'amongst these [the Christians] are men devoted to learning and men who have renounced the world, and they are not arrogant'.[46] The eschatological goal of Islamic domination, beloved of some Islamists and certainly of many who damn and reject Islam, is given expression in Sura 2.193 – 'And fight them on until there is no more tumult or oppression, and there prevail justice and faith in God'. However, this verse goes on to admonish: 'But if they cease, let there be no hostility except to those who practice oppression'. So, is an expectation of triumphant domination a necessary line of interpretation?

Perhaps one of the most problematic verses is that known as the 'sword verse' (Sura 9.5) which ostensibly commands Muslims to fight anyone who refuses to convert; but if they do convert, then mercy is to be shown: 'Fight and slay the pagans wherever ye find them, and seize them, and beleaguer them, and lie in wait for them in every stratagem (of war); But if they repent, and establish regular prayers and practise regular charity, then open the way for them; for God is oft-forgiving, Most Merciful'. However, as we will see when discussing Christian extremism, the sentiment and dynamic of this sura is directly paralleled in the extremism of the Spanish Inquisition: the religious other, if not willing to submit and convert, was banished or tortured and killed; and certainly 'backsliders' – those who showed themselves to be manifestly 'not regular' as referred to in the sura, were excoriated and, most often, executed. A range of other Quranic texts exhort the divine approval of the way of fighting, despite evident reluctance (cf. Sura 2.216). Others advocate asserting superiority and subjugating those who pay the *jizya* (poll-tax), primarily Jews and

Christians who live within an Islamic realm as *dhimmis* (Sura 9.29). Yet others assert that unbelievers must not, and will not, get the better of the believers (Muslims), and indeed Muslims are enjoined 'to strike terror' against them with the promise of divine reward for effort spent in so doing (Sura 8.59–60). This finds echo in Sura 4.74–77, with the addition of labelling the opponents of Islam as the 'friends of Satan' – a motif which is echoed in Sura 9.73 and repeated in Sura 66.9: 'O Prophet! Strive hard against the Unbelievers and the Hypocrites, and be firm against them, their abode is in Hell – an evil refuge indeed.' Such verses as these, together with many that extol a generic struggle in the cause of God – which can be open to many interpretations – form a fund of motif, image and injunction which can be lifted out of context, or applied within a different, new, context, so lending scriptural support to Islamic ideologies of extremism.

Conclusion

Scriptures can be both positively and negatively inspirational. An apparent positive text can have 'a dangerous subtext or underside that has been ignored' and narratives normally positively regarded can evince a 'shadow side'.[47] We have seen how there are texts that provide models, tropes and motifs for religious violence and allied extreme behaviours and attitudes. The role and model of the ancient Hebrew zealot Phineas provides a source for lone-wolf extremists across all three religious traditions that we are here concerned with. There are multiple hermeneutical perspectives that can be applied to biblical texts and so to the ideologies of violence that they spawn. Yet the fact remains, as Collins points out, that the Bible 'has contributed to violence in the world precisely because it has been taken to confer a degree of certitude that transcends human discussion and argumentation'.[48] He goes on to suggest that 'perhaps the most constructive thing a biblical critic can do toward lessening the contribution ... is to show that such certitude is an illusion'.[49] Elsewhere, Collins helpfully points out that

> most of the biblical endorsements of violent human action are set in the context of early Israel, even if they were written later ... In the literature of the Second Temple period, however, the focus is often on the future rather than the past. The late prophetic and apocalyptic literature is not necessarily less violent in its rhetoric than Deuteronomy or Joshua, but it has less emphasis on human action and more of the expectation of the eschatological judgement of God.[50]

By contrast, the apocalyptic literature of the Hellenistic and Roman periods tends to promote faithful waiting for divine intervention, and a new factor is introduced: the hope of resurrection. In such a new religious belief and worldview context, 'martyrdom becomes an option, because the reward of the righteous is not in this world but in heaven'.[51] Collins makes a further critical point:

Both Deuteronomy and the apocalypses fashion identity by constructing absolute, incompatible, contrasts. In the older literature, the contrast is ethnic and religious, but regional. In the apocalypses, it takes the form of cosmic dualism. In both cases, the absoluteness of the categories is guaranteed by divine revelation, and therefore not subject to negotiation or compromise. Herein lies the root of religious violence in the Jewish and Christian traditions.[52]

It is scriptural texts, and their interpretation, that provide a source of ideological succour for religious extremism. Collin's observation is particularly pertinent in respect of Jewish and Christian extremism, to which we now turn.

CHAPTER 5
THE JEWISH EXPERIENCE OF EXTREMISM

In April 1978 an Orthodox reserve soldier, Israel Lederman, shot and killed a Palestinian at close range. There was no provocation and, indeed, the victim was randomly chosen. Lederman simply hated Palestinians as inherent enemies of God and of the Jews. He acted an elimination of this negatively construed 'other'. Following a term in prison, Lederman later threw boiling tea on a left-wing Israeli Jewish MP. His rejection of a despised 'other' was extended to those of his own kind perceived as sympathizers of the 'other'. A few years later, in February 1982, Yehuda Richter, an American-born Orthodox settler ambushed a busload of Palestinians on the West Bank 'in an effort to stop the Israeli withdrawal from the Sinai as stipulated in the peace accord between Egypt and Israel'.[1] Previously Richter had attempted an arson attack on the offices of a Palestinian newspaper and in April 1982, along with several comrades, he protested the evacuation of the Sinai by threatening to commit suicide. Then in February 1983, Israeli society experienced an event of lethal Jewish violence directed at a group of fellow-Jews. Yona Avrushmi, a young Jerusalem resident, attacked a 'Peace Now' rally protesting Israel's involvement in the First Lebanon War. Regarding his victims as Jewish traitors, Avrushmi killed one and wounded nine others with a hand-grenade attack. He was sentenced to life imprisonment. In May 1990 a former Israeli Defence Force soldier, one who had been dishonourably discharged, acted as a lone-wolf terrorist by executing seven Palestinian day labourers who were waiting at a bus station. Dressed in an IDF uniform, and carrying an M16 assault rifle, the former soldier, having confirmed their Arab identities, simply lined them up and shot them. This act provoked riots in the West Bank, resulting in further seven Palestinian deaths. The former soldier claimed that his actions were intended to avenge the Intifada, as well as to assuage personal humiliation felt by Jews. A few years later, in April 1995, Michal Hilel in the company of two friends, all right-wing extremists, murdered a Palestinian taxi driver. At the time Hilel was pursuing the route of becoming a pious Jew. His terrorist act was born of right-wing political and religious extremism.

On another occasion, in May 2003, four religiously orthodox (*Halakha*-focused) Jewish settlers were arrested while endeavouring to booby-trap an East Jerusalem Palestinian girls' school. Eventually known as the Bat Ayin Underground, the group was linked to a series of terrorist acts during 2001 and 2002 which resulted in the deaths of eight Palestinians. Then in August 2005, Eden Natan-Zada, a soldier who was recorded as 'Absent without Leave' boarded a bus in the Israeli–Arab city of Shefar'am. Armed with an assault rifle he shot into the bus, killing four and wounding eight others. He was promptly and summarily lynched by a mob from the nearby town. Significantly, at the time of the attack he was, like Hilel, undergoing a process of *hazara betshuva*, that is, becoming an observant and pious Jew. Once again, fundamentalist orthodox religious sensibilities were closely connected to violent extremist acts. And in October 2009, an American-born settler, Yaakov 'Jack' Teitel, was arrested, then convicted on a variety of terrorist charges that spanned some twelve years. At the time of his arrest, he had a considerable weapons arsenal. His terrorist activities included the murder of two Palestinians in 1997, the booby-trapping of the home of a renowned Jewish liberal intellectual, 'and seriously wounding a follower of the Christian "Messianic Judaism" movement by means of an explosive package'.[2]

Such religiously motivated terrorist events as outlined above would appear to represent a comparatively new mood of Jewish extremism. As Aran and Hassner rightly note, there is a particular context to be taken into account, one which pitches Jewish extremism (*Gush Emunim*) and Muslim extremism (*Hamas*) as in effect interdependent mutual reactionary movements. In this regard,

> Jewish violence cannot be understood outside the context of the Arab–Israeli conflict, in which Israelis were both acting and reacting. Moreover, Jewish religious violence is confronted by a Muslim counterpart. Hamas and Gush Emunim are not merely in direct conflict but also share an implicit dialogue and a certain interdependence. The protagonists engage not only where Israeli settlements abut Palestinian settlements but also at sacred sites, where their conflict takes on a far more profound and blatant religious dimension. This is especially so at holy places claimed by both religions, particularly when these are located in politically contested areas.[3]

Nevertheless, it remains a fact that all the perpetrators were, indeed, religiously observant Orthodox Jews. Furthermore, a considerable portion was associated to some degree with the yeshiva (Jewish seminary) world, and many were characterized by forms of 'super-religiosity' although they comprised only a relatively small minority of Israelis.[4] Yet, significantly, none of these acts of Jewish violence were perpetrated by non-Orthodox Jews. However, many that were not born Orthodox were either 'born-again' Jews (*hozrim betshuva*) or in process of becoming 'observant' (i.e., strict Orthodox) Jews.[5] In other words, when identifying the type of Orthodox Judaism that is most frequently associated with Jewish religious extremism, we are talking about a particular form of Jewish religious fundamentalism. For instance, in their detailed study of Jewish fundamentalism, Heilman and Friedman identify the so-called 'ultra-Orthodox' Jews, or *haredim* – those who are even more strict than the strictures of Orthodoxy and who 'in many cases distinguish themselves not only from non-Jews but also from most of their coreligionists' – as the 'real' (assertive, even impositional) Jewish fundamentalists, indeed extremely so: 'These Jews believe in the *fundamental* truths of their religion which they assume is unchanging'.[6]

Jewish religious violence associated with this fundamentalism is a relatively recent phenomenon. Its genesis lies in the interconnected events of the 1967 Arab–Israeli

War and the emergence in Israel of a 'new form of Religious-Zionism epitomized by Gush Emunim (the Block of the Faithful), an orthodoxy that tends to religious as well as political radicalism'.[7] The first led to the consequence of occupying territories previously in the hands of Palestinians and the accompanying claims to annexation as a result of conquest; the second abetted this process by the active promotion of Jewish settlement. In an echo of the ancient biblical 'ban', the vanquished are metaphorically, if not really, eliminated from their possession of territory that, while conquered militarily, is regarded religiously as belonging to Israel by divine right. This was and is reinforced by the rise in religiosity as exemplified by the Gush Emunim, whose members 'exhibit stringency in studying and observing the commandments of the Torah while also pursuing expansionist and militant attitudes. They are the champions of the Whole Land of Israel policy, suffused with a messianic spirit'.[8]

As the examples cited above demonstrate, for the most part, Jewish religious violence today largely 'appears in connection with Israeli settlement policy in the West Bank and with efforts to promote a Greater Land of Israel agenda'.[9] As Selengut points out, 'Jewish messianic settlers in the West Bank believe that the whole of the Biblical Land of Israel is a Jewish promised land bequeathed to Jews for eternity'.[10] It was his willingness to cede sectors of this land that led the assassination of Prime Minister Yitzhak Rabin (more on which below). It is not any economic value to the land which signifies its importance to the Jewish settlers on it, rather the reclaiming of it as 'sacred territory'. However, Muslims hold a similar claim: 'In the traditional and orthodox Muslim view, Palestine and its holy sites are part of Dar al-Islam, Muslim territory never to be ceded to non-Muslims'.[11] In this case it is quite clear. It is religious ideology that drives both Jewish and Muslim extremism in relation to the West Bank – an example of what we discuss below as mutual extremism (see Chapter 8). Thus the 'conflict and violence is not over territory or economics but about sacred visions and eschatological expectations'.[12]

Furthermore, the most extreme case of anti-Jewish violence ever experienced by Jews themselves, the European Holocaust (*Shoah*) of the twentieth century, cannot be underestimated as an underlying context to the nature and drivers of contemporary Jewish extremism. This is not to offer any sort of excuse for acts of Jewish extremism as such, rather to highlight this factor which not only plays a large role in wider Jewish perceptions and perspectives but is also grist to the mill of extremist Jewish rhetoric and rationalizing ideologies. As such, it sits alongside the biblical material examined above and in particular the model of zealotry found in the story of Phineas. There is also an ongoing messianic motif and an allied complex pattern of the interpretation and reinterpretation of such models and motifs that play a major part. These involve not only changing patterns of biblical interpretation but also developments related to post-biblical history and violence. For following nearly two millennia of, on the whole, Jewish pacifism and political quietism, a radical change has taken place with the emergence of the modern Zionist movement and, since the early 1970s, a further shift wherein 'this secular brand of Jewish violence was overshadowed by a new brand of Jewish religious violence'.[13]

Israel is the first of two modern nation states founded on the basis of providing a homeland to an otherwise disenfranchised religious community. The other is Muslim

Religion and Extremism

Pakistan. Although structured as a democracy, religion is ever-present in the public sphere: 'Not only are nationalism and religion interlocked in Judaism but in Israel religion and state are inseparable'.[14] Biblical language, motifs and imagery suffuse public discourse and provide a prime referent for extreme Jewish ideas, rhetoric and actions. As Aran and Hassner wryly note: 'National political controversies concerning aggressive Jewish initiatives, particularly towards Palestinians or Israeli secular leftists, often sound like medieval theological disputes or halakhic sophistry worthy of a yeshiva setting, even when they take place during a parliamentary debate'.[15] So as we explore the issue of Jewish extremism, we begin with the key model of zealotry derived from the biblical story of the priest Phineas.

The Phineas model of zealotry

A zealot is someone whose actions are described and defined 'as religious violence aimed against those who are perceived as opposing the divine will, particularly by violating the boundaries of the collectivity and thus threatening its identity'.[16] We came across Phineas, and the model of zealotry stemming from his action, in the chapter dealing with biblical extremism. Phineas provides a 'legendary role-model in Judeo-Christian mytho-history, and his epic deed became a morally, if not legally, binding precedent among Jewish and Christian Old Testament devotees' often regarded as 'a quintessential ideal of monotheistic (basically Western) religious virtuosity'.[17] Phineas and his story have provided a paradigm that persists. And, indeed, it has resurfaced today in new ways – as seen in instances of Jewish extremism, and as we will see too with respect to Christian extremism. However, Judaism has also enacted a counterpoint to zealous extremism. While on the one hand there are biblical endorsements of violence that aim to resist and overcome evils of one kind or another, and so are regarded as legitimate in promoting 'the way of God', yet, on the other, rabbis in large measure held that 'the biblical treatment of zealotry amounts to undermining authority, law and order, thus leading to anarchy'.[18] The act of Phineas may be read in two ways: as offering zealous support for the way of God, or as a moral caution in respect of the dangerous anarchic undermining, in the end, of the true way of God. Thus at the same time as we recognize the mimetic impact of the model of zealotry upon Jewish sensibilities and the propensity to extremism on the part of some, we need also to acknowledge that in the context of the development of post-biblical rabbinic Judaism a non-violent ethic which contrasts with the motifs of biblical Hebraic violence was developed and advocated by the rabbis. Judaism has long been dominated by a tradition of non-violence which only serves to highlight, of course, the nature and reality of Jewish extremism – for the most part definitely marginal. Nevertheless, in the twenty-first century, as with other extremisms elsewhere, that which was previously marginal seems to be creeping ever more towards the centre, with the risk and prospect of the formerly marginalized extreme becoming the dominant motif of a central overriding fanaticism.

Gideon Aran has pointed out that the Palestinian Talmud actually argues against Phineas. Such zealotry is 'contrary to the rabbinic spirit' (Jerusalem Talmud, Sanhedrin, 27:2).[19] The rabbinic tradition regards Phineas as manifesting a disruptive and problematic spirit which it 'does not mandate as a practical requirement'.[20] But clearly its inspirational efficacy continues to bear fruit despite the fact that the 'basic point made by the dominant Jewish tradition concerning zealotry ... is that it is a sublime principle which is hardly translatable into actual behavior'.[21] Nevertheless, a ruling of the Mishnah that 'he who cohabits with a heathen woman is punished by zealots' (Babylonian Talmud, Sanhedrin 82a) indicates a contrary pro-violence view whereby the zealous act is expected rather than merely tolerated.[22] However, in their jointly authored article, Aran and Hassner point out that

> tradition qualifies and effectively annuls this important and revealing rabbinic decision. The traditional convention is to introduce this passage into the peculiar category of 'this is religious law but the rabbis do not so instruct' ... the ruling regarding zealotry is one of those rare cases referred to in the Oral Torah in which there is a general consensus about the legitimacy of a certain behavior in principle, but it is modified by the fear that license for such behavior would be expanded beyond acceptable bounds.[23]

Hence the invitation to undertake an extreme zealous act is so restricted that it is virtually impossible to put into practice. Furthermore, additional time-bound restrictions place onerous limitations on the possibility of enacting true zealotry. Hence, significantly,

> zealotry is a matter of a clear-cut specific moment. The sages declared religious violence that is initiated a few seconds too early or terminated a few seconds too late to be illegitimate. Thus the distance between the most elevated zealous act and sheer murderous criminality is miniscule, but nevertheless critical. The Talmud contends that a zealot who approaches religious authorities to ask for their advice and sanction should not be granted such a license: 'If the zealot comes to take counsel, we do not instruct him to do so' (Sanhedrin 82a). That is, zealotry has to be an individualist and spontaneous act. A person who commits religious violence can be defined as a zealot only in retrospect, never beforehand.[24]

Jewish rabbinical sages employed a number of strategies to curtail any propensity to violence and extremism. For instance, in respect of a theological strategy, the focus of responsibility for contemporary affairs was transferred from the spatio-temporal realm to that of the transcendental or 'heavenly' realm of the divine: 'The Jewish collective and the individual were absolved of the need to take an active role in history'.[25] Further, Jewish experience was cast in terms of a moral context: the consequences of past rebellions, which ended in disaster and exile, were by and large regarded as divine punishment for the community's transgression of religious law. Communal disasters were the result of communal sinful disobedience or the ignoring of the will of the

Almighty. In response, pious Jews, in coming to terms with their concrete circumstances, directed their attention away from political circumstances and realities by focusing their piety and religious life on ritual behaviours and contemplation. The political realities had to be simply endured. Indeed, 'since persecution was divinely ordained, failure to submit to God's instruments (the Assyrians, Babylonians, Greeks, or Romans) merely invited further suffering and delayed redemption'.[26] Consequently, the focus of Jewish concerns was turned towards the outworking of the covenantal relationship with God and the resultant tensions between God and Israel, and away from the immediate concerns with the enemies of Jews and responsive or reactive engagements in military and other clashes. This 'also led to significant halakhic innovations, including a moderation and restraining of the laws of war' which included 'changes related to the regulation and humanization of war' and placing 'limits on violent criminal penalties'.[27] So despite the long list of offences given in the Hebrew bible that mandate capital or other severe punishment, in reality the rabbinic tradition would only enact the death penalty in the most rare and extreme cases, and then only after exhausting complex legal considerations. Jewish life and piety seemingly neutralized the extremist excesses that the biblical heritage appeared to allow, if not require in some circumstances.

Post-biblical violence

The development of rabbinic Judaism is itself a post-biblical phenomenon and influenced, especially, by early post-biblical events. Lying outside the Hebrew biblical record, and constituting a comparatively unique phase in post-biblical Jewish history, the period from the second century BCE to the second century CE, inclusive, contained no less than four Jewish revolts against political overlords. These were: the Hasmonean revolt against the Seleucid Empire (167–160 BCE); agitation against the Romans (66–73 CE) concluding with the infamous revolt at Masada; the Kitos War, or revolt of the Diasporas (115–17 CE); and the Bar Kochba revolt, also against the Roman Empire (132–136 CE). These revolts have three characteristics in common. First, a combination of nationalism and religion, including the desire to overthrow a foreign occupier and establish the self-rule of political sovereignty and religious autonomy; second, a messianic spirit that infused and empowered the revolutionary rhetoric and action; and third, a two-edged sword of violence directed to the external enemy on the one hand and, on the other, 'inwardly at political and religious deviants and collaborators who were seen as insufficiently radical'.[28] Together, these provide alternative models within Jewish history that may be called upon to endorse Jewish acts of extremism and violence today. They are now supported by the Dead Sea Scrolls, which are ancient Jewish texts discovered only during the mid-twentieth century. These texts 'are replete with violence, concentrated particularly in the scroll about the "War of the Sons of Light against the Sons of Darkness" (The War Scroll)', which 'offers a detailed Manichean account of a brutal confrontation in the future, between Israel and a coalition of nations that will result in redemption'.[29] Such sentiment contributes to the contemporary coalition of Israel and supportive allies in the West, abetted by non-Jewish, pro-Israel and pro-Zionist Christian religious groups that pitch the survival of Israel in the face of Arab and wider Islamic hostility as an apocalyptic outworking of an eschatological destiny.

However, it is also the case that, on account of the level of violence involved in these revolts, including that which was inwardly directed, and because the rebellions involved ended in catastrophe for the Jews militarily, politically as well as religiously (with, in two occasions, the destruction of the Temple and concomitant exile of the people), Jewish historiography remembers such revolts as unmitigated traumatic disasters for Jews and Judaism. For, indeed, 'the violence resulting from repression of these revolts exceeded by far the violence initiated by Jews'.[30] Thus, since this period, Jewish tradition has tended 'to relegate this interlude to oblivion or to regard it with loathing'.[31] Nevertheless, for modern-day Jewish extremists, there is in this fund of historical memory a supply of motif and model for contemporary adaptation and application. But perhaps of more pressing interest and wider applicability is the phenomenon of messianism and, with that, the motifs of martyrdom and mysticism which came into prominence in the Middle Ages.

Motifs of messianism: martyrdom and mysticism

Bearing in mind that the sine qua non of the Jewish concept of the Messiah is one who is divinely sent to restore the greatness of Israel and redeem her people, during the European Middle Ages there was from time to time the distraction, comfort and even hope provided by forms of Jewish messianism that in turn was precipitated by the strictures under which Jews often had to live. However, it was often the case that any tendency to garner messianic sociopolitical strength that might challenge the status quo was countered by an even greater tendency to suppress any such expression or pursuit of an active messianic vision on account of the disasters that had befallen as a consequence of living out this vision in the past.

> This conspicuous dissonance exemplifies the distinction between the messianic idea and messianic movement. The former is a religious tenet, memory, or aspiration, an abstract principle, or an imaginary, hypothetical, or proscribed model, as depicted in sacred texts. The latter is a historical initiative that takes believers from the religious into the political realm with the intention of inducing profound change.[32]

From the close of the Second Temple period (530 BCE–70 CE) and the subsequent two millennia of dispersed Jewry down to the contemporary era and the establishment of the state of Israel, the trajectory of messianic quietism has been interrupted only by occasional moments or incidents that stand out as mere curiosities. So it would seem a likely source of Jewish violence had been entirely muted. But not quite.

Religion and Extremism

The seventeenth-century Sabbatean movement within the Ottoman Empire galvanized a particular Jewish communal identity around the figure of Sabbatai Sevi. It certainly stirred the pot of discontent, but in the end did not produce a violent reaction. Nevertheless, many were arrested and imprisoned for posing a threat to the authorities – in this case the Turkish Sultan. Jewish messianism coughed briefly into life, revealed itself as at least potentially and problematically violent, then settled back into quiescence. However, it stirred again in the form of East European Hassidism in the eighteenth century, although any prospect of political messianic activism was sublimated by a focus on inward piety and the fervour of a strict religious identity and praxis. Indeed, this highlights two criteria that show whether or not Jewish forms of messianism will likely lead to violence. First, whether the messianic vision is a gradualist, moderate and conciliatory one or if it is revolutionary, total and confrontational. Second, whether the vision is set within a belief that God alone is responsible for redemption, or if human beings play an active role in it. A related question concerns whether the messianic process is inevitable as such, or if there are preconditions that require the collusion or initiative of human agency which need to be met. Not unlike certain Christian conceptions, there are within Judaism some rather violent apocalyptic concepts of redemption that require a dramatic conflagration and the destruction of any forces resistant to the messianic salvific process. Opposition to this process is construed as manifesting evil per se. Furthermore, alongside trajectories of messianism, the Middle Ages also saw developments in the tradition of Jewish martyrdom which took a leaf from Christian experience.[33] However, the violence of this martyrdom was not simply to do with the obvious effect on the one who chose to be a martyr, nor on any consequences or impact of that act on immediate others, including the martyr's family. Significantly, for Jewish appropriations of martyrdom, the effect and appeal was in self-determination: 'The martyr … appropriated the prerogative of killing from his opponent, thus exercising mastery over his own death'.[34] This motif is given clear exemplification in the Bar Kochba narrative. It has recurred from time to time in the context of brutal persecutions of Jews down through the centuries. However, perhaps of more significance from the perspective of understanding Jewish extremism is the fact that 'by undergoing a noble death that sanctifies the name of God, the martyr provoked the divine to avenge his death, unleashing God's violence against his opponent'.[35] Vengeance may be the prerogative of God, but the extremist can foment it and, if need be, enact it on God's behalf.

One particular variant within the rabbinic tradition is that of Jewish mysticism, for which the Lurianic Kabbalah is significant. For, while it endorses a discriminatory attitude towards Gentiles and can also be read as supporting violence against non-Jews, it has had a considerable impact upon the advocacy of violence within Judaism. This is because of the way it linked mysticism with messianism. According to this Jewish mystic tradition, a primal catastrophic event ushered evil and chaos into the world, which requires divine repair (*tikkun*) that involves the redemption of the world and, in particular, Israel. It is not only a matter of a cosmic process – the struggle and eventual triumph of good over evil in respect of the future of the universe – but it also 'delegates a seminal role for the individual Jew': redemption involves necessarily the human contribution of improved religious behaviour which 'unites the mystical and the messianic goals: perfecting the world (*tikkun olam*)'.[36] Thus a mystical intersection is created: 'The redemption of God and the cosmos from a state of fragmentation, the redemption of the nation from its exile, and the redemption of the individual Jew's soul'.[37] This in turn results in a proto-nationalist and activist stance placed as a duty upon individual Jews and on the Jewish people as a whole. It requires, furthermore, separation from non-Jews and, indeed, actively 'discarding them'. Only so can the Messiah be ushered in. This is further reinforced by that strain of Jewish messianism which equates the rebuilding of the Temple – so producing the 'Third Temple' of Judaism – with the coming of the Messiah. Thus, fulfilling the commandments is not simply a personal matter of obedience and piety. It is freighted with cosmic significance, including the divine command to conquer the land and make it their own by settling on it. This gives a measure of transcendent, even cosmic, significance to the treatment of Palestinians and so abets Jewish extremism.

The mystical strain of Judaism, with its kabbalistic roots, encourages placing the Arab–Israeli conflict within the context of such a cosmic drama: violent events of the present reflect that which is 'beyond the immediate and apparent, something spiritual and sublime'.[38] Concrete existential exigencies are conjoined with metaphysical assumptions and perspectives. An extreme perspective results the perpetration of violence against the other who must be overcome, even eliminated, in order for a cosmically and theologically significant goal to be attained. Indeed, the religious hard-line approach holds the view that Jews in Israel are necessarily at war with Arabs, for there cannot be any peace until the ancient biblical land, as bequeathed by God to the Jews, is fully redeemed by Jewish occupation and the Arabs have all gone. This is on the basis that 'Jewish faith is inextricably linked with the land, and ... the liberation of the land is a prerequisite to spiritual liberation'.[39] This biblical land is regarded as sacred to Judaism by divine right, with the implication of an absolute obligation to fully and exclusively occupy the land. To that extent, at one level, Jewish extremism is intensely pro-Jewish and coincidentally anti-Arab, or anti any, including Muslims, who oppose the Jewish claim and heritage. The notion of sacred space in this regard is salient. Jewish occupation of the biblical lands 'is overtly tied to humiliation and a justification for violence'.[40] Jewish sacred history is replete with many examples of extreme violence and this history provides, for current Jewish extremists, both a source of strength and models that can be superimposed on current contexts perceived in like fashion of 'defying humiliation and rising up against persecution'.[41]

Contemporary Jewish violent extremism

Elliott Horowitz argues that there is a widespread view within contemporary Judaism which holds 'that biblical Hebrews were as fearless as their modern European descendants were timorous' and that such perceptions have fed modern Jewish zealotry in striving for the State of Israel. Thus, for example, when Arab riots broke out in Jaffa in April 1936, although there were many Jewish voices calling for a response in kind, 'others argued that such violence would be counterproductive and/or contrary to Jewish tradition'.[42] Indeed, prior to the 1970s, religious Jews contrasted with secular Jews in that the former abstained from violence while the latter were quick to espouse it to promote the obtaining of political goals. Since then, however, it is religious Jews who have committed 'all ideologically-motivated violent acts' with justification given in religious terms, 'while secular Jews tend to refrain from such violence'.[43]

In 1974 the radical New York rabbi Meir Kahane, who had founded the Jewish Defense League in the 1960s, began a right-wing party in Israel known as the '*Kach*' (Thus) party. By 1988 this party was banned as too extreme. Kahane's platform was that Israel should not relinquish any land to Palestinians. Indeed, his 'statements about Arabs were compared word for word with those of Hitler about Jews and were found to be surprisingly similar'.[44] His key ideological position was that of 'catastrophic messianism', or 'the sanctification of God', meaning that 'the Messiah will come in a great conflict in which Jews triumph and praise God through their successes' and that whatever 'humiliated the Jews was not only an embarrassment but a retrograde motion in the world's progress toward salvation'.[45] Thus Jews could respond to humiliation with violence if need be. Indeed, as Juergensmeyer notes, this meant that 'insofar as Jews were exalted and their enemies humiliated, God was glorified and the Messiah's coming was more likely', and this implied, in turn, that those to be humiliated 'included any who came in the way of the movement toward re-establishing the biblical nation', namely Arabs on the one hand, and secular – that is, non-religious – Jews, on the other.[46] Indeed, even a secular government is the enemy. As non-Jews, Arabs are deemed to have no right to live in Israel. For the sake of their own dignity, they should leave voluntarily. If not, they need to be encouraged, even forcefully, to do so. Kahane, who himself met a violent end when he was murdered in downtown Manhattan in November 1990, saw no problem with enacting violence to achieve a divine aim and, indeed, regarded any group or individual 'deemed to be the enemy might justifiably become the object of violent assault, even if he or she might have been an innocent bystander. In a spiritual war there is no such thing; all are potential soldiers.'[47]

There are three cases of Jewish extremism in recent times that deserve special mention. Each was carried out by religious Jews 'and rationalized in traditional Jewish terms … none of these cases can be understood fully without relating to their religious, traditional, Jewish core'.[48] And in each case an ethno-nationalist perspective is 'combined with inspiration and mandate rooted in scriptures, rites, and collective memories, inherited from times past and remote places'.[49] The first is known as the Jewish Underground. Referred to by Israeli media in the early 1980s as the Jewish Underground in the Territories, it comprised a group of yeshiva graduates – all highly religious, observant Jews – who targeted Palestinian individuals and institutions in the West Bank in a series of terrorist attacks. This included killing three Islamic College students with a hand grenade and booby-trapping the cars of several mayors of Palestinian cities. One influential member of the group, a student of medieval Jewish mysticism and an expert in the esoteric texts and rituals of the Kabbalah, led the plan to destroy the Muslim Dome of the Rock on Jerusalem's Temple Mount, referred to as 'the abomination'. Such an act, had it been carried out, would doubtless have provoked a massive Muslim response and led to a conflagration. But for the religious plotters, this would amount to the Armageddon that inaugurates the expected redemption of the people of Israel. Inherent to the messianic schema underlying the plotter's rationale was the belief that the Dome of the Rock radiates 'magical spiritual power' into the Muslim world that has the effect of 'robbing the Jews of their uniqueness and superiority'.[50] Its destruction would thus 'bring about the fall of this hostile power and the disempowering of the wicked'.[51] Although failing in the intention, the fact that an anti-Muslim hostility was fomented not just in political terms (Israeli vs. Palestinian) but also in unmistakeably religious terms, is not to be underestimated in its significance.

The second event of note was, in fact, a successful anti-Muslim attack in the mode of a terrorist suicide mission. In February 1994 a recently arrived American immigrant, Baruch Goldstein, who was a deeply pious medical doctor, an admirer of Rabbi Kahane and a Kach activist, and who also served as a military reserve officer, shot twenty-nine Palestinians at prayer at the mosque within the Tomb of the Patriarchs (in Hebron). When his assault rifle jammed, he was overpowered by survivors who killed him with their bare hands. Occurring on the Jewish holiday of Purim, which commemorates events found in the biblical Book of Esther, his actions were soon celebrated by some Jews in Hebron as righteous revenge against Palestinian terrorism. Goldstein was effectively proclaimed to be a martyr, for his actions 'sanctified the holy name of God' and this was linked with a desire to effectively force God to avenge his death. Indeed, Goldstein's extremism operated at two levels – the righteous killing of Palestinians on one hand, and on the other, 'his allegedly noble death was also presumed to provoke God into killing many thousands more'.[52] It did not; but still his grave became a pilgrimage destination site for Jewish sympathizers.

The third act of extremism was the assassination of Yitzhak Rabin, the then Prime Minister of Israel. In an attempt to bring about a just and peaceful resolution to the vexed issue of Jewish and Palestinian coexistence within Israel, the prime minister had agreed, in the mid-1990s, to the transfer of control of much of the West Bank to the Palestinian Authority. This bold move attracted much support from Jews seeking a lasting and just peace with their Palestinian neighbours, but also deep hostile criticism from a wide range of opponents, including those whose views – and in this case, actions – inclined towards more hard-line and extremist ideological positions. A mass rally in support of the peace initiative took place on 4 November 1995. At its conclusion, Yigal Amir, a graduate from a yeshiva high school who had served in the army and at the time was a law student at Israel's national-religious Bar Ilan University, shot and killed Rabin. Although acting alone – indeed claiming to do so 'on orders from God'[53] – Amir reflected the opprobrium of the radical, or extremist, right in Israel that regarded Rabin as a 'traitor' due to his signing of the interim peace accord enabling the transfer of authority.[54] Jewish right-wing policies and extremists instead advocated the annexation of the territories by Israel. They implacably opposed any Jewish withdrawal and their subsequent handover to Arab Palestinians. In his defence, Amir claimed justification of the 'pursuer's decree' of Jewish legal precedence favoured by militant rabbis. This is a principal that morally obligates a Jew to halt someone whose actions are regarded as presenting an immediate danger to Jews. This was applied to Rabin's action of allowing the Palestinian Authority to expand into the West Bank.

Other supporters of Amir, and the extremism he enacted, regarded Rabin as having committed treason, for which the punishment is death. Thus Amir had stopped 'a runaway train'.[55] In Jewish tradition there is a provision, albeit rarely applied, of the *din rodef* that allows not only the direct target to commit self-defence by striking pre-emptively but also permits – even obliges – a third party, namely someone who sees what is going on, to prevent the imminent threat even by the killing of the putative perpetrator. This would attract no guilt, since the action was undertaken in good faith to save Jews. And the key to understanding such an action is that it involves the perceived necessity of 'taking an instant violent initiative without a rabbinic mandate'.[56] Indeed, at his trial Amir stated: 'I acted according to *din rodef*... I did this not as a punishment but as a prevention'.[57] Rabin was regarded as the threat, one who by his conciliatory actions was setting Jews up to be killed by Arabs. So in effect, Rabin himself could be viewed as about to murder Jews, albeit indirectly. However, Israeli security authorities at the time presumed that Amir was not acting alone and that there must have been rabbinical authorities who would have provided sanction for the assassination, the point and focus of this form of Jewish extremism. They were mistaken for, indeed, the

> urgency of saving a life relieves the would-be killer from the need for judicial sanction and the killer is exempt from penalties in court after the fact. Because Premier Rabin's peace policy was perceived as spilling Jewish blood, he had to be dispatched immediately. Amir took on this holy mission for the sake of the land, the Torah, and the name of God.[58]

He needed no further support or sanction for his act. Mark Juergensmeyer has noted, in regard to the extreme acts of both Goldstein and Amir, that their actions were justified – by themselves and others – on the basis of 'Jewish theology, historical precedents, and biblical examples'.[59] And all cases we have thus far noted manifest the underlying biblical model of zealotry, a model which has been taken up in the contemporary cause of Zionism.

Zealotry and Zionism

Juergensmeyer comments that, in the months before the assassination of Rabin 'there had been a great deal of discussion ... about the religious justifications for the political assassination ... of Jewish leaders who were felt to be dangerously irresponsible and were de facto enemies of Judaism'.[60] The context for such discussion is that of messianic Zionism which takes a cosmic view of the divine purpose to which the Jewish people are called, namely that the redemption of the world is contingent on their actions in creating the necessary conditions for God's salvific action to take place. The foremost actions include the rebuilding of the Temple and making it ready to resume its ritual activities and to ensure that not one piece of the divinely given land is yielded. It is thus regarded as 'heretical to give up the least bit of biblical land' (that is, the West Bank) to the non-Jewish 'other'.[61] The roots of Zionism lie in the European post-Enlightenment period when Jews were emancipated and so enabled to participate fully in society. However, although now liberated from a ghettoized existence, ironically this emancipation had the effect of threatening Jewish identity by way of promoting values of secularism and individualism: the cohesion of the traditional Jewish community was severely tested, and at times clearly ruptured. Thus 'Jews were faced with a choice between several fundamentally new options: assimilation; joining European nationalist, liberal, or socialist movements; varieties of reformed Judaism; and Orthodox Judaism ... The remaining option was Jewish secularism, especially of the ethno-nationalist brand, that is, Zionism.'[62]

From its inception Zionism tended towards an assertive, even aggressive and at times violent stance. This reflected the inspiration and influence of other European nationalist movements of the time and it reacted against the long traditions of diasporic rabbinic Judaism that had promoted spirituality, quietism and passivity. The Zionism that emerged in the mid-nineteenth century and came to focus early in the twentieth, sought liberation from this claustrophobic heritage and asserted, in contrast, values of 'pride, power, physicality, masculinity, assertiveness, and militarism'.[63] The self-image that was actively promoted was 'away from a people characterized by persecution and subordination' to that of 'a "muscular Judaism" whose members toiled the land, excelled in gymnastics, and bore arms'.[64] The golden-age epochs that beckoned were those of the ancient biblical and the Second Temple eras: 'The common denominator of these two phases was not merely Jewish territoriality, physicality, and sovereignty but also Jewish violence directed both inward and outward ... Zionism appropriated elements of Jewish tradition that embodied Jewish violence'.[65] The practice of observing a commemorative fast day (*Tisha B'Av*), which remembers the various times when Jerusalem was destroyed, was set aside. The great military and conquering heroes of old, together with the Maccabees and, in particular, the Masada zealots were to be celebrated instead as the models of the modern assertive secular Jews: 'Religious Jews were relegated to a relatively marginal role'.[66] This period of Zionist identity and polity lasted down to the 1970s. However, in glorifying ancient biblical texts for political purposes, there is a 'supreme irony' in that this ideological use of the Bible 'distanced Orthodox Jews from their secular counterparts'.[67]

> This was part of a greater challenge that Zionism posed. Orthodox Jews had to contend with a Zionism that monopolized the definition of Judaism and that practically fulfilled the prophetic vision of founding a Jewish state. The religious right's response to this challenge in the mid-1970s was a mystical messianism in which empirical reality was perceived as hiding another reality, more profound and sublime. This hidden reality, they argued, was in fact a redeemed reality. Secular Jews were said to be unaware of their true inner nature, which was alleged to be very sacred.[68]

Religion and Extremism

So by the last quarter of the twentieth century, Jewish religious extremism had emerged in the form of a religious Zionism that reinterpreted secular Zionism as, in fact, responding to and working from a messianic motivation. Therefore Zionism is in reality a religious movement, in spite of any appearances to the contrary. Religion and nationalism were now symbiotically entwined and this new religious Zionism 'shifted the Bible's center of gravity towards the tribal, ethno-nationalist aspect, together with a cultic facet that sought to emphasize rituals that were previously considered archaic'.[69] Religious Zionism has since become increasingly prominent within the Israeli institutions of government and the military: 'While religious-Zionists make up only 10–13% of the Jewish population in Israel, in 2010 Orthodox soldiers accounted for between one third and one half of the School for Officers' graduating cohort'.[70] Indeed, research by an Israeli military sociologist 'has argued that the outright "religionisation" of the army, especially of particular fighting corps, is related to the disproportionate use of lethal force in the Intifada in the Territories, as reflected in the high number of local Palestinian casualties'.[71]

Significantly, contemporary Jewish extremism has been influenced by a 2009 Israeli book, which is a compilation of quotations from a range of classical Jewish texts focusing in particular on rabbinical rulings, in effect provides a putative licence for extreme violence enacted by Jews against non-Jews. It argues that the biblical prohibition against murder, for example, 'applies only to the murder of Jews by Jews, not to the murder of Gentiles by Jews' – even a righteous Gentile, 'as long as he has not converted to Judaism'.[72] Indeed, Gentiles were construed as belonging to two groups: 'Those who can be killed with impunity, and those who respect the seven Noahide laws, who are tolerated, yet whose killing has no legal implications for the perpetrator'.[73] But it is not only with respect to the actions of individuals that the book has had an impact, but also in regard to dealing with inter-communal tensions, specifically of Israelis and Palestinians. Anyone in the camp of the 'other' deemed to encourage or support 'the persecution of Israel is considered a rodef and is thus a valid target for killing'.[74] And this extends even 'to the killing of children, since they might join the enemies of Israel in adulthood'.[75] In removing texts from their originating context and in so doing giving them a fresh emphasis as well as a new public airing, this book constitutes a significant item of contemporary extremist rhetoric, making old ideas freshly relevant and ancient motifs of extremism capable of being applied to contemporary contexts.

Conclusion

Although, to be sure, the trajectory of recent history, including the very real threats and security challenges faced by Israel, has come to dominate the Jewish experience and impact contemporary Jewish mentalities, extremism and violent actions are by no means the full story of either Israel or Judaism. Certainly, as has been noted, 'secular, nationalist, Jewish violence found expression in two modes: the execution of state policy in the form of wars, military operations, and counterterrorism; and domestic political violence in the form of political assassinations, sabotage, and rioting (which came dangerously close to civil war at certain times)'.[76] One distinct category of Jewish religious extremism in Israel, largely internally directed, is, as we saw above, the Ultra-Orthodox or *haredim* who take a strict and puritanical line to what it means to be a Jew. Their targets tend to be fellow-*haredim* who belong to rival factions, as well as secular Jews, tourists, missionaries and the secular Zionist establishment as such. They also take umbrage at driving on the Sabbath, immodest dress, archaeological excavations that defile Jewish tombs, autopsies and much contemporary advertising.

Where extremism seems to be gaining in prominence it is, by definition, always something relatively marginal: that which is other than the norm. The situation of contemporary Jewish extremism is by no means without challenge.

> The classical issue of Jewish self-questioning regarding the place of violence in Jewish tradition finds expression in four current dilemmas faced by Jews in Israel and in the Diaspora: intra- versus extra-Jewish violence, the relationship between committing violence and being subject to violence; definitional issues surrounding Jewish violence; and the place of Jewish violence in the Israel Defense Forces (IDF). All four issues are manifested in bitter public debates that have both ethical and political implications.[77]

Nevertheless, it is also the case that, reinforced by the memory of the Holocaust, and underscored by the deeper purpose of Zionism – to establish a secure, independent, homeland state for Jewry – there is a motif of victimhood that is dominant within 'both the political and the religious discourse in Israel and the Diaspora' cultivated especially by the Ultra-Orthodox factions and somewhat 'ironically ... still present among secular right- and left-wing Israelis as well'.[78] This motif is also effectively supported by the 'close relationship and substantial overlap between religious and ethno-national association'.[79] For, in contrast with other world religions, being Jewish religiously equates to membership of a particular ethno-cultural group – the Jewish people, often regarded as a racial category. Thus Jews worldwide are caught up with the plight and possibilities of Israel by virtue of their Jewish identity, whether or not they are supportive of Israeli politics as such. Furthermore,

> Jewish collective memory and collective identity as victims of violence has two implications. On the one hand, it has led Jews to be acutely aware of issues concerning violence, leading to toleration and moderation. On the other hand, a distinct minority of Jews use their own victimhood as a license to inflict violence upon others by way of compensation or revenge. Some Jewish individuals and institutions have used or abused the Holocaust as an explanation and legitimization for Jewish violence directed against non-Jews (mostly Palestinians).[80]

Even with – perhaps because of – the centrality of Israel to Jewish identity, it is wise to distinguish between Judaism as the religion and Zionism as a political platform. Each can have multiple expressions, and internal contestation between them is a mark of the ongoing vigour and energy of what it means to be Jewish. And, to be sure, 'Jewish tradition includes an abundance of material that has clearly violent implications but also a profusion of materials that support a non-violent ethic. Jewish religious motifs are as apparent in the past and present struggle against Jewish violence as they are in justifying such violence'.[81] There are many Jewish peace activist movements in Israel and elsewhere, movements that promote the ethics and values of peaceful coexistence and resist the justification as well as the acts of aggression on the basis of what is found within the ancient sacred texts. They eschew the otherwise predominance of today's extremist Jewish ideologies and activities. Interestingly, in echo of the analysis above of the relationship of fundamentalism to extremism, Aran and Hassner comment: 'It would seem that religious groups and political groups can change their character and shift from quietism, tolerance, and reconciliation to violence and back'.[82] They also observe that, paradoxically, 'whereas some critics of Israel see Zionist violence as the actualization of the violence inherent in Jewish tradition all along, other critics see Zionist violence as a deviation from the "non-violent traditional Jewish way"'.[83]

> The topic of Jewish religious violence has become the primary bone of contention in the conflict between religious (mainly right-wing) and secular Israelis.... religious violence is not merely a historiographic question but primarily an issue concerned with Jewish identity. This question preoccupies Judaism not only in the present but in the past as well. The Jewish tradition itself asks "is Judaism violent?" This question was traditionally hard for Jews to evade since it was often asked not only by Jews but also by non-Jews, especially Christian neighbors and rivals.[84]

Violent Jewish extremism is both an ancient and a contemporary phenomenon. It has had multiple forms of expression as recorded in the biblical record, and it has emerged in new forms and modalities in recent times. Yet extremism is more than violence. There is arguably more evidence of extreme attitudes and viewpoints than instances of extremist violent acts as such. And certainly, without the existence of such attitudes, much of recent extreme actions taken in the name of Israeli security and the protection of Jews might have not proceeded, or perhaps not gone quite so far.

CHAPTER 6
FORMS OF CHRISTIAN EXTREMISM

The problem of religious extremism is often focused on the question of religious violence, as we saw in respect of Jewish violence. As a human phenomenon, violence has widespread application from times of war to the acts of 'militant extremists on the fringes of civilization'.[1] It infests religion; indeed, extremist violence 'is perpetuated by zealous groups and individuals from within major religions of our time, and, perhaps even more devastating, in the name of religion within the most developed and advanced societies on our planet. Christianity is no exception'.[2] Adherents of a religion are often the last to recognize the reality of their religion's extremism and violent tendencies. For religions normally have to do with life-affirming and supportive values of peace, harmony, justice, and the like. And, as already noted, religious adherents would normally regard any violent extremists to emerge from their ranks as other than even marginal – they are most often regarded as having abandoned their religion and its core values altogether. The extremist is typically regarded as an apostate, a denier of the religion. But, in reality a religious extremist is one who acts out of religious motivations and justifies his or her actions with recourse to religious teachings, interpretations of religious texts and generally the application of at least a variant ideological position that falls within the range of cognitive expressions of the religion. The intrinsic link and identity cannot be brushed aside. This is as true for Christian extremists and Christian violence as it is for any other: Christian terrorism is that which is 'committed by groups or individuals who appeal to Christian motives or goals for their actions'.[3]

A popular form of American Christian extremism 'based on selectively used biblical verses or a reinterpretation of certain verses to create an alternate version of the Christian religion' has been referred to as 'freewheeling fundamentalism'.[4] One variant, associated with some forms of Christian extremism in North America, is known as 'Dominionism', for it involves 'the belief that the world should be governed through a theocratic Christian dictatorship'.[5] These types of Christian extremism present a mirror image of some current types of Muslim extremism (of which more below). This is no accident, for there are forms and dynamics of extremism which, in being manifestations of dimensions of religious fundamentalism, are found as common threads across different religions. The chief identifying element is that they express some form of impositional absolutism. And, in the case of Christianity, it is certain biblical motifs and genres that come to the fore, including apocalyptic literature, which express 'an intrinsic connection between present forbearance and eschatological vengeance'.[6] Indeed, within the Christian New Testament, a passage from the letter to the Romans (Rom. 12.19–21) expresses a paradox reflective of this apocalyptic line. Vengeance is meant to be left to

God; it is the Christian's duty of forbearance to offer succour to an enemy and yet, even in so acting with apparent charity 'you will heap burning coals upon his head'.[7] In other words, the divine vengeance will be exacted in and through the succouring action. John Collins notes that both earlier and later apocalyptic literature shapes 'identity by constructing absolute, incompatible contrasts':

> In the older literature, the contrast is ethnic and religious, but regional. In the apocalypses, it takes the form of cosmic dualism. In both cases, the absoluteness of the categories is guaranteed by divine revelation and is therefore not subject to negotiation or compromise. Herein lies the root of religious violence in the Jewish and Christian traditions.[8]

Extremism, and its associated violent behaviours, is not new to Christianity. The first three centuries of the Christian era saw Christians substantially the victims of the extremist violence of others. Subsequently, Christianity has fomented its own forms of violence and spawned its own examples of religious extremism. Following an historical overview, I will examine the theological rationale for such extremism. How and why does this particular monotheistic faith produce extremism and even incline, at times, to terror? The intention is not to be exhaustive but rather to be suggestive and provocative with respect to teasing out an understanding of extremism and the propensity for deadly and destructive actions to which it may lead, in this case with special reference to Christian-related instances. I will outline some contemporary examples and apply a 'Five Point Profile' drawn from the exposition of religious fundamentalism to further tease out the nature and form of Christian extremism.

Christian extremism: An historical review

For approximately the first 300 years of its life, the Christian community was often subject to violence. Martyrdom arose in the context of Roman persecution of Christians and the abjuring of Christianity by the religious and political authorities of the Roman Empire. Christians suffered waves of persecution, which intensified during the latter half of the third century and came to a climax early in the fourth under the emperor Diocletian. Among the more well-known of the Christian martyrs during this era is the philosopher Justin, who converted to Christianity and died in Rome in 165 CE. Thereafter he has been ever known as 'Justin Martyr'. The Christian Church was forged in the context of being the victim of extreme reactions to its very existence. This included state-sponsored persecution and varying acts of mob violence. But then things changed. A new Roman emperor, Constantine, decided that instead of feeding Christians to the lions he would be better off, politically speaking, if he employed Christian fervour and zeal – not to mention its growing attraction and popularity – in the service of the empire. Overnight Christianity went from outcast to most-favoured status. And subsequently, Christianity, once the subject of religious and political extremism, has demonstrated its

Forms of Christian Extremism

own propensity for expressions of extreme belief and behaviour. Christian extremism emerged as an intrinsic part of Christian history.

Once Constantine had made of Christianity a licit religion, the Church quickly emerged from the shadows of society and took on the mantle of power and prestige. No longer need Christians fear the prospect of being fed to lions. Official acceptability and associated ease of movement allowed for both consolidation and growth so far as the emergent ecclesial establishment was concerned. But that also provided a new climate in which diverse opinion and interpretation could flourish. And this in turn meant that, as differing views were expressed, some sort of determination as to which was correct – 'orthodox' – and which was incorrect – 'heterodox' or 'heretical' – had to emerge. In a nutshell, the contours of orthodox, or normative, Christian faith and identity developed in the shakedown of determining what was genuine and authentic over against that which could be viewed as 'heresy', such as Gnosticism[9], Marcionism[10] and Montanism,[11] for example. At the same time, this paved the way for embroiling the Church within the larger political canvas: the emperor was concerned that unfettered theological dissension would foment Christian disunity and so undermine the imperial desire for a homogenous religious institution which he could champion and to which he could relate, and which would undergird his own imperial authority and the political unity and stability of the empire. So, with a theological agenda having to do with the concept of God and the understanding of the figure of Jesus in relation thereto, and also with an accompanying political agenda to uphold stability within the body politic, Constantine convened the first great meeting of Christian leaders (that is, bishops) from throughout the empire – the first ecumenical council of the Christian Church as such. This was held at Nicea in 325 and led eventually to the formulation of what we now know as the Nicene Creed. Other meetings produced further refinements and other doctrines and dogmas – authoritative Church teachings – which have contributed to the development of Christian identity and its own internal options and points of distinction and diversity. The details of this historical development need not detain us here. What is important to note is that Constantine's initiative began, in effect, the long relationship between Church and state that at varying times has led to the involvement of the apparatus of the State in the cause of ecclesial (Church) unity – or at least in the imposition of sanction against those who would dissent from that unity – and the imposition of religious sanction in the cause of political unity.

An example of the former is the eventual reaction of St Augustine to the schism brought about by the challenge of Donatism, which was an early extremist viewpoint vis-à-vis Christian self-understanding. Spanning the end of fourth century and the beginning of the fifth, Augustine was the key forerunner of medieval Western theology and, indeed, he influenced the thinking to emerge in and through the sixteenth C Reformation. Ordained a priest in 391 he became Bishop of Hippo (in North Africa) in 395. His considerable skills and talents were soon put to use in the need to respond to a series of significant issues. One was regarding what do to about a theological dissension that was rooted in the last great persecution of Christians (in the years 303–5). During this time many Christians – including bishop-leaders – were forced to surrender copies of their precious scriptural texts to be destroyed; refusal meant torture at least, frequently also death. There were many martyrs. But equally many – including bishops – acquiesced in order that the community of believers would not be without leadership. Dissimulation has ever been resorted to – by Jews, Christians and Muslims – in times of extreme threat and danger in order to preserve life. Fidelity to the life of faith can resume once the danger is past.

The Latin for 'handing-over' (*traditore*) is the basis for the term 'treason'. Following the era of persecution, some Christians of a more strict or puritan ilk – perhaps among the first who could be said to illustrate and enact an extreme form of Christian faith – called into question the post-persecution authority of bishops who had surrendered the scriptures. Could such bishops validly administer the sacraments? Were episcopal consecrations (the making of bishops), that had been carried out by them, authentic? The puritanical dissenting group answered such questions in the negative and, in reaction to the perceived laxity whereby the Church allowed a *traditore* bishop to continue, had another priest, Donatus, consecrated as a rival bishop. An alternative Church was then established under his name – the Donatist Church in North Africa. This was in existence still at the time Augustine became himself a bishop. Significantly, the dominant stress on preserving the unity of the Church became the overriding concern. Augustine's action, in essence, was to argue that there can be only one true Church, namely the Church Universal (*catholic*) in the light of which the so-called 'Donatist Church', being no more than a local group (hence technically *non-catholic*) was ipso facto guilty of forsaking the true universal (catholic) church. Thus individual Donatist Christians could be legitimately subject to sanction in the attempt to persuade them of the error of their position and the need, for the sake of their eternal salvation, to return to the bosom of the true Church. An allied doctrine to have emerged by now was that it is only in and through the sacramental ministry of the Church Catholic that the benefits of the salvation won by Christ could be accessed by faithful mortals.

The problem of what to do about hard-line Donatists – that is, those who would not listen to reason, not respond to rational persuasion – led to Augustine sanctioning the use of State force to bring about an ecclesial (church) outcome. The Donatists were forcibly brought into line. Property was confiscated. Fines were imposed and enforced. In other words, at this juncture the notion that forceful – and so, by extension, violent – means could be legitimately applied to effect sacred ends was introduced. This set up a paradigm legitimizing extreme and violent behaviours in the service of religious aims and, vice versa, the application of the violent behaviours of an extreme form of Christian faith that in various contexts, and at various times, has served political ends. Thus extreme forms of Christian religiosity have been varyingly enacted down through the ages. Augustine's innovation marked the critical switch for Christianity from being a persecuted movement to becoming a persecuting one. A line of justification that would wreak havoc in later centuries was laid down. Such persecution meted out by one group of Christians, intended to compel a 'return' to the true faith, 'inevitably involved both ecclesiastical and civic concerns … Punishment … was an act of charity … persecution an act of benevolence'.[12] Although Augustine advocated a relatively mild form of coercion in respect of recalcitrant Donatists, 'medieval persecutors increasingly turned to violence against religious minorities', for example, Jews, and also schismatic movements such as the Cathars as well as, indeed, any others considered 'deviant'.[13] Augustine had 'argued from scripture and from experience that coercive means used against heretics and schismatics are justified because of the ends they sometimes achieved: the return of lost Christians to the community of charity that is the Church'.[14] This convincing line of reasoning proved dangerously open to wide range of interpretation and application. For example, three papal initiatives expressed the persecuting mentality of Christian extremism at the time:

> Pope Lucius II's bull *Ad abolendam* (1184), which established episcopal inquisitions and called bishops to hand unrepentant heretics over to secular authorities; the decrees of the Fourth Lateran Council in 1215, in which Pope Innocent III called on Jews and Muslims in Christian lands to wear distinguishing clothing; and Innocent IV's bull *Ad extirpanda* (1252), which authorized torture as a means to combat heresy.[15]

Christian orthodoxy emerged as something more than the articulation of right belief in contrast to false opinion; it became also a badge of communal cohesion and political identity. The sense of preserving not just the unity, but also the 'political security' of the Church at all costs was here established and would be used to powerful effect. To eschew orthodoxy became equivalent to committing treason, with equally severe consequences. Heterodoxy was not just a matter of an alternate view; along with outright heresy this challenge to emerging normative – that is, orthodox – theology had to be ameliorated if not exactly neutralized. In short, one could say that in terms of post-Constantinian Christianity, there is evidence from within the life of the Christian Church of the exercise of extreme behaviours with a view to ensuring orthodoxy of belief, or thought, that reinforced the context of a religious 'normativity' and political stability, and which therefore must necessarily issue in assured conformity with respect to both attitudes and behaviours. The absence of these 'norms' was perceived as a threat to the status quo of good order and true religion. And such an anomic situation cannot be allowed to persist, lest it lead to anarchy and the breakdown of society and social order. Such was the reasoning which, in fact, has applied until relatively recent times – and, in some quarters, applies still.

As well as the example noted above, there was a widespread use of anathematizing and banishment of dissident individuals, and the ostracizing of dissenting groups and alternate emerging traditions, for example, those who demurred from Chalcedonian Christology,[16] such as the Nestorians. The eventual use of papal armies and the inquisitor's rack to bring to heel those who would challenge and threaten, by virtue of being different, the status quo became for a time quite de riguer. All such actions undertaken by Christian authorities express intensity of concern and perspective with respect to issues of religious identity, normativity (or orthodoxy) of belief and practice, and general consistency and conformity. Thus an exclusive perspective predominated, one which tended to equate religious and societal identity: to be a member of the body politic was to hold a certain religious – Christian – commitment and identity, and vice versa. It is only in recent times in the West that religious belief has been dissociated from national, or political, loyalty. Throughout the Medieval period, the Church in the West pursued policies and behaviours that give evidence of an intense concern with rightness of belief as a mark of true identity and so belonging to the body politic which was also effectively identified with the ecclesiastical (church) body. This intensity of perspective was applied to the maintenance of the status quo: those deemed heterodox were marginalized if not eliminated; those at the margins were treated hostilely, such as the Waldensians of the twelfth century and the later followers of John Hus (1369–1415). Those who were deemed heretics were regarded as opponents of the faith, and so thereby of God, and therefore forfeiting all rights and dignity, even that of life itself. Intensity of religious outlook and an excluding narrowness of understanding resulted in Christian engagement in violent acts. Extremism had, to that extent, moved from the margins to occupy the central ground.

Change initiated by the sixteenth-century Reformation of the Church in the West, while initially promising release from some of the more violent and repressive practices that had evolved through the Middle Ages, in fact spawned new and equally intense acts of extreme behaviours and accompanying extreme belief perspectives. Martin Luther's rail against the peasants and his deprecation of Jews stand out as examples; the Christian ethic of compassion and love seem conspicuously absent. The French Protestant, John Calvin, imposed a rigid form of Christian life upon the citizens of Geneva on the premise that Church and State share the same foundational authority and final responsibility. He was not averse to enacting extreme punishments, such as amputations and even death, in accordance with Levitical prescriptions.[17] And in his view it is the duty of the Christian to obey the law of the State as both an expression of obedience to God and an acknowledgment that even the State institution is under God. The voice of Augustine echoes down the centuries. Even post-Reformation Western Christianity, born out of an emerging ethical concern for the health of the ecclesial body, together with the dawning renaissance within wider society, was not immune to the trajectory of religious intensity spawning terrifying extreme behaviours. For, as the Reformation unfolded, rather than a reformed but essentially united Church being produced, the floodgates were opened to allow for an ever-increasing diversity of Christian identity, self-expression and social self-organization. The so-called 'radical reformation' – developments such as the increasing number of protestant denominations and 'Free' Churches that occurred within reformed Christianity in the seventeenth century and beyond – exacerbated the tendency to fissiparous diversification of the Christian community: 'An odd collection of pacifists and violent revolutionaries, eccentric individuals and tightly knit communities, biblical literalists and those who followed the inner voice of the Spirit'.[18] Denominational diversity proliferated. Although this meant, arguably, a diffusing of religious intensity by virtue of a multiplicity of Christian identities, each claiming their place in the greater scheme of things, nevertheless an increasingly competitive praxis emerged. The radical view saw the Church as inherently corrupt since the time and efforts of Constantine: thus reform of the institution was inevitably inadequate; the papacy was beyond redemption. Only a return to the first-century roots of faith, and a whole new beginning with respect to church life and order, would do. But the consequent diversity of protestant orthodoxies led to a state of mutually condemned heterodoxies. A new age of fanaticism and bigotry had come about; Protestant versus Catholic, Arminian versus Calvinist, Baptist versus Anglican and so on.

The stories of the various Christian denominations and groups to have emerged out of the theological and ecclesial freedom ushered in by the Reformation, such as the Anabaptists, are replete with tales of hostile reception, violent reactions, marginalizing responses and the imposition of extreme outcomes. Christians became adept at burning each other at the stake on the basis of condemnation as heretics, a practice that continued down to the modern period. The English Puritan revolution, for instance, made much use of biblical analogies drawn from the Old Testament as the basis for justifying its particular stance. Indeed, 'Oliver Cromwell drew a parallel between his revolution and the Exodus and proceeded to treat the Catholics of Ireland as the Canaanites'.[19]

Yet as the age of Reformation gave way to the emerging Modern period, so there arose a new ethic of tolerance and, of course, the mutual security of secularity. Christian diversity was working out its own modalities of coexistence, a development that would result in the twentieth century's ecumenical movement and the plethora of interdenominational cooperations. One expression of this new diversity is the neo-Protestant grouping that consists of relatively new churches or denominations which, in effect, began as and often continue to be 'protesting' both the Roman Catholic and the (historic) Protestant positions and traditions. They see themselves as, by and large, providing a corrective to the churches and denominations which are perceived to have departed from the true way of being Christian and/or being 'Church'. Churches in the neo-Protestant group have mostly arisen since the nineteenth century. Many are identified as Pentecostal or charismatic and all would be theologically conservative if not fundamentalist, and at times give voice to quite extreme expressions of Christian belief and understanding. One such, of which more will be commented on below, is the Brethren group which was initially a nonconformist development out of Ireland and west England (hence its name 'Plymouth' Brethren) of the early nineteenth century. The division into 'Open' and 'Exclusive' branches occurred in 1849. There are no clergy as such; leadership and administration is undertaken by elected 'elders'. The ethos is conservative/fundamentalist, but not charismatic or Pentecostal. The Exclusive branch, however, is more assertively or hard-line fundamentalist than the Open branch. The history of violence by Christians against someone perceived as a threat, or as a theological 'enemy' – such as both Muslims and Jews during the Crusades – is matched by a history of intra-Christian violence such as Catholics versus Protestants, especially in Europe, and a legacy of reciprocal killings down to Northern Ireland in the twentieth century, 'locked in a brutal struggle in which religious identity provided the grounds for murderous violence'.[20] And sometimes this violent extremism is directed simultaneously within and without as when, for example, 'Yugoslavia crumbled in the 1990s, Orthodox Christian Serbs and Catholic Croats vented murderous rage against each other and their Muslim neighbors'.[21]

Religion and Extremism

The dawn of the twenty-first century is arguably dominated by the contemporary postmodern context where tolerance is widely affirmed: multiple identities within many dimensions of human existence are deemed acceptable by society at large, even if it is still contentious within some quarters of the Christian community as well as within other segments of society. For the most part, mutual acceptance of 'otherness' is promoted, and certainly mutual respect in regard to differing intra- and extra-Christian identities is advocated. By and large the Christian Church has become positively disposed to the values and expressions of plurality and liberality within the secular context. This has been one consequence of the rise to prominence of the ecumenical movement whose barrier-transcending ideology has captivated not only the Eastern Orthodox and Western Catholic churches but also the historic protestant churches and the more recent emerging churches in Africa and elsewhere, who have joined with other churches in being members of the World Council of Churches. But, at the same time, signs of growing retrenchment and reversal abound.

There is increasing evidence from within the wider Christian community globally of resurgent intentional religious identity expressed often in terms of increasing exclusivity and fundamentalism. The perception of Christianity being targeted by hostile regard of other faiths, or by a resurgent anti-religious sentiment from within an increasingly vocal secularized society, is clearly leading to the promotion of mutual hostility: the religious 'other', as perceived opponent, is increasingly named 'enemy'. The gospel injunction in that respect – to love even one's enemy – is conspicuously absent. The age of tolerant acceptance and mutual regard seems in danger of usurpation by a rising tide of hegemonic hubris and condemnatory dismissal of difference. Extremism as such is not of itself new within the purview of Christian belief and action. Whether in respect of the assertion of institutional authority or the insistence on acceptance of formularies of belief, it could be argued that, indeed, the history of Christianity – at least in the West – has been one of an exclusivist and excluding religious system until the eventual rise of free thought, the autonomy of the individual and the secular contract that allows for the coexistence of worldview pluralities within wider society. But nowadays even this is under threat by both the rise of competing new exclusivist religions and, in part as a reaction thereto, the rise of new and renewed forms of extreme Christianity, in some cases resulting in violent and terrorizing behaviours. In response to Islamic aggression, for example, Christians have attacked mosques and Muslims in Nigeria. In reaction to postmodern liberalities in Western societies (such as North America), some Christians have been moved not only to protest but also to engage in extreme violent actions including murder. The religion of Christianity can be said to produce forms of terror, albeit in some contexts and circumstances. How is this so?

Christian extremism: A theological rationale

At first glance it might appear counter-intuitive to even suggest the possibility of a theological rationale for any form of Christian extremism. But, in fact, whenever Christians, or the Church, have acted in extremis, and wherever in contemporary times people of Christian persuasion enact an extreme form of this faith in respect of both belief and practice, then there is – even implicitly, but most often explicitly – some form of theological justification at work. Whether or not such justification is valid is not, at this point, the issue. The fact remains that Christian argument in support of impositional fundamentalism or extremism, and even the enacting of terrorizing violence, has been at play ever since Augustine called upon the force of the State to compel a theological outcome – the elimination of a rival schismatic church. Papal armies did likewise to the Cathars[22] and the inhabitants of Tabor,[23] among others – although not always successfully. And in the case of the Taborites, their early success against the might of Rome only abetted the development of *their* own form of extremism.

More recently another example can be adduced from that of apartheid in South Africa – and in this case the prospect of the eventual overthrow of a Christian extremism is also signalled. For, indeed, apartheid has ended, although not necessarily its underlying theology entirely. Nevertheless, for the most part, ever since the 1982 Belhar Declaration made by the Dutch Reformed Mission Church,[24] the theological rationale for apartheid premised on a racist hermeneutic of scripture that produced 'false absolutisms' has been steadily dismantled. Without doubt many non-white Christians suffered terror at the hands of the extremist Christian whites, all because of a specific theological position taken by the dominant Dutch Reformed Church and others, a position not unlike that found today in the Christian Identity movement in the United States, namely that certain races of people are created by God as inferior to other races. Scriptural justification is adduced, generally on the basis of select key passages and the interpretation given, and a line of theological reasoning applied to produce the theological worldview that then explains and justifies concomitant actions of repression and oppression.

This same methodology can be discerned at points throughout the history of the Christian Church, and its manifestation in different cultural milieux. Very often it is a combination of theological items – such as salvation and eternal destiny – with a mix of metaphysical presuppositions (the concrete existence of the locales of heaven and hell, for instance), scriptural literalism in respect of undergirding the presuppositions (these locales are what the Bible is talking about, literally) and a juristic reading of the will and action of God (to administer reward and punishment), that has led the Church in former times to enact the torturer's art in an attempt, by the imposition of physical suffering, to lead a soul back from the brink of damnation to the certainties of salvation. Better a short burst of pain and torment now than an eternity of the same. So, a mixture of worldview motifs and religious sentiments were combined to produce a theological rationale for extreme religious behaviour and belief which, for a period, occupied the centre-ground rather than existing only at the margins of Christianity – at least in the form of the Western Catholic Church.

Much the same can be said for various contemporary and historically recent and relatively more localized extremist groups and movements such as the Ku Klux Klan, and even the Nazi ideology of racial superiority. Each of these drew from the Christian extremism wellspring. One led to the terrorizing of blacks in the United States in the name of a Christian understanding of identity and racial relativities. The other led to the terrorizing of various human and cultural alterities – Jews, homosexuals, gypsies and the mentally handicapped, among others – in an attempt to bring about a supposedly divinely sanctioned destiny for a pure and superior race. Nazi ideology does not spring to mind as an obvious example of Christian extremism, but it certainly derived a large measure of ideological support and was promoted among the German people as, indeed, the fulfilment of a divine plan for the ordering of the world. Examples such as these serve to highlight the twin trajectories of extremism, namely, marginality and fanaticism.

Contemporary Christian extremism

The Exclusive Brethren is an example of a fundamentalist Christianity that recently demonstrated a transition from a hard-line assertive stance to that of an active impositional phase in respect of some contentious and duplicitous underhand political activities, at least within New Zealand, albeit from which it has since resiled.[25] Although there was no violence, no terrorism as such, involved – the paradigmatic shift did not go that far – nevertheless the actions taken did exemplify a change in the direction of an impositional extremism. There are other Christian groups and movements, however, for whom there is no compunction in going the full way in terms of manifesting extremism. I have in mind the Christian Identity movement, The Church of Jesus Christ Christian/Aryan Nations, and the Phineas Priesthood, which I will discuss in turn.

There are, of course, many other examples that could be cited, such as the infamous Ku Klux Klan (KKK) in the United States, or various sectarian groups and churches, such as New Zealand's Gloriavale Community or Destiny Church, which would be reduplicated in many other countries in one way or another. For in these cases their extremism is more theological, being instances of passive and assertive fundamentalism rather than impositional as such. By contrast the KKK was manifestly an extremist group that imposed its ideology and meted out violent acts with the impunity of Islam's Taliban or ISIS movements of more recent times.

The Christian Identity movement

Christian Identity (CI), an American successor to the British Israelite movement, is a form of highly racist, right-wing and socially conservative Protestant Christianity. It 'combines poisonous antigovernment politics with an apocalyptic, end-of-the-world vision' and advocates the view that 'the United States is a divinely gifted white Christian holy land to be conquered through an apocalyptic battle against the Jewish-controlled U.S. government, race traitors, and deviant sub-groups'.[26] It is not a single church or institution as such, but rather an 'umbrella concept' ideology shared among a number of different church groups on the far right of Protestant Christianity, in regard to which a wide variety of specific theologies, or theological emphases, may be found.[27] Nevertheless, in essence CI preaches the gospel of an Aryan Israel, that is, the 'gospel' of a non-Jewish Aryan (or white) Christ. Wesley Swift of the New Christian Crusade Church, Los Angeles, was one of the first and most important CI preachers. Theologically, CI subscribes to a literalist reading of the Bible, the plain word of God revealed to the faithful. The Bible is the ultimate authority, albeit as read and interpreted through the lens of CI ideology. CI adherents believe in the real presence and existence of the devil, or Satan. And as 'Satan' is not regarded as an abstraction or metaphor but rather as a real being, a conflict dynamic is set up between the righteous and the fallen. It is also important to note that CI, on the whole, refers to God not as Jehovah, which is the Anglicized form of the Hebrew name (YHWH); rather, it uses the Hebraic 'Yahweh' form, thereby co-opting the Israelite name for God as its own, so underscoring the claim to be the true Israelites (which, for CI, the Jews most certainly are not).

One of the major theological platforms of CI beliefs is 'Two-Seed theology', which holds that while Cain and Abel both had Eve as their mother, Abel had Adam as a father but Cain was fathered by the serpent that seduced Eve in the Garden of Eden. From Cain are descended all the 'unclean' races, particularly the Jews, who are therefore regarded as the children of Satan. Thus Jews are not only genetically conditioned to oppose the sons of Abel (i.e., the Anglo-Saxon races); they are equally beyond all redemption. There are, however, two mutually oppositional divisions within the CI movement: 'hard-core' and 'soft'. Hard-core CI holds strictly to the belief that Jews, quite literally, are descended from the devil – a view that had wider popular adherence only in Europe's Dark Ages, perhaps. The Christian gospel is meant for Aryans (pure-blood whites) only, for a spark of the Aryan God exists in the white race; non-whites, by comparison, are 'mud races' such that for whites to breed across these races is to extinguish the divine spark: 'The Original sin ... is miscegenation, transgressing God's order of creation that every living thing should only be with its own kind'.[28] To mix race genes is to mongrelize creation, for the result is that a God-given purity is rendered impure; hence resistance to the prospect of such impurity is by way of exclusion: races are to be kept apart. Arguably, it would seem hard-core CI issues in a form of racial Gnosticism; racial hierarchies are embedded in aetiological myths. Politically, CI regards Christianity and National Socialism as necessary correlates and theologically God is understood to call his people to trigger the apocalypse so as to usher in the end of the age. In this regard the true Israel will be God's army in the apocalypse and meantime, an elite cadre, the Phineas Priesthood (of which more below), who hold a dispensation to punish transgressors of divine law are mandated to execute divine justice. CI members 'expect to partake in the global cleansing' of the earthly war of Armageddon.[29] Thus CI, at least in its hard-core variant, holds an eschatology of imposed purification. Indeed, in a 1990 direct linking of CI to the Phineas Priesthood, the hard-core CI ideologue, Richard Kelly Hoskins, 'suggested that individual zealots could atone for Israel's transgressions by assassinating homosexuals, interracial couples, and prostitutes'.[30] Undeniably, hard-core CI results in violent extremism; it is in effect an ideology of Christian terrorism. It expresses, par excellence, an ideological rejection of diversity.

By contrast, soft CI regards Jews as only allegorically descended from Satan. The negative value remains, but it is not underpinned by an aetiological myth believed historically or genetically true. For soft CI, Israel is a guide for the nations and others will benefit from the Aryan Christ. Politically, National Socialism is regarded as a secular diversion. Soft CI 'rejects as misguided the hardcore theology of violence'.[31] Yet broadly representative sermon titles include 'Preserving Our Racial Self Respect' premised on the theme of being divinely separated-out; 'Who Are the Israelites?' to which the answer is 'The White (Adamic) race' – not the Jews; 'The Race Identity' premised on the notion that contemporary secular education in America is aimed at diluting (i.e., mongrelizing) and so destroying the white race: the plot to destroy America involves 'surrender to the sovereignty of an super imposed government, greater than ours ... by submission ... and made up of a majority of people who are not of our race' (hence immigration is opposed); 'Racial Streams and their Biblical Destinies', which is premised on the idea of racial differentiation by divine decree; and 'Was Jesus Christ a Jew?' to which the answer is a resounding no.

The Church of Jesus Christ Christian/Aryan Nations (CJCC/AN)

During the late 1970s, following the death of Swift, the original Church of Jesus Christ, Christian (so called to make the point that Jesus was not a Jew), was changed to the 'Church of Jesus Christ Christian/Aryan Nations' (CJCC/AN), with CJCC being the religious arm, and AN being the political arm. The new leader, Richard Butler, moved the Church from California to Hayden Lake, North Idaho. There he built a complex which would evolve to be the centre of a large, influential and politically successful organization in that many different types of white supremacists and 'the radical White' would gather there. Hayden Lakes would become the rallying-ground for many of the US hardline white supremacists such as William Pierce (author of *The Turner Diaries*), Louis Beam, author of the seminal essay *Leaderless Resistance*, and Glen Millar who was KKK Grand Dragon and head of the White Patriot Party.

Theologically, Aryan Nations, in common with the CI movement more generally, has its roots in British Israelite ideology which was born, in part, out of the phenomenon of British Imperialism and the propensity for many, especially aristocratic, Englishmen to see their world-spanning empire in theological terms – the British were obviously God's chosen people, just like the Israelites. In 1794 one Richard Brothers, a Royal Navy Officer who self-styled as a prophet, published *A Revealed Knowledge of the Prophecies and Times* in which he asserted that the English nation was descended from the prophets and notables of the Old Testament. Brothers was committed to a mental asylum for eleven years, between 1795 and 1806, and upon release spent the remainder of his life waiting his crowning as 'Prince of the Hebrews' in a New Jerusalem. He died in 1824. After Brothers, others picked up the essential theme and during the nineteenth century added an increasingly complex theological and linguistic rationale. Here we have a further clue to Christian extremism as such: the juxtaposition of a theological perspective with a self-perception of superiority and biblical-like chosen status. Further, while not actively antisemitic, the British Israelite movement did lend itself to antisemitism in that it denied the essential 'Jewishness' of the Jewish people and negated the integrity of their identity. The Church of Jesus Christ Christian/Aryan Nations has played a significant role in the shaping of some forms of Christian extremism. Although eventually sued out of existence, the name continues to be used by others along with the continuation of regarding Jews and the American Government – also referred to as the Zionist Occupation Government (ZOG) – as the implacable enemies of the CI movement.

The Phineas Priesthood

Of specific interest for our purpose is the nebulous Christian extremist movement known as the Phineas Priesthood (PP), another group that draws heavily on CI ideology and is prone to violence. The Phineas Priesthood is not an organization as such, having adopted the modus operandi of participating in a leaderless resistance. Ideologically, PP opposes interracial intercourse, the mixing of races, homosexuality and abortion. It is also marked by its antisemitism, anti-multiculturalism and opposition to taxation. There is no governing body as such, no formal gatherings, and no membership process. One becomes a Phineas Priest by simply adopting the beliefs of the Priesthood, and acting upon those beliefs. As we saw above, the PP name comes from an account in the Hebrew Bible – 'Old Testament' – where it is recorded (Num. 25) that an Israelite priest, Phineas, grandson of the High Priest Aaron, killed an Israelite man and a Midianite woman while they were having intercourse in the Tabernacle, by running them through with a spear. In the Bible, Phineas is commended for having prevented Israel's fall to idolatrous practices brought in by Midianite women as well as putting a halt to the desecration of God's sanctuary. Today, members of the PP use this deed as a justification for undertaking violent actions against interracial relationships and other forms of alleged immorality. PP members are identified in the United States as at least potential terrorists on account of, among other things, planning to blow up Federal buildings, abortion clinic bombings and bank robberies. The PP ideal is the underlying model and motivation of so-called 'lone-wolf' terrorists and extremists such as Timothy McVeigh, responsible for the bombing of a Federal building in Oklahoma in 1995, and Anders Breivik who carried out a massacre in Norway in 2011 (more on Breivik below).

At one time the official homepage of the World Headquarters of Aryan Nations included a call for 'a new generation of "Phineas Priests and Priestesses" to rise up and enact divine judgment like their Islamist counterparts in the Middle East'.[32] Paradoxically, PP recognized and acknowledged an ideologically parallel movement and held it up as an inspiration to action. The targets, task and reward of PP are clearly identified. 'Those who disobey are outlawed by God. God has specified the outlaw's punishment. The Phineas priests administer the judgment, and God rewards them with a covenant of an everlasting priesthood'.[33] This provides a link from the biblical narrative to modern extremists in that a 'post-biblical image of "Phineas Priests" who have committed acts of violent racial and moral purification out of righteous jealousy for "God's Law", and which summons a new generation of white Christian zealots to similar action', is celebrated and advocated.[34]

By early twenty-first century, the PP had emerged as the ultimate badge of honour within American Christian white supremacist culture, 'for those who rise up to enact militant racist terror in the name of God'.[35] However, the biblical referent provides not just a name, and a foundational narrative of justification, but also a biblical–theological rationale for extreme actions – the meting out of divine judgement – on anyone deemed to have transgressed biblical laws and norms in respect of social behaviours and life. Reference is made to Psalm 106 which praises Phineas for executing divine judgment in response to Israelite laxity. But this biblical reference is with respect to religious, not racial intermixing, deemed an affront to God.

The racist interpretation and application of Christian extremists as exemplified by PP ideology is a later expansion of the root motif. The putative appeal of this ideology is that 'it provides a biblical-interpretive set of unifying terms for an otherwise extremely disparate and centreless movement'.[36] It promotes a righteous elitism in that it endorses the taking of militant racist action which sees the actor as joined to 'that spiritual priesthood of those zealously jealous for God'.[37] Indeed, it 'asserts that such militant action is for the good of the larger social whole' and that the Phineas priest can be valorized as, in fact, acting selflessly 'on behalf of the children of Adamic-Israel (that is, white Man)'.[38] Furthermore, anyone contemplating taking such lone-wolf action and who might – quite naturally – experience some hesitation or inner conflict is encouraged to dispel such feelings by interpreting them as markers of 'a grievous paralysis brought on by generations of complacency in the face of lawlessness'.[39] A 'new and open hagiography, a story of a royal priesthood of saints who have been jealous with God's jealousy' is created wherein the actions of the individual militant extremist are situated 'in the context of a larger apocalyptic battle ... Phineas acts are seen as potential sparks aimed to ignite the world in an apocalyptic racial holy war between the Aryan children of God and the non-white spawn of Satan', whoever these may be.[40]

Christian extremism: A five-point profile

Eugene Gallagher notes that an extremist group which 'defines its mission as "religious" is claiming a very powerful form of legitimacy' for this claim, and its outworking in actions may, for example, 'become particularly problematic and threatening to the social order when a group also espouses a strongly anti-government ideology'.[41] Thus, if 'such a group acts or threatens to act on its principles, the need to evaluate its claims to religious legitimacy becomes urgent'.[42] Gallagher is clear that religious sensibilities lie at the core of many radical, or extremist, right-wing ideologies; in effect, they represent forms of religious – indeed, here, Christian – extremism. Our concern is with religion when it provides primary sanction for an extreme, even violent, resistance to the status quo. With some minor modifications, the second half of the overall sequential paradigm of fundamentalism outlined above provides, I suggest, a five-point profile of religious extremism which can be usefully introduced here. In so doing it offers an ideological template that may be helpful in assessing the relative propensities of otherwise 'fundamentalist'-oriented religious groups to yield to extremist ideologies and perhaps then to terrorist engagement. This profile can of course also be applied to other religions and their extremisms, but here the focus is on Christianity.

Point 1 – contextual scope

Religious fundamentalism, as an identifiable ideological trajectory, begins to turn towards the extreme end of the paradigm, I suggest, at the point where there can be discerned evidence of an 'Inclusive Contextual Scope' where ideological exclusivism conjoins with an inclusivist polity. We can see this with respect to the ideology of the British Israelite movement, an ideological forerunner of the CI and the American Aryan Nations movements. The juxtaposition of an encompassing theological perspective with a self-perception of superiority and biblical-like chosen status such that the contextual scope of the ideology is quite exclusively inclusive: empires are all-embracing; rivals – negated others – are necessarily shut out.

Point 2 – condemnatory stance

Next, there is the evidence of a 'Condemnatory Stance': deprecatory attitudes and values which are given clear and vociferous articulation. This not just a matter of voicing an opinion. The weight on the word 'stance' indicates an ideological intention: it is in the expression of judgemental values that assertive fundamentalism displays its real position towards any who would dissent from within or oppose from without. Denigration, deprecation and ultimately denial of rights, whether in regard to virtually any other (particular groups or categories of people such as Jews, Muslims, Blacks or gays or even the world at large), or focused on specific others, flesh out this element of the profile. It is the depth and intensity of expressed condemnation that marks an extremist ideology.

Point 3 – negative value application

Third, as the next logical point of development towards outright extremism, there is the direct application of negative values expressed in the condemnatory stance where alterity, or 'otherness', is often given specific identity and deeply 'otherized' by virtue of being cast as 'satanic', or at least significantly and intentionally labelled in some nugatory fashion. In this regard, the superiority of the fundamentalist's self-identity is asserted. This gives rise to a combination of hostile perspective towards the excluded 'other', and accompanying rhetoric with either direct or indirect – often symbolic – action enjoined. This is exemplified, for instance, in the CI movement.

Point 4 – explicit action justified

Not only is the particular religious ideology that corresponds to this typological template undeniably extreme, it is also poised to take the final steps to outright acts of terrorism.

For at this juncture the ideology at play has come to the point where explicit actions are given unequivocal justification: impositions in respect of the negatively valued, and so condemned 'other', are sanctioned with both the advocacy and the potential action of violence towards that other legitimated by recourse to a 'higher ideal' or 'greater authority'. So a platform of justification is established, at least in the mind of the extremist. This may be seen in the example of the PP, which draws heavily on the ideology of the CI movement but is even more prone to violence.

Point 5 – enacted violent extremism

The manifestations of contempt, as expressions of negative judgements and the negation of the 'other', will at this juncture be instantiated in various overt and contemptible behaviours – intimidation, coercion, violent and destructive actions directed at non-human symbolic targets – or else manifest in respect of forms of organized intentional terrorism directed at human subjects: the terrorizing of a targeted population, or even the elimination of a specific one. Violence, both real and symbolic, is the outcome of the ideological trajectory of religious extremism. This can be exemplified by actions undertaken by the Branch Davidian sect outside of Waco, Texas in 1993 and of the bombing of the Federal Building in Oklahoma City in 1995. Indeed, 'religion unequivocally provides the ground and the motivation' for actions of those extremists who consciously model themselves as militias.[43] One good example is the *Field Manual of the Free Militia* which 'is systematically organized to accomplish its pedagogical goals, functioning virtually as a catechism for the instruction of initiates'.[44] In pseudo-Gnostic style it guides the reader towards 'a simple theory of interpretation that should be applied to any text ... the *Field Manual*'s exegesis is distinctive in depicting Jesus of Nazareth as a role model for the militias', and it concludes by suggesting that 'a close look at the Bible will show that Jesus Christ was not a pacifist and that he approved of the justified use of deadly force'.[45] For the *Field Manual*, the 'sacred history' of the United States teaches the same lesson as the Bible: deadly force in godly and principled opposition to tyranny is not only acceptable but necessary. Thus the 'volatile mix of religion and politics is more the rule than the exception on the contemporary radical right'.[46]

Conclusion

It is the five-point profile as adumbrated above, I suggest, that best illuminates the theological rationale for the variant forms of Christian extremism. For it is not a matter of discerning which biblical texts are utilized – that depends on the nuanced ideology of the extremist group. Whatever are looked on as key texts, these are read in the context of an 'exclusive inclusivity' – the extreme perspective is not an armchair option but an exclusive view inclusively applied. This goes together with a stance of active condemnation that seeks to deny, even eliminate, the 'other', howsoever identified. And within the horizon of belief that the extremist's worldview is indeed divinely sanctioned, actions undertaken that are commensurate with that belief are legitimated. Whether in terms of biblical reference, recourse to the tradition of the faith – or its disavowal – or in appeal to a new application of reason and contemporary experience, there will be indicators of narrowness of narrative indwelling and perspectival absolutism that will confirm the views espoused as not just merely fundamentalist but, in fact, indubitably extreme. The potential scope of Christian extremism is quite wide.[47] Historically, Christianity has known extremism in a number of guises, as indicated above.[48] Often these have involved the application of violence for political and spiritual ends or the engagement in violent clashes in respect of competitive theologies and so on; this is a matter of historical record. Both marginalized and fanatical variants of the faith have arisen and have themselves been the subject of repressive and extreme measures. Aran has noted that with respect to religious violence, Judaism has traditionally pursued 'a qualified and reluctant attempt to diffuse the sting of zealotry' whereas 'the essence of the contemporary "protestant" (Christian, especially US) treatment of the zealotry complex … is an enthusiastic adoption of the text concerning zealotry, adding it to the cultural reservoir of authoritative argumentations that support existing inclinations towards religions violence'.[49] In today's world there is evidence of an upsurge in fundamentalist mentality and groups within Christianity sufficient to support the contention that fundamentalist extremism is not just the province of Islam, nor of Judaism. Clearly Christianity is able to produce its own extreme ideologies and related actions. Christian fundamentalism can and does yield extremism of one sort or another; Christian extremism can and has yielded violence and terrorism both throughout its history as well as in recent times.

CHAPTER 7
TRAJECTORIES OF ISLAMIC EXTREMISM

In 1529 Muslim armies of the Turkish Ottoman Empire were besieging the ancient city of Vienna: the enemy was at the gate. And with Vienna being a southern European entrance, there was a real sense that the then Islamic enemy was indeed attempting to storm the gates of Europe. Targeting the Twin Towers of Manhattan in 2001 was the dramatic twenty-first century equivalent of the medieval storming of the gates. The great secular city was unable to repel the invader, but neither was it overrun. Attacks on embassies, the bombing of transport infrastructure, the targeting of locales of commerce and communal congregating, internet hacking and the disruption of computer systems are the contemporary equivalents of an enemy assaulting the ancient gate. A sense of siege by, once again, an Islamic enemy would seem for contemporary Western society to be a mark of our own age. And a question inevitably arises: Is Islam inevitably associated with aggression and militarism? Is the religion itself really so 'extreme'? The answer is both yes and no. And both are qualified – the 'yes' by dint of history and contemporary revivalist Islam, or 'Islamism', the 'no' in respect of essential principles and the proprieties of Islamic piety. Look closely enough at the Christian history of violence and warfare – the contrast between it and Islam is really not so different. Christian emperors, kings and armies have engaged in battles for a mixed bag of religious and political motivations down through the ages, all the while seemingly justifying aggressive and extreme actions on the basis of biblical warrant and theological argument. Islamic rulers and armies have done likewise. But it is not the relative extremism of otherwise 'normal' situations of warfare that is our focus here. Contexts of war fought for predominantly political and other expediencies are not that of the religious extremism we are here concerned with.

In times of absolute surety of identity, cause and rightness – with the power and might to back that up – extremism can certainly be manifest at the institutional 'centre' of a religion, emerging at moments when religious fanaticism has held dominant sway. And, as we have noted, extremism is ever known and manifest at the margins, with dissenting groups seeking change to the status quo, or simply seeking to break free from it; or with those who take it upon themselves to judge their fellow-religionists as in some way deficient and believe themselves to be divinely mandated to mete out a supposed divine judgement upon them directly. How many extremists, both Muslim and Christian, have declared they were acting on, or acting out, the direct will of God? And it is this manifestation of extremism that stands in stark contrast to the normative streams of peaceful piety that can be found in all the three Abrahamic religions. At the heart of Islam is 'Salaam' – 'Peace', and the root meaning of being Muslim is to be in peaceful submission to the will of Allah (God). But principles and piety inevitably run up against the harsh realities of realpolitik on the one hand, and the pressing claims of competing interpretive frameworks on the other. What is occurring today is, from one perspective, simply the present out-working of embedded tensions between humble piety and hermeneutical hubris: religion is ever subject to varying, even contradictory, interpretations and Islam is no exception.

A disquieting paradox of our time is that we have so much information but so little knowledge. And without right knowledge there can be no right action. There was plenty of information, as it happens, about Umar Farouk Abdulmutallab, the so-called 'underwear bomber' who attempted to sabotage, as a suicide mission, an American Northwest Airlines flight on Christmas Eve 2009. But nobody knew precisely what he was up to. So no interception took place. Happily for the passengers, the explosive device he had secreted on his person failed to detonate. Not long before, there was a growing record of US Army Major Nidal Malik Hasan's interactions with extremist Islamic ideology, but no capacity to assess that as a portent of extreme behaviour. So again, no intervention took place and, in a carefully premeditated attack, on 5 November 2009 he shot and killed thirteen soldiers and injured thirty-two others at Fort Hood, Texas, where he worked as a psychiatrist. Receiving a capital sentence for this act of extremism, he languishes now on military death row. It was a matter of sheer good luck that Umar's underpants bomb did not explode. Was it simply bad luck for Fort Hood that Hasan was based there? For information to become actionable knowledge, the dots, as they say, need to be joined. Specifically, what that means is that data has to be interpreted. The data that we need to attend to today are basically two: Islamism – as the driving ideology from which Islamic extremism, and so terrorism, springs; and the Islamic extremist and terrorist movements or organizations themselves. Our focus here is with the former.

Islam: Perception and reality

In today's world it is Islam itself that is often perceived by many as a threat. This generally goes with an absence of discernment and knowledge that distinguishes otherwise normal Muslims and normative Islam from that which is extreme – the Islam of Islamists. Certainly it is the case, as David Cook observes, that radical Islam, or Islamist extremism, comprises 'a network of movements or a tendency within the larger field of Islam that seeks to radically reform Islam as a whole, and to drive it to a new stage of world predominance'.[1] It is this intense and extreme form of Islam, in a variety of manifestations, but particularly that of the recent emergence of ISIS in the Middle East, which 'seeks to create doctrinal boundaries to delineate exactly who is a Muslim and who is not, then to bind Muslims together into one state'.[2] The historical development of Islam has been immensely complex, producing internal diversities as well as differing modalities of interaction with other religions and their peoples. Within a century or so of its inception, Islam presented to Christianity not simply a rival world religion but a rival worldview and world power. Islam was first treated by Christians as a heresy – implying that it spoke the same religious language but that it derived alternative, and thereby false, religious conclusions. The history of interaction of these two faiths has been nothing if not chequered. And today they represent, together, over half the population of the globe in terms of religious affiliation. But it is a mistake to think that whereas Christianity is manifestly diverse – with its great divides between East and West, Catholic and Protestant, and the many variants and denominations even within these – Islam is by contrast a monolithic unity and that all Muslims think, believe and act alike. Far from it.

A wide spectrum of humanity adheres to Islam. Indeed, over a billion people – representing many different races and cultures – are Muslim. Within this human diversity there is certainly found the unifying idea of a universal Islamic culture (*adab*) which in theory unites Muslims across the divides of ethnicity, language, culture and so forth. Ideologically, Islamic nations do constitute one vast notional socio-geographic and religious entity, the world of Islam – *dar-al-Islam* – to which minority Muslim communities elsewhere are associated to form an overarching single religious community – the Ummah. The Islamic Ummah, in this idealistic sense of a singular community of faith, is spread across some four dozen countries where Muslims form the majority, and throughout many other lands where Muslims are in the minority. In many of these latter cases, individual Muslims are often members of minority Islamic communities within the larger, usually secular, society. Yet diversity is perhaps a greater reality than popular rhetoric from within the world of Islam, and the uncritical perception from without, allows. For, contrary to the ideology of the one worldwide Islamic Ummah, there have been, and are in fact, many Muslim 'worlds', or particular major communities, that have existed through time – empires, kingdoms, caliphates – or which exist in the present. Broadly speaking, Islamic identity contains within it a tension, even a dialectic, between singularity and diversity. Muslims everywhere, of whatever race and culture, are united in the requirements of belief and duty, and this is given concrete expression and realization on a daily basis. To that extent, Islamic identity is something overt and obvious, and apparently a single unity. But diversity of Islamic identity is found in terms of geographic location, ethnicity, language and accompanying histories that have defined and determined one group of Muslims in distinction from another – including the great Sunni–Shi'a divide, and also within those two blocs which have each given rise to variations and sectarian alternatives of one sort or another. Specific Muslim identity is highly variegated and often rooted in terms of location of birth and ethnic or national or other historical factors. Islam presents itself as a universalizing global religion yet, for instance, in countries such as Turkey, Malaysia and Indonesia, ethnic identity equates with religious identity. One can be a Turkish citizen and hold a religion other than Islam, but one cannot, by definition, be an ethnic Turk and not be Muslim. Similarly, ethnic Malays and Indonesians are, by definition, Muslim. Against the notional singularity of the Ummah, undergirded by a religious ideology of unity (*tawhid*), there is today a multiplicity of national and other Islamic entities and identities. Pluralist reality coexists in tension with the ideology of a global communal unity. The tension between the reality of socio-political diversity and the ideals of religious unity is an inherent problematic within the world of Islam.

Muslims in different parts of the world are seeking today to recover and assert their religious identity. Islamic communities are seeking to shape their destiny according to Islamic ideology. This is happening all across the abode of Islam – *dar-al-Islam* – involving countries as different as Turkey, Afghanistan, Iran, Pakistan, Nigeria, Somalia and Malaysia. And none of these is ethnically or culturally Arabic. It is happening both within the normal peaceful processes of social evolution and development, as well as in the headline-grabbing excesses of radical and impositional forms of Islamic resurgence with its jihadist rhetoric and accompanying militaristic and other extremist actions. And there is a deep inherent tension between conservative tendencies (the maintenance of the received tradition of religion) and radical tendencies (the return to the roots of religion). Each can engender change, yet each can resist further novelty: it all depends on context and circumstance. The conservative may call for revitalization of institutions and the revival of religious sensibilities and in the process may be labelled 'fundamentalist'. But this could apply equally to the radical who critiques the sociopolitical status quo and advocates revolutionary change in order to regain true values and the realignment of the institutional expression of Islam.

Prior to the modern era, the most powerful Islamic blocs had been the Safavid empire in Iran, the Mughal empire in India, and the Ottoman empire radiating out from Turkey. The spread of their impact was felt not only in Europe but also in North Africa and Asia.[3] But then came the aggrandizement of an economically powerful and consumer-hungry West. The advance of colonization and the spread of European civilization – warts and all – are not to be underestimated in regard to their impact upon the contours of the Islamic world. Ever since Napoleon Bonaparte's incursion into Egypt in 1798, the world of Islam has been continually subject to a relentless 'onslaught' from the West with the most infamous recent example of the Iraq war which, albeit momentarily, was couched in the language of a 'good' Christian-West crusade against an 'evil' Islamic empire. But the roots of Muslim reaction to the imperial intentions of the West go back to the late nineteenth and early twentieth centuries. Outcomes and impacts have been starkly noted.

> The grabbing game reached its climax in 1920 at the end of World War I when British troops occupied Damascus and Baghdad, once the two most powerful centres of the Umayyad and Abbasid Caliphates. Everywhere Muslims found themselves utterly defeated and thoroughly demoralised. More shameful was their sense of religious subjugation at the hands of Christians, whom they had always regarded with contempt. The loss of political power was understandable; but what irked them was the superior behaviour of the new rulers whose forbears they had always vanquished in the past.[4]

Whereas the ruling Muslim cliques often acquiesced, fanatics and puritans rebelled. European influences became ever more pervasive and persuasive. Furthermore, 'Christian values were presented in a way which made many Muslims doubt whether theirs was, as the Qur'an had proclaimed, "the best community" '.[5] Secular Muslims – Muslims who abide by the principal of the separation of the power and authority of religious and state or political institutions – tend to go with the flow of change and modernity, Muslims pursuing a more resurgent and self-assertive agenda – nowadays referred to as Islamists – resist and react, with a further distinction in modus operandi obtaining between political Islamists and militant Islamists. It is the latter who are of particular concern here. More broadly, however, what is often in Western discourse and literature referred to as Islamic fundamentalism is actually more militant forms of Islamism, including aggressive political Islam (although we need to acknowledge that categories of distinction are often porous, if not fluid). In this context, as applied to Islam, the term 'fundamentalism' or, better, the phrase 'fundamentalist movement'

> refers to modern political movements and ideas, mostly oppositional, which seek to establish, in one sense or another, an Islamic state. The model for an Islamic state is sought by these movements in a 'sacred history' of the original political community of the faithful established by the Prophet Muhammad in Medina in the seventh century and maintained under his four successors, the *Rushidun*.[6]

The term 'fundamentalism', even in its Christian origin, refers to the notion of clinging to an exclusive set of 'fundamental' beliefs and presuppositions in distinction from a wider range of belief and interpretive perspective. As noted already, in its application to Islam, fundamentalism, qua denoting an affirmation of fundamental beliefs, would seem to lack any real discriminatory power: almost by definition, Muslims as such are 'fundamentalists'. Interpretation of the 'fundamentals' of Islam has never admitted a wide range of options. The parameters of belief are tightly proscribed. Thus religious resurgence is more a matter of 'holding the line' against a perception of loss; of more diligent application and overt assertion of a faith and practice that, in its essentials, has not greatly changed, if at all, since its inception. Although there is a tenor of strictness and discipline that adheres more or less naturally to Islam by virtue of the very nature of the religion, the headline-grabbing excesses are just that: an excess of fervour and zeal rather than an expression of the essence of this religion.

In recent centuries many Muslim nations, or nations previously dominated by Islamic rule, found themselves in submission to a Western colonial power. But that submission has since been cast off. The political response to the collapse of colonialism, and a way forward for Islamic communities, has very often been to embark on one form or other of nationalism and socialism. Muslims often assert that their religious culture needs no alien influence: Muslim civilization was the leading light of the world during the golden dynastic age of Islamic learning and political ascendancy. Another political dimension, of course, is the fact of the State of Israel and Islamic perceptions of Zionism. Andrew Rippin has suggested that, ironically, Israel may yet serve as the grit of irritation that produces the pearl of beauty insofar as Zionism has 'led to a strengthening of Islamic identity'.[7] Contrariwise, it could also prove to be the Achilles heel of an Islamic inability to accommodate Israel and instead succumb to, in the end, a self-undermining absolutism of the rejection of this co-religionist 'other' in counter to a long-standing tradition of inclusion. Rippin also acknowledges that the existence of Israel represents, for many Muslims, an eternal reminder of the decline of Muslim civilization. A difficulty is posed for many Muslims by the existence of the State of Israel as a product of the modern era. Winter puts it more starkly: 'If the Crusader intrusion resembled an attempt to defy God's purpose ... the Zionist movement presented a still more shocking challenge', one which has provoked a response that is a mirror image of the zealotry of Judaism in its reckoning that resistance to Zionism is acting in the righteous cause of God.[8]

However, Akbar Ahmed argues that Muslims can, logically, be neither anti-Judaism nor antisemitic, for that would be to deny their own religious heritage and would beg the question of the ethnic origins of Islam. But Muslims can be, and indeed are, opposed to Zionism on the grounds that it was 'politically organized in modern Europe, was basically alien, a foreign import, to the Middle East'.[9] The scene is thus set for a 'clash of civilizations', to use Samuel Huntington's celebrated phrase, in the cause of protecting cultural identity and values. And more than anything else, the modern electronic media can represent within the Muslim world a symbol and agent of cultural invasion and value displacement. This can be so even though, at the same time, this media is an agent of the promotion of a transnational Islamic identity and, of course, a tool in the armoury of extremists. The 'real' world and the 'virtual' world intersect today in a manner and depth that has some alarming consequences and none more so than when extremist religious ideologies are in the frame. The range of ideological options within the Islamic world has included, at one end of the spectrum, the call of the radical Islamist for total Islamization whereby the Muslim concept of the divine law, Shari'a, governs every part of life. At the other end, Muslim modernists have advocated the abandonment of the early Islamic politico-religious ideals in favour of the privatization of religion, which is the model of Western secularism and, of course, anathema to the dedicated Islamist. Between modernist reform and Islamist revivalism there are many variant positions on the spectrum of ideological option that may be – and often are – taken. Our focus here, however, is with but one: Islamism.

Islamism: An extremist ideology

Although it is true that for centuries Muslims have 'striven ... to express their belief through creative expression and progress in the arts, science, technology, and education', it is also the case that, in the last half-century or so, and especially in the twenty-first century, 'Islam has also been shaped and redefined as a result of violent attacks perpetrated by its followers'.[10] Much of this Islamic violence has been a manifestation of Muslim difficulties in dealing with the effects and impacts of the modern age. Milton-Edwards notes that 'Muslim history, as constructed and interpreted by scholars such as Bernard Lewis, is the redoubt of bloodshed ... Violence appears to anchor Islam, and fundamentalist discourses that resurrect the past and speak to Muslim identity in the present are seen as evidence of this enduring and threatening attachment'.[11] But as with any religious violence, it is an expression of an ideological extremism found within the religion as one among many options of interpretation and application. In this regard, Rippin delineates three major groupings or categories of Muslim response to the modern age: Traditionalist, Revivalist (sometimes referred to as 'Fundamentalist') and Modernist.[12] William Shepard classifies the variant responses as Islamic secularism, modernism, Islamism, traditionalism and neo-traditionalism.[13] My own attempts to delineate the ideological options that have predominated within the Islamic Ummah during the modern era suggest the broad groupings of Traditionalism, Modernism, Pragmatic Secularism and Islamism.[14] It is this last ideological option that throws up Islamist, or Islamic, extremism as such. Muslim tendencies to reform and modernism have, in recent decades, been eclipsed by the rise of Islamism ideologically, and more latterly by the allied actions of Islamic extremism. Islamists ideologically assert Islam as a revolutionary option and jihadist programme whose goal is to destroy the social structure of the world, whether in respect of a specific local context or some grandiose claim to the entire world as such, and build it anew. The old order is typically construed as 'man-made', with the new designated as the application of a God-given order. Jihad is thus revolutionary action in a transcendent cause. In the view of the Islamist extremist, Islam is not a matter of optional belief but is inherently a total and totalizing socio-ideological system. This is the essence of the paradigm that has motivated the pattern, found throughout Islamic history, of popular overthrow of Muslim governments deemed corrupt and un-Islamic: jihad is taken up as a tool of social salvation; deep disaffection finds resolution in assertive jihadist action, including at times assassination. For example, Karen Armstrong cites the assassination of Egypt's president Anwar Sadat on 6 October 1981 as the first (in recent times) such 'act of Islamic terrorism to grab the world's attention'.[15] Not unlike the context of the assassination of Israel's Prime Minister Rabin, this was an 'inside' job: a devout Muslim, reflecting the sense of betrayal then felt by the 'devout element of Egyptian society'[16] in respect of policies of Westernization and the pursuit of détente with Israel via the Camp David accords, took eliminative action.

Jihad may be viewed as a Muslim liberation struggle to be engaged in on multiple fronts, and terrorism becomes viewed as a legitimate tool of jihad. As Tim Winter has observed, 'Despite the willingness of mainstream jurists to redefine their reading of the Koran to reduce or abolish the scope for offensive war, the concept of jihad remains firmly part of Muslim discourse'.[17] We need to note, however, that jihadism, and the related term jihadist, is an imperfect descriptor that has multiple meanings. Certainly, it has been taken up by many terrorist groups to describe themselves and their activities, and it is the common appellation favoured by security services and commentators. Pete Lentini regards jihadism as an ideology that instrumentalizes jihad, making it to be a form of insurgency against agents of the secular state, particularly in Muslim-majority countries, in order to implement Sharia-based systems of governance. Thus, in referring to a Muslim terrorist as a 'jihadist' or 'jihadi', the response to this form of Islamism is then located within the framework of an existential battle between the West and Islam. The ideological battle is located exactly where the extremists want it to be and discussions are then, as Lentini notes, 'no longer about the murder of innocents in terrorist acts; they are about theology'.[18] And this theology can empower extreme acts of revenge:

thus, for instance, a British Muslim slays an English soldier in London on the grounds that the British government's involvement in Afghanistan exemplifies the fact that it is the British politico-military might that is arraigned against Islam and Muslims everywhere; the fight for Islam is ubiquitous.

Islamism essentially contends for the application in a society of Quranic principles and values as expressing the divine will through the law – Shari'a – and the dismissal of all else. Islamism pushes beyond the conservative tendencies of predominant Traditionalist interpretations and applications of Islam. It tends to use select authoritative sources of the past to legitimize changes in the present. It 'refers to the movements and ideologies that claim Islam, as they interpret it, as the basis for restructuring contemporary states and societies according to an idealized image of Islam's founding period ... Hence, Islamists talk of the need to return to Islamic roots and a "golden age".'[19] John Esposito summarizes the ideological framework of Islamism as follows.[20] First, it holds strictly to the position that Islam is a total and comprehensive way of life. Second, the failure of Muslim societies is due to their departure from the 'straight path of Islam' and their following a Western secular path; this underscores their problematic context of being in *jahiliyya*, the state of ignorance of God and God's laws and ways. Third, the renewal of society requires a return to Islam and the advancement of an Islamic religio-political and social reformation or revolution; a Muslim society must be in its entirety intentionally, not casually, Islamic. Fourth, Western-inspired civil law codes must be replaced by Shari'a, which is the only acceptable blueprint for Muslim society. Fifth, although Westernization of society is condemned, modernization as such is not – that is to say, science and technology are accepted, but they are subordinated to Islamic belief and values. Finally, the process of Islamization requires organizations or associations of dedicated and trained Muslims: onward, Muslim soldiers – to borrow a catch-phrase from Christian evangelical piety – is here both a watchword and a modus operandi.

A singular defining characteristic of Islamism is the concern to gain political power: religion is not confined to the realm of the private and personal, but is necessarily in the public domain and so carries with it an active concern for the political life of the society. Therefore obtaining the controlling interest in politics is critical for Islamists 'if they are to reshape society, politics, the economy and culture in accordance with what they deem to be God's ultimate will.'[21] Rippin notes that, for such extremists, 'reliance on text ... opens up possibilities of independent reasoning through the rejection of authority by that very process of the return to the text and the ignoring of traditional interpretations of those texts'.[22] Thus the way is cleared for the revivalist to adopt radical, even relatively novel, strategies and policies on the basis of a closely reasoned Islamic ideology that is grounded in the primary texts. And such Islamists – one only has to consider here the well-known position of the most recent expression of Islamism, namely ISIS – are often characterized by concern for the socio-moral decline of Muslims and, in response, advocate an intentional return to the origins of the religion and the shedding of all accretions of legal and mystic traditions. They tend to reject the predeterminist outlook of popularist or traditional Islam and are inclined to effect, or at least attempt, revivalist reform through armed insurrection and imposition. An Islamist movement will use the authority sources of past tradition to legitimate present-day change from an unsatisfactory state of affairs to that of an ideal of what should be the case.

The goal of establishing an Islamic state is viewed as a necessary precursor to achieving an Islamic society per se. Hard-line and impositional Islamic extremism calls for a strict application of Shari'a under which all Muslims – indeed, often, all members of the society regardless of personal religious identity – should live; and also for the creation of an Islamic state in which Muslims can live free from needing to account for the religiously 'other'. Ironically, while a typical trope of contemporary Islamist rhetoric is to refer to Israel and Zionism on the one hand, and the West and Christianity, on the other, as 'Crusaders' to be equally opposed and vanquished, such Islamist extremists can themselves be viewed, ideologically, as 'crusading' by virtue of giving expression to a crusader mentality in their advocating of opposition to all colonialism, and especially Zionism. They live by an imperative, namely, that an Islamic government is not simply an alternative but is in fact a divine requirement which, in complete submission to Allah, there is no hesitation in obeying. The radical Islamist will not hesitate to criticize Muslim governments perceived as not following Shari'a. Political leaders judged to be atheists or apostates are thus subject to the full imposition of jihad. There have been plenty of examples of this in recent times; one only has to think of the Taliban, al-Qaida, ISIS, Boko Haram or al-Shabab. They also tend to be *a priori* oppositional in that opposition to Muslim governments is often extended to the religious establishment (that is, ulema, mosques, and so on) that are deemed to have been co-opted by the status-quo government. All this means that radical Islamists view their programmes for divinely sanctioned change, and the actions taken to bring this about through undertaking jihad against unbelief and unbelievers as, in fact, a religious duty. Such Islamists are radically exclusive to the extent that Christians and Jews are generally regarded as unbelievers, rather than as 'People of the Book'. They are ranked along with any other religious group regarded as apostate, such as the Zaidis and others in Syria as was the case recently, together with similar judgements on other non-Muslim religious groups elsewhere.

The Middle East is a diverse and complex region. In terms of the worldwide Muslim population it represents only a minority. But in terms of influence on the wider world of Islam, it remains the ideological hub and rallying heart. The Middle East has given to the wider world the legacy of Islamic political life, one where religion is integral to both social policy and political praxis, among other things. Mahmud Faksh argues that no Arab state is actually 'democratic' in the normal (that is, 'Western') sense of that term. 'In no single case is government based on the consent of the governed, with constitutional rules and procedures guaranteeing participation and access to power by all groups'.[23] But Islamic states and regimes do not always sit comfortably with Islamist ideology and goals. Indeed, they are often in deep opposition. This has provoked two models, or modalities, of action in respect of the stance taken by Middle East Islamic regimes towards the political threat posed by dissenting Islamist groups. On the one hand there is the inclusionary model which aims 'to co-opt Islamists into conditional participation in a political process which is in essence managed by the state' and on the other hand an exclusionary model which seeks 'to deny Islamists the opportunity to influence society, primarily through repression'.²⁴ Most dictatorial rulers resist, to a greater or lesser degree, the inclusion of the general populace in decision-making processes. They also tend to distrust open and free communications. Hegemonic control is the order of the day. With regard to Islam, Faksh is trenchant in his critique.

> Modern Middle Eastern states have grown increasingly supreme in the lives of their people, overwhelming civil society and inhibiting freedoms. The political area is controlled by the dominant elites presiding over increasingly centralized state authority. They are intolerant of independent tendencies outside the realm of their fiefdoms and are bent on barring the citizenry from open political participation.... this has been the established practice from Morocco to Saudi Arabia: by and large, demands for political reform and popular involvement have either been suppressed or gone unheeded.²⁵

The political situation in the Middle East is nothing if not fluid, although in large measure the fluidity continues to be contained by way of very controlling, if not repressive, governance. Reactionary Islamists, who rail against controlling regimes perceived as the inherent oppositional 'other' par excellence to 'true Islam', generally advocate 'a return to the Qur'an and a purified Sunna so that Islam might be revitalised' and, furthermore, that 'this could only truly happen if Islam became the constitution of the state'.²⁶

It is often the case that, as with the transitions noted in the exploration of the phenomenon of fundamentalism, Islamic revivalism takes on, at some point, the more extreme contours of radical Islamism which may later moderate once the revolutionary overthrow phase has passed, as was the case, for example, in Iran. And Islamic extremism is noted for five themes that ground its ideology. The first is the fusion of religion and politics, which is the expression of the holistic view of Islam as 'both an ideology and a system of life comprising religious, legal, and moral aspects in accordance with God's commands' and leads to the conviction that the 'establishment of an Islamic order is prerequisite to the actualisation of Muslim life'.²⁷ The second is the notion of divine sovereignty or rule (*hakimiyya*) which expresses a cardinal principle of Islamism wherein the political order is subservient to the rules of Shari'a: human rulers and political leaders are merely God's representatives and are to be judged according to the fidelity and integrity of their representation. The third theme is that of Islamic authenticity being asserted in response to *jahiliyya*, the state or condition of spiritual ignorance and specifically of being ignorant of God and God's will.

The new *jahiliyya* against which Islam is pitted is the seduction of Western culture and values viewed as inherently antithetical to Islamic culture and values. Islamic universalism (as in the idea of the Ummah), over against nationalist particularism (*qawmiyya*), constitutes the fourth theme. A shared element in Islamic revivalist discourse is the 'restoration and reassertion of Islamic authenticity in response to Western hegemony'.²⁸ The contemporary *jahiliyya* is viewed as an expression of secularity and nation statehood within the world of Islam. Therefore, any and all forms of nationalism, including pan-Arab nationalism, are rejected: 'The bond of religion is the heart of community solidarity'.[29] Indeed, for the true Muslim Ummah, 'the only relevant bond is the religious bond, which supersedes all other affiliations. The Islamic state therefore is not nationality-based; it is an ideological Quranic-based state that transcends race and nationality'.[30] The fifth and final theme, one that is found throughout much extremist Islamic literature and rhetoric, is that of jihad. This is a critically important theme. The dynamic and comprehensive interpretation of this core religious motif gives a sharp edge to revivalist ideologies. All the above themes are found exemplified in, for example, the phenomenon of ISIS or the Islamic State.[31] Militant Islamists generally pursue destructive and destabilizing strategies in the interests of waging a war of attrition – such as with Boko Haram in Nigeria, for instance. The extremism of ISIS also issues in an all-out war to capture and defend territory with the aim of physically establishing a new Islamic State or Caliphate.

As the current sociopolitical order is totally rejected, such Islamists continue the struggle for as long as it takes: surrender is unthinkable, compromise anathema: anything less than the achievement of the goal is tantamount to apostasy. However, it is the nature of this phenomenon that militant groups are highly competitive, fractious and often mutually exclusive. As a movement, militant Islamism is highly fissiparous – rivalries, competition and shifting allegiances are de riguer, as with the tension between al-Qaida and ISIS, for example. And shifts of policy and praxis can also occur, as with the Egyptian Muslim Brotherhood (*Ikhwan*) formed as a militant extremist group in the late 1920s, which later pursued more constructive and social-supportive strategies. The original aim of the Brotherhood, whose influence has extended well beyond Egypt, was the reform of hearts and minds, to guide Muslims back to true religion and away from the corrupt aspirations and conduct created by European dominance. Emerging initially as an Islamist movement inspired by Sayyid Qutb (1906–66), who viewed twentieth-century Egyptian society as in a state of *jahiliyya* requiring, in effect, to be conquered afresh for Islam, in the decades since its inception the Brotherhood has played a significant political role. But it is presently outlawed in Egypt on the basis of its inherent Islamist policy and agenda; its pedigree as a militant impositional extremist group remains a bone of contention. Qutb was, and still is, a major intellectual force behind Islamic extremism. He advocated 'a return to "pure Islam" and a move away from the materialism of the West which he perceived as contaminating Islam', for it is Islam alone that can provide a universal social system applicable to all humanity and which 'will cure all the ills of the modern world'.[32] The roots of this extremism lie in the absolutism of just such an interpretation and application of Islam. For example, Bassam Tibi notes that Qutb, as the 'intellectual father of Islamic fundamentalism … who inspired Bin Laden, was also the one who claimed an Islamic world order to replace the present one'.[33] A key concern with Islamic fundamentalism is thus that it poses a real challenge to national security in a wide variety of contexts 'inasmuch as it proposes to topple the existing order' and further, that this is no theoretical challenge but rather 'a very concrete one posed and practiced by … *jihad*-fighters willing to sacrifice their lives'.[34] Indeed, Islamist movements on the whole contrast with other Islamic groups in respect of the organization and discipline, among other factors, which they bring to bear in order to fulfil their intentions: 'Their emphasis on discipline, loyalty, and training as well as social-activist programs (has) resulted in more cohesive and effective organizations'.[35]

Islamic extremism: Fundamentalism and terrorism

The rash of Islamic terrorist activities recently carried out or attempted within Western countries – including North America, Australia, France, Germany and England – is cause for grave concern and demands very careful analysis and reflection. The surrealistic drama of hijacked aeroplanes assaulting the grand edifices of modernity may have been replaced by the more pervasive and insidiously terrorizing small-scale targeting of transportation infrastructure and the innocents of cities – nightclubs, restaurants and open places of public gathering – who happen to be there at the explosive moment. But either way the calculated randomness of such anarchic activities can achieve no other end than the fomenting of disorder and social panic. There may be an associated rhetoric of the meting out of punishment in respect of the transgressing of divine justice, but even this serves to reinforce the fact that this is no more than a petulant terrorism enacted out of what can only be described as a frustrated fundamentalism, the temper tantrums of a cognitively challenged worldview. It marks the descent of a religious ideal into the clutches of criminality. Nonetheless, criminality and anarchic disordering in regard to current acts of Muslim extremism, at least, rest in a variant – if not virulent – fundamentalist Islamist ideology. Any analysis of contemporary Islamist extremism that ignores the roots of this religious fundamentalism has missed the point entirely.

But before we proceed further in an exploration of Islamic fundamentalism and extremism, a cautionary note needs to be sounded. As Ron Geaves has appositely noted, 'to label any Muslim as fundamentalist who takes his or her religion seriously, adhering to the *shari'a* where possible and living by the words of God as transcribed in the Qur'an and the Prophet's example, is ludicrous and provides support to the views of Muslim critics of the term who argue that it cannot be transferred from Protestant Christianity to Islam'.[36] Reliance upon scriptural revelation is standard practice within Islam which can lead, uncritically, to assuming that this makes Muslims fundamentalist in a pejorative sense. Of the difficulty of applying the term 'fundamentalism' to Islam, Geaves notes that in place of using the term, many scholars today choose to use other terms, such as revivalists, reformists, jihadists, Islamists and Islamic militants.[37] The application of the term 'fundamentalism' needs to be considered and it must be recognized as a technical term, as per the examination of it in Chapter 3. The majority of Muslims would most likely qualify as 'passive fundamentalists' in accordance with the critical exposition of the phenomenon of fundamentalism. Fundamentalism as such, in its wider application beyond its origins within Christian discourse, is by no means synonymous with extremism, let alone terrorism; rather it is a certain form or 'phase' of fundamentalism – impositional – which, as a religious phenomenon, can and does apply to many different religious contexts, including Jewish and Christian, as we have seen, and now also Islamic.

Fundamentalism, as applied to Islam, is better understood in the hard-line and impositional sense – where the religious 'norm' is suffused with an absolutist perspective that issues in extreme ideological interpretations and applications of those norms. And there is no one unified extremist or Islamist position within the world of Islam; diversity reigns here, just as it does within the worldwide community (Ummah) of Muslims. One Muslim critic of elements of contemporary Islam, Syrian-born Bassam Tibi, takes the view that 'Islamic fundamentalism strongly rejects (the) spirit of religious pluralism, dismissing it as a heresy threatening the neo-absolutist claim for the dominance of political Islam throughout the world'.[38] He further asserts in respect of the 'challenge of fundamentalism as a threat that results in creating disorder' that this 'is not only posed to the West and to its civilization, but also to decent Muslims – men and women – who suffer the intolerance and totalitarian views and practices of the Islamists'.[39]

However, Tibi tends to view fundamentalism per se as primarily, if not solely, a political phenomenon that is first and foremost 'an aggressive politicization of religion undertaken in the pursuit of nonreligious ends'. Thus fundamentalism is only secondly and 'superficially a form of terrorism or extremism'. Tibi represents a different understanding on fundamentalism and its relation to extremism than I have proposed. Nevertheless he issues a salutary warning.

> In the long run the Islamic fundamentalists are far more dangerous as ideologues of power than as extremists who kill ... Fundamentalism is a *Weltanschauung*, or worldview, that seeks to establish its own order, and thus to separate the peoples of Islamic civilization from the rest of humanity while claiming for their worldview a universal standing.... Islamic fundamentalists challenge and undermine the secular order of the body politic and aim to replace it with a divine order ... Certainly Islamic fundamentalists will not be able to impose their "order" on the world, but they *can* create *disorder*, on a vast scale.[40]

Tibi thus views religious fundamentalism more as a political ideology based on the instrumentalizing of religion for sociopolitical and economic goals, albeit in the pursuit of establishing a divine order: 'This ideology is exclusive, in the sense that it attacks opposing options, primarily those secular outlooks that resist the linking of religion to politics.'[41] But for Tibi it is the political ideology, not the religion linked with that ideology, which is the point at issue. I suggest such an assumption of a deep dichotomy between religion and politics is problematic. For much religious fundamentalism, and certainly Islamic fundamentalism, has championed the inherent linking of religion and politics: the necessary symbiosis of Islam as religion and Islam as civilization is the default position which Tibi seems, in effect, to be overlooking. Certainly, as a devout Muslim, Tibi is deeply concerned about the identification of Islam *per se* with fundamentalism: 'Islam as a religion is definitely not a threat, but Islamic fundamentalism is.'[42] He is most concerned about the blurring of the distinction between Islam and Islamic fundamentalism in the media: 'It is important to not only distinguish clearly between the two but also to make clear that the phenomenon [that is, religious fundamentalism as such] is not restricted to the Islamic world.'[43]

Tibi regards current Islamic fundamentalism as an outgrowth of tensions that hold between the secular worldview of Western cultural modernity and the monotheistic worldview of Islam. It is these tensions which can become a source of international sociopolitical conflict. Nevertheless it is an interpretation and application of religious sources that predominate in the forming of Islamist ideologies, and Tibi acknowledges that. 'In their writings ... Islamic fundamentalists present themselves as true scripturalists, though they invoke the scriptures in a highly selective manner.'[44] Furthermore, such Muslim fundamentalists, strictly speaking, 'are not traditionalists; their ideal is the selectively perceived and arbitrarily purified state of seventh-century Islam'.[45] That such Islamists go beyond the Qur'an is given credence by an Egyptian example of a sheikh, a legal scholar, who was a 'renowned authority on the Islamic concept of human rights' and who declared in a fatwa (June 1993) – published in a London-based Arabic newspaper – that 'every Muslim who pleads for the suspension of the *shari'a* is an apostate and can be killed. The killing of those apostates cannot be prosecuted under Islamic law because this killing is justified.'[46] This is an articulation of an extremist position. As Tibi asserts, nowhere in the Qur'an is there support for such a fatwa: 'There is not one revelation in the Qur'an that sanctions the killing of *murtad*/apostates. The command to slay reasoning Muslims is un-Islamic, an invention of Islamic fundamentalists.'[47] Tibi's critique is trenchant and far-ranging, although he does tend to gloss the religious basis and component of Islamic fundamentalist ideology. He provides an example of the critical scholar who nevertheless underplays the religious dimension. It is the ideology of *religious* fundamentalism as such that needs to be addressed if there is to be any sustained successful counter to the contemporary threat of Islamist terrorism, or indeed of any terrorism that arises out of, or in conjunction with, a particular religious milieu. And one element of that is exploding the myth that extremism and extremists are born solely of circumstances of poverty and social deprivation and that they are reacting politically to socio-economic stimuli. This may be a contributing driver; it is by no means the principal cause.

What 9/11, for example, and the subsequent bombings in Madrid and then London 7/7 (2005) revealed is that extremist suicide-bombing Muslims, enacting out their jihad, are by no means the poor, oppressed and dispossessed of this world. Whatever their lot in life, they were well educated for the most part; they had sufficient affluence to travel with impunity; they had access to sophisticated technology. Indeed, in the aftermath of the London bombings there was increasing evidence of the recruitment of young affluent middle-class Muslims to the radical Islamist cause. A joint Home Office and Foreign Office dossier on 'Young Muslims and Extremism' placed likely recruits in two categories: those well educated, especially in the engineering and IT (Information Technology) fields, together with those who may not be unintelligent, but who had emerged in their youth as underachievers, often having already come to the attention of authorities in relation to criminal activities. Such young Muslim men have enjoyed all the benefits and opportunities of the contemporary globalized industrialized world. These are not the warrior peasants of old, intent on sweeping out the corrupt and decayed administrations in order to inaugurate a renewal of their society. There may have been an echo of that ancient Islamic paradigm motivating Pashtun tribesman of the Taliban. It is most certainly not the agenda of an al Qaeda terrorist cell or an ISIS-inspired lone-wolf extremist. Extreme actions are not being called for in the name of a societal reformation and the overthrow of a present sociopolitical evil. Evil is being employed for no more reason, practically speaking, than a cruelly quixotic tilting at the windmill of Western society per se and in the attempt to bring about an idealized Islamic State in the form of a new Caliphate – or to punish those who would seek to thwart it.

It is clear that some initially quite locally focused groups, in terms of the outworking of jihad, are now linked to international extremism. Boko Haram in Nigeria, Al-Shabab operating out of Somalia and groups in Libya and other parts of North Africa on the one hand, together with groups in Southeast Asia on the other, come to mind. Jihad is today globalized. The war on terror is a war of ideology; in particular, it is a war against the dominance of certain religious fundamentalism and extremism. And, interestingly, by virtue of being 'extremist', individuals who carry out terrorist atrocities in the name of a religion are often disowned by the community of faith with which they are otherwise identified. Their actions, in the case of Muslim extremists, are condemned as un-Islamic, as contrary to Quranic dictate and as inimical to normative Islam. Alongside this rejection of aberrant behaviour there is also a direct and outright denial by some – possibly many – from within the Muslim community of any Islamic link to the situation in the first place, and even an attempt to redirect responsibility elsewhere – such was the case with reactions to 9/11. Such paradoxical and absolute denial of Islamic-driven extremism and terrorism is based on an ideological stance which goes, in effect: 'Given that such terrorism harms Muslims and besmirches Islam, any true Muslim could not possibly commit it.' Straws of denial and deflection are being desperately clutched at by some. On the one hand there is a refusal, on ideological grounds, to believe fellow-Muslims could even commit such acts of terrorism; on the other hand, Islamic extremists will target Muslim and non-Muslim alike on equally ideological grounds. One result is that the many moderate and peace-loving Muslims in Western secularized communities are tired of being held hostage by the acts of other Muslims.

So what is driving contemporary globalized Islamic extremism and terrorism? Is it just a contemporary sociopolitical aberration in a religious guise? Are these little more than the anarchists of our age? Arguably, when the matter of attending to public discourse is pressed, a potential measure of the propensity to terrorism can be identified in terms of a scrutiny of certain forms of Muslim rhetoric, namely when there is unequivocal advocacy of the view that, vis-à-vis an Islamic context, 'passive oppression' – as evidenced within the United Kingdom, for example, by a foreign policy of non-action in Kashmir or Chechnya – has been eclipsed by an intentional 'active oppression' against Muslims and Islam. That is to say, in regard to the advocating of Islamic rhetoric, military interventions in Afghanistan and Iraq, the West's so-called 'war on terror' or whatever else may be deemed to express 'active oppression' are regarded by Muslims as, indeed, acts perpetrated against Islam per se and not simply responses to localized radical actors who happen to be Muslim. Acts against Muslims in a specific context are thus interpreted as acts conducted against Islam generally and universally, thereby calling forth and legitimating, qua the logic and rhetoric of jihad, an aggressive Islamic response. Where such rhetoric of advocacy and argumentation is fomented there may well be a case for pre-emptive countering action on the part of the authorities concerned. The problem, of course, is that such action only reinforces the rhetoric.

Conclusion

The message of Islam is believed to have been addressed to all humankind. For the Islamist, this means every person who believes in the message becomes, ipso facto, a member of the 'Islamic party' or the 'party of God', which is engaged in an inherent struggle to put in place a new civilization explicitly based on the 'word of God'. For it is certainly the case that Muslim tendencies to reform and modernize that emerged in the late nineteenth and early twentieth centuries have been eclipsed in recent decades by the rise of Islamism, and more latterly by globalized and internationalized Islamic extremism. And Islamism, as naming a form of Muslim extremism, is a multifaceted phenomenon. It involves piety, but increased devotion does not just focus on religious observance. It also looks to the application of social, economic and political values. The critical factor is that in the understanding of an Islamist it is *Islam*, and not a secular ideology, which shapes attitudes and directs actions. Islamism involves a high-level conscientization process and a deeply held intentionality. Further, there are many disquieting elements associated with it that act as catalysts for revival, together with a wide range and number of attempts to make Islam politically relevant. John Esposito, in commenting upon the ideological worldview of Islamism, or Islamic revivalism as he prefers to term it, states:

> At the heart of the revivalist worldview is the belief that the Muslim world is in a state of decline. Its cause is departure from the straight path of Islam; its cure a return to Islam in personal and public life which will ensure the restoration of Islamic identity, values, and power ... radical movements assume that Islam is not simply an ideological alternative for Muslim societies but a theological and political imperative.[48]

Four options of potential response are possible. The first is the way of rejection: following the model of jihad as a sacred struggle to fight against, and overcome, the forces of antipathy and threat. The second is the way of withdrawal: following the model of *hijra* that is, leaving the territory which is no longer under Muslim rule. Directly opposite is the third way, which involves the embrace of secularism and Westernization, viewed as movements of positive modernist reform. Here the values of Islam are coupled with taking up the practical advantages of the colonizing culture and power. The fourth way, Islamic modernism, attempts to bridge the gap between Islamic traditionalists and secular reformers. However it is the emergence of Islamic extremism – Islamism – that has today eclipsed even these. Certainly, 'Islamic movements prepared to engage in religiously justified violence have done much to bring Islam to public attention and to increase the propensity of the Western media to resort to stereotyping.'[49] Geaves argues the need 'to place "Islamic fundamentalism" within the framework of liberation movements' within the context of 'the relationship of religion in the role of nation-building in the post-colonial era'.[50] To be sure, in order to fully understand the machinations of Islamic fundamentalism and extremism in any given situation, 'the wider political, social, economic and cultural contexts framed within the context of both recent and more distant history' need to be taken into account.[51] The focus here is not on any specific situation in detail but rather the broader dimensions of the ideological elements underlying any given manifestation of Islamic extremism. Recent Muslim history is certainly a field ripe for the study of Islamism.[52] More recently there has been a flood of publications tracking the development and studying the impact of al-Qaida on the one hand and ISIS on the other. Al-Qaida, for instance 'conceived itself as a militant vanguard institution, mounting counteroffensives on behalf of the Muslim community' which 'had been weakened by the influence of savage nonbelievers, whose ways are debased and irreligious'.[53] The common cause of Islamic extremism is to recover and revive 'proper Islamic faith' grounded 'in the sacred discourse revealed by God through his prophet'.[54] In essence, it is a cause common to all pious and intentional Muslims, but the modus operandi of the extremist is to absolutize their particular interpretation and operative understanding, and so the application of 'proper Islamic faith' to the exclusion of all other options. And as we have seen, this is the hallmark of impositional fundamentalism underlying and promoting religious extremism as such.

CHAPTER 8
MUTUAL EXTREMISM: REACTIVE CO-RADICALIZATION

An increasingly widespread atmosphere of antipathy in respect of a religious 'other' perceived as a threat is undeniably abroad in the world today. On the one hand there are examples of secular anti-religious sentiment seeking to eliminate religion from the public sphere: religion is relegated to the sphere of private indulgence. On the other hand, where societies and nations are more overtly religious, or where religion still holds a significant place and role even within a modern secular state, there are increasing instances of inter-religious hostilities as well as hostility expressed towards a specific religion. Instances of Islamic extremism, for example, can provoke a reactionary extremism from parts, at least, of the non-Muslim world, including from both Christian and Jewish quarters. At the same time, Muslim extremism is frequently advocated within the Islamic world in response to a perception of an aggressive and impositional non-Muslim world – and again, particularly with respect to the Jewish and Christian worlds. Furthermore, there is the growing widespread phenomenon of Islamophobia (see further in Chapter 9) which gives expression to Jewish and Christian as well as secular reactions that are themselves manifestations of extremism. I also note, but do not elaborate, other reactionary contexts such as the Buddhist–Muslim tensions in Myanmar (Burma) and southern Thailand, and both Hindu–Muslim and Hindu–Christian conflicts in India. A vicious circle of mutual extremism is at play. In this chapter I will explore the notion of 'reactive co-radicalization' in respect of the phenomenon of mutual rejection and exclusionary response that is currently evident in many parts of the globe.

The problem of religious extremism is not only in respect of the proven potential of any one religion to produce it, but also with the phenomenon of a reaction to such extremism that itself is extreme. This seems, alarmingly, to be on the rise within societies that, at least since the middle of the twentieth century, have pursued policies of liberal tolerance and multicultural acceptance. For instance, we see this today with respect to Islamic extremism and the demonstrable radicalization emerging within and from the political right-wing of Western secular countries, and increasingly impacting or involving sectors of the Christian community within them. Historically speaking, religious violence, for example in Europe, is nothing new; but it is now many centuries since it was a prominent, even daily, feature. The Wars of Religion are happily long past; the era of ecumenical détente is well and truly established so far as the intra-religious Christian context, that once fomented the violent clashes of mutual discontent, is concerned. And the Christian turn to positive internal (inter-Church or ecumenical) relational engagement has been extended into the interfaith arena. Interreligious engagement in the cause of peaceful coexistence and human societal betterment are now well embedded.[1]

The wider setting for this development of comparative 'peace and goodwill to all', namely the rise of secularism with its multiple expressions in both political and social terms, has always had three beneficial effects. These are: the muting of religious power and political aggrandizement, the allowance of diverse non-religious political life, and the acceptance of diverse religious identities and the accompanying legislative framework allowing, albeit within some boundaries, the free expression and practice of the diversity of religions and faith identities. Thus can the multiplicity of religious identities and political platforms coexist and, indeed, intermingle without precipitating warfare, violence or the terrorizing of populations. Negative behaviours, previously all too often ascribed to religious motivations, are meant to be a thing of the past. The secular contract allows for peaceful diversity – in religion as well as politics. Today, however, a variety of religiously motivated extreme actions and reactions abound, some physically violent and others not so – but nevertheless still at the extremities. And as a feature of this there is, arguably, increasing evidence of an expression of mutual discontent – wherein two religious and/or political groups are given to mutual hostility, nugatory attitudes and allied behaviours of rejection. How may the dynamics of this discontent be best understood?

Often, there is a temptation to view the underlying extremism of such mutual discontent as really beyond religion, largely on account of various social, political and economic factors, among others, that may have played a part in fomenting any given situation that yields to religious extremism. But are such contexts and allied actions so extreme that they are really removed from the religious orbit? Or are they to be understood, also and sometimes especially, from within the frame of religion? If so, might this allow for strategies for their amelioration to be devised by regarding the religious dimension as much a part of a potential solution as it is a part of the underlying problem? These are challenging issues and they raise difficult questions. To be sure, terrorism has many root causes as well as differing frameworks of self-understanding. Extreme behaviours, including the violent acts of terrorism, are born of many factors. Religion, in varying forms, is increasingly in the frame as a critical component of contemporary terrorism and political violence.[2] In the case of religious or religiously motivated actors, one factor is that of the religious ideology that embeds – that is, doctrinally or intellectually undergirds – the justifying narrative. Religion is by no means the full story, of course, but religion is not to be discounted and may even emerge as the lead factor – especially where there are obvious links between the terrorism and a given religion. Today, however, a new form of religious extremism has emerged, arguably one which portrays itself as, paradoxically, being a counter to a perceived extremism which is posited as a real and imminent threat. The perceived and manifest antipathy of one towards the other is reciprocated; discontent is mutual.

In the contemporary world, the two protagonists expressing such mutual discontent are, broadly, elements of the Islamic world and elements of the Western 'Christian' world, even though, especially in regard to the latter, there is no such 'world'. Rather there is a varyingly secular sociopolitical context which nevertheless still draws upon, reflects and is nourished to a greater or lesser degree by a Christian cultural heritage and value legacy if not a still-active religiosity. And even though the term 'Islamic World' has a real and concrete referent or cluster of referents in respect of societies that would identify themselves as part of *dar-al-Islam*, there is great sociopolitical variability within that world. In reality there are multiple identities and a great diversity of actors and agents from within each of these 'worlds'. But for the sake of discussion and manageability, I shall for the moment work with these two protagonist 'sets'. Accordingly, I address the issue of explicating the concept of reactive co-radicalization as both a hermeneutical tool and heuristic device. The genesis and trajectory of the expressions of discontent, as an expression of religious extremism, can perhaps be better understood by way of this concept. Before proceeding further, though, the key term – radicalization – requires some minimal discussion and referencing.

McCauley and Moskalenko view radicalization as an aspect of 'increasing extremity of beliefs' as well as behaviours supportive of conflict and violence: 'Functionally, political radicalization is increased preparation for commitment to intergroup conflict. Descriptively, radicalization means change in beliefs, feelings, and behaviors in directions that increasingly justify intergroup violence and demand sacrifice in defense of the ingroup.'[3] On the other hand, scholars such as Dalgard-Nielsen[4] and Lentini[5] regard radicalization as involving a drive for comprehensive change: politically, culturally and socially. For the former, radicalization refers to a development that precedes and so justifies violent or otherwise extreme actions; in respect of the latter, violent behaviours are more of a tool of the radicalization whose objectives legitimate the actions: ends justify means. I incline more to the former, on the basis that religious extremism which can be spoken of in terms of radicalization certainly has to do with a process of change to beliefs, perceptions, feelings and other drivers of behaviour, both psychological and ideological. In the two cases I discuss below, my contention is that each arises out of processes of radicalization involving sets of guiding ideas (theology, ideology) that varyingly impact persons whether individually (as with Norway's Breivik) or collectively (as with those Swiss who voted against Muslim minarets). In terms of behavioural specifics there is no comparing these two cases: one enacted death, the other simply a denial. Yet each gives evidence, I suggest, of a process of radicalizing of values, beliefs, attitudes, and so on, that, relatively speaking, resulted in some form of extreme outcome including the rejection of the diversity that is, indeed, represented and presented by a specific 'other'. While for many it would be the Breivik case only that would be classified as a genuine example of extremism, my contention is that what we mean by 'extremism' needs to be understood more broadly, and more processively, rather than as simply the manifestation of an atrocious act.

Not all acts of violent extremism are committed by Muslims, but the combination of, on the one hand, media reports of instances of Muslim extremism and terrorist events (more often within and towards Muslim lands and communities than directly outside *dar al-Islam*) together with, on the other hand and also thanks to the media, widespread awareness of Islamic rhetoric of a more aggressive and extreme ilk, means that Islam today presents as a sharp problematic on many fronts. For instance, the question of the relationship of 'Europe' (as a cipher of cultural and secularized Western Christian identity) and 'Islam' (as a byword for an assumption of impositional religious ideology, presumed to be inimical to democracy) is a pressing and fraught one. Discourse focuses often on the term 'jihad' and posits Islamic jihadism as the main threat to European democratic values. For many this gets easily generalized to Islam per se, with resultant fear, antipathy and rejection expressed, as will be discussed below when we turn to Islamophobia.

My interest lies in the theological or ideological-religious dimension that so empowers extremist positions, and how that might now be playing out within Europe as well as further afield, including in North America as well as Asia. As I have discussed above, contending with diversity per se as simply the value-neutral fact or state of affairs is the underlying issue to the problem of exclusivist extremism which lies at the heart of so many troublesome religious – and other – ideologies. The rejection of diversity is made manifest in varying expressions of intolerance – the denial of diversity and the rejection of alterity.[6] This is expressed in many contemporary situations within society – with respect to gender identities, racial or ethnic groupings, as well as with religious allegiance and identity. Such rejection may be regarded as a matter of attempting to maintain a state of uniformity and a defence of 'tradition'. And in the process, a justifying narrative is enjoined. For without it there would be no rationale, no excusing, extreme expressions and allied behaviours.

Within the realm of religion, discussions and analyses of fundamentalism can elucidate the nature of extremist ideology and behaviours. Anna Halafoff usefully notes the general belief of fundamentalists that 'humanity has lost its way and fallen into moral decay and materialism by disavowing such guidance in the pursuit of freedom'.[7] She goes on to note the reaction of religious extremists to diverse expressions of contemporary secular plurality. As we saw above, in my own analysis of fundamentalism I identify three interrelated sets or phases, namely passive, assertive and impositional. Passive fundamentalism tends to 'mind its own business' so far as the rest of society is concerned, assertive fundamentalism perhaps somewhat less so. But it is of the essence of impositional fundamentalism to impose its views and demand that its programmatic vision be implemented. An impositional fundamentalism wants to see things change to fit its view of how things should be, and will take steps to make its views dominant and, if need be, act imposingly to bring about change – by covert or overt interventions, including fomenting revolution or enacting terrorism. Thus, at this juncture, fundamentalist ideology holds that extreme actions, including violent behaviours and even terrorism per se, may be contemplated, advocated and engaged. Denial of alterity, the devaluing and dismissal of 'otherness' as such, leads to the dehumanizing and demonizing of the negated other. The ideological sanctioning of a programme of imposition leads naturally to the legitimation of extreme behaviour, even violence. I will see how this applies in the two European case studies of extreme reaction to the fear of Islamic extremism. Each in its own way demonstrates reactive co-radicalization.

Among a number of possible cases that could be considered, I wish to focus on two – the 2009 Swiss ban on the building of minarets and the 2011 Norwegian massacre carried out by Anders Behring Breivik. These are examples of what I have come to think of as the extremism of mutually reactive co-radicalization. By this I mean the phenomenon whereby, it would seem, the awareness by one party that another is fomenting a threatening extremism then precipitates, within the first party, a reactive move in the direction of a like radicalization even though, paradoxically, the perceived initial extremism of the second party is eschewed and denounced. This is the basic pattern of mutually hostile nations, whether in hot or cold warfare mode, of taking account of each other's political posturing and military capacity and attempting to ensure that the other side does not gain advantage. It is a fundamental dynamic of international relations that leads to policies of active (as in contemporary United States–North Korea), sometimes mutual (as in United States–Soviet era) deterrence. But whereas such dynamics belong not inappropriately to state actors, what I am here focusing on is a similar dynamic applying to non-state actors who nevertheless may seek to influence, or in some way represent, the state – more usually with respect to what it is believed the state ought to be, rather than what it is. This dynamic certainly applies to these selected cases. Further, both expressed a form of focused anti-diversity and gave evidence of the politics of cultural and identity threat. The Swiss case issued a message of implicit exclusion; the Norwegian affair enacted a displaced elimination. The Swiss took fright at four minarets in their country and resolved that no more should appear; Anders Breivik killed fellow-citizens as a means of expressing the rejection of Islam on the grounds of this faith being a cultural and religious threat to European identity.[8]

Switzerland: No minarets

Since late November 2009, the erection of Muslim minarets in Switzerland has been forbidden. Switzerland, by virtue of a citizen's referendum (*Volksinitiative*), voted with an absolute majority (57.5% as against 42.5%) to ban the erection of any more minarets. Populist concerns were picked up and fanned into fires of fear by the right-wing politicians eager for grass-roots support. Xenophobia and racism played a part in the negative discourse, alongside anxieties associated with immigration and asylum-seeker concerns, and diatribe about foreign-born criminals. However, for the most part, the attention of the angst was Islam itself; the minaret was the focal symbol so far as the discourse about Islam was concerned.[9] At the time of the vote, there were some 200 mosques in the country. The oldest, an Ahmadiyya mosque built in 1962, is in Zürich. The largest, built in 1975 with Saudi funding, but open to all Muslims, is in Geneva. Of the 200, only four had minarets. However, two mosques had sought planning permission to erect minarets, and it was their applications which sparked a right-wing reaction aimed at, and eventually achieving, the addition of a single sentence to article 72 of the federal constitution forbidding the building of any more minarets in the country.[10] And this despite the counter advice of the Swiss Federal Council, all the main political parties, the Churches and other inter-religious groups or councils. So long as this addition to the constitution remains, there will be no more minarets built.

Religion and Extremism

Internal religious matters are normally dealt with at the regional or local level – not at the level of the Swiss national parliament, although the state does seek to ensure good order and peaceful relations between different faith communities. Indeed, the freedom of these communities to believe and function publicly is enshrined in law. However, as a matter of national policy, now constitutionally embedded, one religious group, Muslims, is not permitted to build their distinctive religious edifice, the minaret. Switzerland may have joined the rest of Europe with respect to engaging the challenge of Islamic presence to European identity and values, but the rejection of a symbol of the presence of one faith – in this case, Islamic – by a society that is otherwise predominantly secular, pluralist and of Christian heritage, poses significant concerns. Switzerland wasn't exactly at risk of being transformed overnight into a minaret-dominated landscape. So, what was the real issue? Does the ban mark a 'retrenchment into a ghettoized mentality; of a fall-back to an exclusive fundamentalism?'[11] Or is it merely a localized quirk of Swiss democracy? Most Muslims in Switzerland are foreign-born and so not Swiss citizens. At the time there were some 350,000–400,000 Muslims in Switzerland, mainly migrants from south-eastern European countries such as Turkey and the Balkans. For the most part they were very well integrated into Swiss society and quite secular in outlook and practice. Nevertheless, two small highly conservative Swiss political parties[12] promoted the initiative to ban the building of new minarets as a means of registering deep resistance to the very idea of Islam as an acceptable religion, even though there is no denying that the religion is widely present, at least in the main cities. Populist concerns were picked up and fanned into fires of angst, with xenophobia and racism playing significant roles in the discourse. Other European countries have their flash-point issues with Islam – often centred on female attire – however, as Mayer notes: 'The symbolic nature of the minaret … acquired a central place in the political debate in Switzerland … (although) larger anxieties and issues hide behind the minaret question'.[13]

In the event, construed as a symbol of an exclusivist and domineering religion, the response of the Swiss was to enact their own domineering exclusivism by way of blanket rejection of a significant symbolic architectural trope of the religion. But this is not just an isolated affair. The Swiss ban, including the motives and arguments, broadly echo concerns and prejudices widely held throughout western Europe. Lying behind many negative arguments and opinions supporting the ban is the reality that many Swiss clearly hold fears concerning Islam and its perceived and presumed challenge to Swiss democracy. Some are of the view that the rising overt presence of this religion leads them to feel foreign in their own land. Indeed, the anti-minaret lobby argued that the presence of Islam in Europe threatens the secular status quo, therefore Islam should be either 'tamed' or rejected. It is unlikely to be tamed, in the sense of becoming, like the Churches, secularized vis-à-vis relations with the State. Thus its very presence is regarded as threatening the religious freedom of others. The argument of the political parties supporting the referendum stated that the purpose of the motion was 'to ban a religious–political symbol of that which represents the rejection of religious toleration thereby ensuring the freedom of belief for all'.[14] Islam and Muslims were portrayed invariably as religious fanatics, intolerant, unenlightened and thus incapable of integration into Western democratic society. Reference to minarets symbolizing aggression was quite widespread and it was drawn upon by some right-wing politicians. One even claimed that minarets reminded her of menacing rockets.[15] Minarets were spoken of symbolically as both a sign of, and a guardian 'watchtower' for, Muslim belief. This one architectural object was seen to represent symbolically both piety and power – with power emerging as the dominant motif, leading to a climate of engendered fear of Islam. Some distinguished minarets from church towers, referring to minarets as representative of Muslim drive to predominance and power aimed, in the end, at 'the ousting of the entire (liberal) Swiss legal system'.[16]

Swiss discussion also drew on 9/11 as a background context and made references to former European negative interactions with Islam, the general European history of perception and experience of Islam, as well as contemporary migration issues. In short, the negative press and dimensions of Islam were read as descriptive of normative Islam, and so all Muslims per se. Motivation to vote in favour of the ban was largely based on a view that the Islamic world seeks political power not only in Islamic countries, but also elsewhere – including, especially, Europe. One recurring argument held that, on the basis of Swiss society having been founded, in effect, upon certain Christian values and principles, and Islamic values and principles being something wholly different, even inherently oppositional to these founding values, Islam per se (and especially in respect of Islamic law) is entirely incompatible with Swiss society. Significantly, this ignores the reality of the secular contract that obtains in Switzerland: Swiss citizens may hold radically different, even incompatible, religious beliefs, and even take a critical perspective towards the State, but at the same time they concede, implicitly or explicitly, to live within the societal norms of secular tolerance and abide by the legal expectations and framework of the State. Indeed, the State itself guarantees religious freedom in relation to both belief and practice.[17]

The Swiss action has been criticized as, paradoxically, mirroring an exclusivist Muslim stance, such as in Saudi Arabia, towards the religious 'other', which the West often fulminates against. Typically, in the West, the cry is that Muslim countries ought to display towards others (usually Christian and/or Jewish others) the same openness and freedom to practise one's faith that the (Judeo-Christian) West shows towards religious others, including, in particular, Muslims. So Switzerland was acting more like an exclusivist Muslim country than an inclusivist Western one. American media tended to the view the minaret ban as representing not so much a special Swiss case but rather interpreted it in the context of a growing European Islamophobia. Switzerland is regarded as having reacted to something that a considerable portion of European society apparently feels – a generalized antipathy towards Islam. The Swiss vote is an expression of a wider European tension. Certainly, it highlights key problems and questions of cultural identity, rights and political processes, indicating that when it comes to matters concerning Muslims and Islam, democratic processes can yield undemocratic outcomes.

Religion and Extremism

Norway: Reactionary terrorism

On 22 July 2011, Norway witnessed a horrific assault from within.[18] Anders Behring Breivik, then only thirty-two, detonated a bomb in the capital of Oslo, destroying a government building in which several people died and many more were injured. Shortly thereafter he set about executing sixty-nine individuals, mostly young people who were attending a political (Labour) youth camp on the island of Utøya. His intention was to precipitate an uprising against Islam. Writing in the aftermath of the massacre, Egil Asprem commented:

> Anders Behring Breivik overnight became the most famous Norwegian name since Vidkun Quisling made his a global synonym for treachery. The parallel is ironic, for in Breivik's own mind it was a civil war against the "quislings" of contemporary Norway which made it absolutely "necessary" to blow up the government offices in the center of Oslo, and cold-bloodedly murder sixty-nine people, mostly teenagers, one by one, on the tiny island of Utøya.[19]

Breivik's Facebook profile at the time noted his political views as being 'conservative' and his religion as 'Christian'. But when a picture of him posing in Freemasonic regalia emerged, it was, says Asprem, 'as if a collective confusion gripped not only the Norwegian public but the international one too'.[20] This picture is included in his so-called 'manifesto' which he released via email and internet posting shortly before he put his terrorizing plans into action. In this can be found clues and statements concerning his ideology and rationale. The title and symbolism that threads throughout is telling. It carries a Maltese cross on its title page, superimposing a Latin motto.[21] The first half may be translated as 'In praise of the New Knighthood' for it is, indeed, the title of the defence of the Knights Templar by Bernard of Clairvaux (1090–1153). The second is the official title of the Knights Templar themselves: The Poor Fellow-Soldiers of Christ and the New Temple of Solomon.

From the outset, Breivik's text combines a certain form or understanding of Christianity with advocacy of military action and the defence of Europe which results in a vision of a 'new Templar terrorist organization, dedicated to fight Islam, save Europe and kill the traitorous "cultural Marxists" – that is, politicians on the left, their journalist protégés, academics in the humanities and social sciences, and anyone sympathetic to multiculturalism and feminism'.[22] Attacks on such targets are discussed in some detail. Much of this 'manifesto' is actually culled from right-wing blogs. It is, therefore, not the original work of a single mind but more the redaction of diffuse and widespread sentiments through a single-focus lens. A generic fear of creeping 'Eurabia' concerned at the rise of Islam replacing church with mosque and imposing Shari'a law dominates this thought-world. Significantly for our purposes, such concerns are echoed by many established parties of the Right within the European parliamentary system.[23] Breivik may be classified as a 'radical revolutionary conservative' for 'it is the revolutionary aspect which truly sets him apart from the numerous non-violent proponents of similar worldviews and ideologies'.[24] And his massacre took place just ten weeks after the assassination of Osama bin Laden. In effect, it can be said that the so-called '*counter*-jihadist movement' has, this century, produced its first (Christian) terrorist, at least within Europe. But what is of particular note is that the counter-jihadist repackaging of right-wing ideology was largely made possible by the public response to 9/11 because, effectively since then, Islamophobia – fear of Muslims – has become a mainstream ideological response to the presence of Islam. A correlative dehumanizing rhetoric with respect to Muslims has mushroomed in official media outlets as well as in semi-public discussion forums both online and in the form of concerned citizen's gatherings of one sort or another. And, notes Asprem, all of these are 'howling about the invasion of Muslims as well as the "treachery" of liberal politicians' and other community leaders.[25] By naming their opponents 'traitors', the rhetoric ramps up, leading to the justification of extreme action. In this respect some commentators regard the religious dimension of extremists such as Breivik as no more than an epiphenomenal cover; religion is instrumentalized for purposes other than religious. But others see it differently; religion is at the heart of the matter, though not alone there.

Mark Juergensmeyer is one scholar who early on asserted Breivik to be a Christian terrorist.[26] He was likened to the infamous Timothy McVeigh who bombed the Oklahoma Federal Building. One line of reasoning applied is that just as Muslims who are terrorists are referred to as Islamic terrorists so, too, Christians who are terrorists can be rightly labelled Christian terrorists. But is the admixture of religion and politics sufficient to justify the label in each case? Or is this little more than playing with nominalism? Juergensmeyer argues that what religions do 'is provide the "mores and symbols" through which such acts of violence are understood, legitimated, even seen as necessary and good'.[27] And here the religious narrative is most often cast in a context of a cosmic dualism: good against evil, the right and true against the false, God against Satan. But Asprem is right to critique this explanation of Breivik's views. Breivik is in fact focused on the immediate concrete context of Europe, not the cosmos. His is a temporal fight, not a metaphysical or spiritual war. Further, Breivik, in his manifesto, advocates national purity in other contexts, especially Indian as well as north European, against the encroachments of Christian evangelicalism and its cultural tropes.

Breivik presents himself as a 'cultural Christian'; he spurns any evangelical or other specific traditional Christian identity. Further, and in contrast with many Christian right-wing extremists, Breivik is a cultural Christian-Zionist. He is not anti-Jewish. He is a champion of Christian values and the legacy of the Church as a cultural marker. In his manifesto he states that, in fact, the Church he loves 'does not exist anymore because it has been deconstructed' but, he avers, 'I know that it can be reformed and that it again will embrace and propagate principles of strength, honour and self-defence.'[28] So rather than a secularist abandonment of the Church, he wishes to see it reformed as a Eurocentric nationalist institution. Breivik believes that Christianity is 'the only cultural platform that can unite all Europeans, which will be needed in the coming period during the third expulsion of the Muslims'.[29] However he wishes it to be also inclusive, or at least accepting, of distinctive European pre-Christian traditions such as Odinism. Breivik asserts his pagan north European Odinist identity; in effect he is thoroughly modern in claiming legitimacy for a form – admittedly limited – of multiple religious belonging. Nevertheless, for him it is Christianity which is regarded as having the necessary unifying power to stand up to the incursion of Islam and to resist multicultural dilution and 'globalism'. He used his violent actions, and his subsequent trial, as a performative platform aimed at rousing sympathy for his cause and empathetic action to further it. The aim was to provoke a sympathetic enjoining of the masses to fight the good fight, and the broad dissemination of his manifesto.

Interestingly, Breivik's recourse to the Knights Templar as a revolutionary motif is acknowledged by him as a fictional play on the Templar image, but it serves to produce a new 'fact' nonetheless, for the dynamic of the image is the thing, empowering a new reception and action derived from the old motif as carried by the image.[30] Umberto Eco puts it rather well: 'The lunatic is all *idee fixe*, and whatever he comes across confirms his lunacy. You can tell him by the liberties he takes with common sense, by his flashes of inspiration, and by the fact that sooner or later he brings up the Templars'.[31] But although Breivik states that his Templar Order is fictional, nevertheless there is a certain ambiguity for he holds the fictional to be nevertheless exemplary and 'in character'; thus 'his Templar dreams are as much part of his ideology – as motivational fiction, utopian literature, or blueprints of revolution – as any of his paranoid Eurabian fantasies and anti-Marxist rants'.[32] Motivational, utopian and revolutionary blueprints have all been applied as hermeneutical models for appropriating religious texts from time to time, and especially with respect to the Christian Bible.

I suggest that Breivik 'indwells' the Christian narrative – that is, his conceptual and ideological points of reference derive from his imbibing, both consciously and subconsciously, a particular version, and vision, of Christianity. His Christian identity is shaped by the narrative of it that he has internalized. Indeed, I suggest it is such 'indwelling' of a religious narrative which, in large measure, provides religious identity per se, for such identity is shaped and referenced by the data as well as the dynamics of the relevant religion's narrative tradition. So in that sense Breivik is correctly labelled a Christian terrorist whose terrorism is born of a reaction to the perceived threat of Islam, and whose radical response correlates to that of the Muslim extremism he fears – hence his is a reactive co-radicalization. One way of digging deeper into the specificity of the Christian narrative in which he may dwell, and which thus in a limited and apt way marks him as a Christian radical extremist reacting to the perceived radicalism of Islam, is by way of the style of Christian extremist ideology that goes by the name of the Phineas Priesthood, as discussed earlier. The hallmark of this extremist movement is that it empowers the solo actor – the so-called 'lone wolf' terrorist. Breivik is not known to have identified with this movement as such, but his actions reflect its ideology and modus operandi nonetheless. Insofar as the PP is a model applying to some forms of Christian extremism, it locates Breivik's actions as sitting within a very extreme form of Christian-oriented terrorism.

Breivik may well have acted alone, but he is by no means alone either in respect of his motivating sentiment or in the way his actions were received. There is in Europe a fringe – and a not insubstantial one – of rising xenophobia and Islamophobia which was a contributing thread. Furthermore, while many on the right showed evidence of recoiling from Breivik's methods and targets, they nonetheless sympathized with his message: Islam and Muslim immigrants are a threat to European survival. There is no evidence of European far-right extremists having softened their rhetoric in light of the widespread horror at what Breivik did. Xenophobic sentiments abetted by religion-based ideologies feed the emerging phenomenon of reactive co-radicalization. As one commentator has remarked: 'While most European extremists active online sought to distance themselves from Breivik, Russian neo-Nazis and far-right Russian nationalists hailed his killing spree'.[33] And well-regarded New Zealand columnist the late (Sir) Paul Holmes would not be alone when, having given a righteous berating of Breivik's actions, opined: 'Mind you, he's not the only European to worry about Muslim immigration. He's not the only European to feel himself and his culture and his country and his way of life threatened … Islam and the average way it presents itself in the street is imposing; to many it is threatening'.[34]

Another columnist referred to Breivik as the 'Christian Terrorist' who had failed to accept the multicultural and multireligious reality of today's world, insisting on waging war in favour of a Europe preserved for white Christians, fighting to preserve 'our Christian cultural heritage'.[35] The author was reporting, not agreeing, and added: 'There's no denying he's a Christian, albeit one occupying the lunatic fringe of the faith, along with those who murder abortion doctors, picket the funerals of US servicemen, and pray for President Obama's death,' and tellingly acknowledges that 'what is disturbingly clear' on the evidence of Breivik's manifesto, is that 'his rants against multiculturalism, immigration and the so-called 'Islamization' of Europe – isn't all that fringe'.[36] Quite.

Reactive co-radicalization

What might be discerned from these two cases? Clearly each displays evidence of extremism born of a reaction to the presumed threat of Islam.[37] A radical response is enacted that directly correlates to the Islamic radicalization that the respondent objects to. In one case the respondent is an electorate, in the other it is a single extremist. My argument is that the evidence of counter-extremism, in response in these cases to Islamic extremism, together with the more diffused phenomena of rising antipathy towards Islam and Muslims that is a distinct feature within Western society – secular and Christian – points to the paradox of 'reactionary extremism'. Because Islam is perceived as something extreme, reactions to it are becoming also extreme. And this is necessarily so in the eyes of those advocating this reaction. One only has to consider the phenomenon of the newly elected US president enacting restrictive measures with respect to refugees and citizens from a select few Muslim majority nations to see how, in fear of a prospect of Islamic terrorism occurring on American soil, a relatively extreme, and certainly highly contentious, disruptive and arguably wholly counter-productive, measure is taken. In particular, certain forms of extreme right-wing Christian and quasi-Christian religio-political rhetoric posit Islam as an implacable threat fully deserving of all the opprobrium heaped upon it and justifying any exclusionary, if not eliminative, actions that can be mounted against it.

The criminal actions of Breivik and the quixotic Swiss minaret ban are two examples of what I call 'reactive co-radicalization' at work. They are not the only examples. They are among the more obvious and dramatic. One could add to these the frenzy whipped up across the Muslim world in the wake of the widely reported and commented upon *The Innocence of Muslims* video posted on YouTube in July 2012. This precipitated frenetic reactions and widespread protests as it denigrated the Prophet Muhammad. It was eventually removed. And among the reports of increasing acts of anti-Islamic hate speech and allied negative actions, the violent rejection of all things Muslim was in late January 2017 enacted by a lone-wolf ultra-right nationalist and white supremacist against worshipping Muslims in a Quebec (Canada) mosque.[38] In every case the perception of a religious other as manifesting a threat leads to an extreme reaction. The mutuality of radicalization yields the irony of an 'impositional extremism' – even elimination – being enacted against those perceived to be 'impositional extremists' and whose extremism and supposed impositional intentions are denounced.[39]

A key question to ponder is whether counter-radicalization and counterterrorism techniques and processes, presently targeting Muslim communities, need also to be applied to the ideological host communities whence arise Christian (and other religious) forms of reactive co-radicalization. Ironically, in the case of modern Western societies, it is the secularity of a secular society that allows for religious diversity in the first place. Yet today the utopian vision of such a secular society positively predisposed to religious diversity – that is, allowing freedom of religion to all – is under threat from both religious extremism *and* the reactionary forces that may be either religious or non-religious. The point is rather well made by philosopher Martha Nussbaum. With reference to the contemporary upsurge of reactionary intolerance, she observes: 'Our situation calls urgently for searching critical self-examination, as we try to uncover the roots of ugly fears and suspicions that currently disfigure all Western societies.'[40] Nussbaum notes of the burqa and niqab bans implemented in France, Belgium and Italy that the numbers of actual wearers involved is a tiny minority. As with the Swiss minaret ban, such rejections of a couture are more symbolic than real. And there is a further irony: high fashion may even mimic, parallel or otherwise replicate the veiled couture of the rejected Muslims. There are many instances – the ski pistes of the French Alps for example, where women are entirely 'veiled' from sight, and no query is raised that this might suggest something of a cultural threat. And while the burkini may be objected to in some parts of the world, in other areas – especially where there is concern for the effect of too much exposure to damaging sun rays – the couture of female swimwear covering the greater part of the body is on the increase.

Nussbaum concurs that Breivik's expression of extreme rejection amounted to a reactive co-radicalization, albeit one that evoked a disturbingly mixed response from a wider Western public, as noted. His actions were virtually universally condemned but his cause received wide sympathy and his real intention of 'fighting the Muslim invasion' was even celebrated.⁴¹ Interestingly, Nussbaum's remarks were endorsed by the decision of the Norwegian Court:

> Norway's tragedy was not the work of a psychopath ... Breivik writes lucidly and ideologically ... he is an extremist with a paranoid view of the world, but he is capable of articulating a rationale for his deeds that is comprehensible ... Breivik ... used the occasion of his crimes to draw attention to a rationale for violence he would like to commend to the world.⁴²

Nussbaum points out that fear, as a narcissistic emotion needful for self-preservation, is at the same time destructive of both heterogeneity and the acceptance of alterity – especially when based on falsehood and enflamed by propaganda and prejudice or ideologies, whether religious or otherwise, such as antisemitism, for example. 'First, fear typically starts from some real problem ... Second, fear is easily displaced onto something that may have little to do with the underlying problem but serves as a handy surrogate for it ... Third, fear is nourished by the idea of the disguised enemy.'⁴³ She avers:

> Our current climate of fear shows that people are all too easily turned away from good values and laws, in a time of genuine insecurity and threat. Our time is genuinely dangerous ... many fears are rational, and appeals to fear have a role to play in a society that takes human life seriously. Still, at this point, the balance has all too often shifted in the other direction, as irresponsibly manufactured fears threaten principles we should cling to and be proud of.⁴⁴

Fear of the 'other', of difference and diversity, is the root problem. It lies at the heart of the mutuality of reactive co-radicalization.

What we are faced with today in the so-called 'secular' West is increasing evidence of extreme right-wing and quasi-Christian religio-political rhetoric abjuring Islam and Muslims that is drifting ever more steadily towards the centre. Former marginal views are becoming increasingly mainstream. The centre is becoming ever more radicalized. Extremist denouncements and calls advocating and justifying exclusionary or eliminative actions against the threatening 'other' of Islam are increasingly tolerated. Certainly, they are rarely challenged. They are becoming normalized.

Conclusion

To what extent does the phenomenon of reactive co-radicalization pose a threat to West European, American and other Western democratic societies such as Australia and Canada? I have written elsewhere that

> in a threatening context of change and challenge, recourse to the unchangeable and the security of that which is presumed a received tradition of unyielding sameness;

or alternatively the attempt to return a society to such a state once thought to exist in some pure form, now lost or besmirched and so requiring extraordinary effort to recover, lies at the heart of religious reaction that attempts to reinforce an identity lager, and so inclined to take extreme action with those perceived to threaten by way of their transgression of it.[45]

The wider context into which the two cases discussed above, among others, fits is the situation of a putative challenge to social harmony and cultural identity. In societies where there is a long-standing rich diversity of religious identity, such as India perhaps (notwithstanding the contemporary Hindutva context of hegemonic assertion), there can certainly be instances of inter-communal violence. However, in such cases there is perhaps not the same pernicious prospect of wholesale appeal to the maintenance and defence of a singular social identity in the face of the threatening presence of an aggressive 'other'. A long history of cultural and religious plurality militates against the sort of reactive co-radicalization that can now be detected in European societies. For in Western European nations today the preceding – and certainly premodern – cultural identity was substantially, if not totally, Christian. In effect this meant a religious singularity and cultural homogeneity, and so dominating identity over against which deviation and otherness were contrasted, usually negatively so. More comparative research is certainly needed to tease out such contrasting contexts, but I think the distinction between a context of religious singularity and religious plurality is prima facie a valid one. For in respect of the situation out of which the phenomenon of co-radicalization arises, both of the above cases I have focused on are premised on the defence and recovery of a singular, or at least dominant, 'Christian' or perhaps 'Christian/secular-democratic' social identity, in face of a perception of erosion or loss of this identity. And the perceived concerning 'loss' is not on the basis of the loss or decline of religion as such, but rather on the imagined effect upon society of the presence of self-assertive religion in the form of Islam. The presence of this religion is perceived to be a threat to contemporary secularity in a way that other religions are not: it is thus of threatening concern to secularism. And as a long-standing rival to Christianity, it poses, to some of that faith at least, the presence of a threatening other. Either way, the scene is set for a rise in extreme responses to this 'other'.

The Swiss minaret affair is arguably an instance of an extreme democratic act undertaken as a reaction to the perception that the presence of Islam and Muslims transgresses, not simply the landscape, but in fact the very identity of Switzerland as Swiss and, at least notionally, Christian. Anders Breivik widened the horizon of transgressors to include even the children of the political Left, deemed by him to be the fifth column allowing for the transgression of European identity by virtue of the acceptance of Islam and the allied promotion of multiculturalism within Europe. He, too, advocated a reinvigorated Christian-identity Europe. And in both cases certain democratic processes were followed to the letter of the law to the point of questioning whether, indeed, the rights and privileges presently obtaining ought really to continue to do so. The Swiss right wing made full use of the democratic system, with its facility for a popular citizens' referendum that, if won, is immediately written into the constitution. In the case of Norway, it was the due process of democratic justice that ironically enabled a platform for Breivik, at least in the short term, to take centre-stage in the advocacy of his ideology, even as he was tried and found guilty of murder. For at this juncture, the anti-Muslim rationale that is apparent – and which even those abhorring Breivik's actions may nevertheless endorse – only serves to reinforce the rhetoric of Islamic extremism. At the same time, the focus given to Breivik and his cause, courtesy of the democratic judicial process, served to reinforce and elevate like-minded angst about Islam in Europe, and also elsewhere, and promote other forms of extreme reaction to it. Fear of the 'other', of difference and diversity, is the root problem. It is expressed in terms of the mutual discontent, in hostile antipathy that feeds religious extremism. It lies at the heart of the mutuality of reactionary extremism; it is the lifeblood of reactive co-radicalization as I have sought to identify and illuminate. It seems clear that the predominant pattern of reactive co-radicalization is occurring in the context of widespread anxiety about Islam. Accordingly, our discussion of extremism now turns to the issue of the fear of Muslims as such.

CHAPTER 9
EXTREMISM AND ISLAMOPHOBIA

In his inauguration speech, US president Donald Trump declared an all-out war on Islamic extremism: 'We will ... unite the civilized world against radical Islamic terrorism, which we will eradicate completely from the earth.'[1] This pledge was made in the context of an assertion of 'patriotic loyalty' ('We all bleed the same red blood of patriots'), supported by a biblical reference to the benefits 'when God's people live together in unity ... infused with the breath of life by the same almighty Creator'.[2] Jingoism and religion were intermingled to produce a patina of self-confident assertion. This was music to the ears of those who rejoice in the idea of eliminating that which they fear, rather than seeking to discover, at depth and with critical understanding, just 'what the hell is going on'[3] in respect of Islam and Islamism. They revel in the prospect that we, the good guys, are going to trump you (no pun intended!), the bad guys. But tragically, this sort of political rhetoric from the so-called 'leader' of the free world will only exacerbate the phenomenon of reactive co-radicalization discussed in Chapter 8. It will also serve to foment a growing Islamophobia. For such rhetoric, and any accompanying policies and actions, will only serve to reinforce the attitudes and actions of the many extreme right-wing and Islamophobic individuals, political parties and movements that are found throughout the 'free world' today – from Australia in the Antipodes to Norway near the Arctic Circle, and beyond, as well as within America itself. In the end the president may not need to take direct action as such, his policies and values will encourage others to do that – potentially, a licence for extremism against Muslims feared en masse to be, at least potentially, extremist.

This chapter discusses Islamophobia and argues that in many respects it can be regarded, in effect, as a manifestation of religious extremism. It has emerged rather prominently in much contemporary right-wing political parties and movements which have an anti-Islam stance as a major focus. As we saw with respect to the discussion of reactive co-radicalization, we are faced today not only with the problem of being confronted with Islamism and Muslim extremists but also with religious radicalization emanating from a variety of different religions and religious groups or organizations that amounts to a parallel reactionary extremism. Arguably Islamophobia, in some cases at least, presents as a religious extremism equal to – at least ideologically, if not always behaviourally – any Islamic threat, whether merely perceived or indubitably real. Beginning with a wide-ranging discussion on the phenomenon of Islamophobia, I touch on issues of anti-Islamic prejudice and analyse the role ignorance plays in fomenting Islamophobic attitudes. This leads into a discussion of how perceptions of Islam are formed, and the impact of media and political discourse.

Religion and Extremism

The phenomenon of Islamophobia: Meaning and reactions

Paradoxically, the United States of America has some of the best scholars and analysts who do understand the nature of Islamism and just what is going on. But, seemingly, their knowledge and advice is being ignored in favour of long-standing prejudices and presumptions. These include that there is more or less a single radical or extremist Islam to contend with, and that Islam is inherently violent and extreme. Therefore all Muslims must be presumed to be of that ilk – unless they can prove otherwise. An implicit view that Muslims per se are inherently guilty and not to be trusted inevitably emerges to fuel anti-Muslim prejudices. Ignorance trumps critical understanding. Rejection trumps affirmation of Muslim otherness. Prejudice trumps acceptance and tolerance of Muslim diversity. And so an otherwise reasonable concern with those extremists who have, indeed, declared their opprobrium for, and even war on, America and the West is generalized not only to all Islamists of whatever ilk – political or militant – but to all Muslims anywhere, irrespective of their particular Islamic identity and orientation. This generalized and inchoate fear of Muslims is the core of what is meant by the term Islamophobia.[4] To target, militarily, a known and avowed enemy is one thing. To simply identify, by dint of a generic identity association (namely, religion) a whole people as 'the enemy' on the pretext that it is the apparent sameness of their religion that marks them out as a hostile 'other' – irrespective of any protestation or evidence to the contrary – is to give way to a generalized fear or anxiety that, in turn, can – and does – give lead to extreme negative reactions. This happened to Jews in the twentieth century. Antisemitism – effectively a visceral abhorrence, and so demonization, of Jews and Judaism – is a direct parallel to Islamophobia. In the latter case, an otherwise genuine concern at the reality of Islamist extremism provokes an Islamophobic reaction that all too quickly assumes a mantel of inclusive generalization and so an abhorrence of all Muslims and everything Islamic. Paradoxically, the logic of this generic identity association was also used by Osama bin Laden and fellow-Islamists, especially since the 1998 World Islamic Front declaration 'Jihad against Jews and Crusaders'.[5] Bin Laden was a signatory to this document which seeks to assert the eradication of an otherwise well-recognized distinction between combatants and non-combatants. And so reasonable anxiety, concern or fear of an aggressively militant form of Islam is projected onto all Muslims, virtually whoever and wherever, and to Islam as such.

Islamophobia can certainly register as a contentious term, with some doubting whether there is such a thing as a 'phobia' of Islam. However there are others who, in agreeing that there is indeed an anti-Islamic phenomenon, suggest that using the term Islamophobia is a mistake. It has been critiqued as often 'reduced to a phenomenon that is both overly simplistic and largely superficial'.[6] Jocelyne Cesari notes that the term 'Islamophobia'

> is contested because it is often imprecisely applied to very diverse phenomena, ranging from xenophobia to antiterrorism. It groups together all kinds of different forms of discourse, speech, and acts by suggesting that they all emanate from an identical ideological core, which is an irrational fear (a phobia) of Islam.[7]

Nevertheless, the term has gained widespread coinage. Rather like 'fundamentalism', it is here to stay. The trick is to gain a more nuanced understanding of that to which the term refers, and attempts to do just that have been ongoing for a number of years. In 1997 the British Runnymede Trust issued a report which set something of a benchmark, declaring Islamophobia to be the 'dread or hatred of Islam and therefore, to the fear and dislike of all Muslims'.[8] It documented a range of actions whereby Muslims were being discriminated against on the grounds of their religious identity. Islamophobia, rather like xenophobia, names an irrational and exaggerated fear of an 'other' – in this case the Muslim 'other'. In May 2002 the European Monitoring Centre on Racism and Xenophobia (EUMC) released a report that drew upon research from across all then EU member states.[9] Tracking developments since 9/11, the report noted 'an increase in Islamophobia-related incidents' and 'highlighted the regularity with which ordinary Muslims became targets for abusive and sometimes violent retaliatory attacks'; indeed, in spite of 'localised differences within each member nation, the recurrence of attacks on recognisable and visible manifestations of Islam and Muslims themselves was the report's most significant finding'.[10] Little has since changed. As Ihsan Yilmaz remarks, 'Islamophobia includes the prejudiced perception that Islam has no values in common with other cultures, is inferior to the West, and is a violent political ideology rather than a religion as such'.[11] Islamophobic discrimination and attacks have been diverse and widespread in recent years.

> The double discrimination of racism and religious intolerance are frequently evident in attacks against Muslims. Incidents have included bombings and arson attacks on mosques and Muslim institutions in many countries, including Austria, France, the Netherlands, Spain, and the United Kingdom, with attacks on Muslim cemeteries also widely reported. Assaults on individuals ranged from spitting, shoving, or the snatching of women's headscarves, to punches and kicks and lethal bludgeoning, stabbings, and shootings. Personal assaults were often accompanied by shouted insults alluding to religion and ethnic or national origin – sometimes expressing both racism and religious hatred.[12]

And reports of people of other faiths, notably Sikhs, being mistaken for, and so targeted as, Muslims – sometimes with tragic results – have been likewise quite widespread.[13]

Islamophobia thus adequately names a very real and pressing problem that confronts many societies today. For, without doubt, there are many who feel a degree of anxiety – even fear – in respect of Islam and Muslims. And significantly, in extreme cases of this reaction, the fear and anxiety is manifest as a hate-filled negativity with, at times, violent actions taken against Muslim locations – such as mosques; or people – as wearers of burkini swimwear recently discovered on the beaches of France. Negative perceptions and resultant anxieties about Muslims and Islam are generated by a multitude of factors that overlap and interact. They are seldom found in isolation from each other. Simple fear of the stranger – xenophobia – may be one such factor. Ignorance, which promotes the seeing of the unfamiliar as 'other' can also contribute to a fear of the outsider, as we will explore further below. Fear or anxiety about that which is different, of that which is not us, is often based on the absence of true knowledge and, instead, the presence of limited and biased information. The imagination creates a picture of what is presumed to be true. Judgements, attitudes and actions are premised on that. Other factors, such as concerns regarding immigration impacting employment and disrupting existing cultural norms, or of refugees harbouring terrorists, also weigh in. And, it should be added, the West's ancient discourse concerning the alien nature of Islam, both religious and cultural, with its apparent opposition to Western post-Enlightenment values, is another contributing factor when it comes to plumbing the roots and reasons lying behind contemporary Islamophobia. In short, the focus and phenomenon that manifests as Islamophobia

> is an ideological position current in Western societies that negatively positions Islam and Muslims as the Other – as a problem to 'us' – which takes different forms and produces various effects. The ideological meanings of 'Islam' and 'Muslims', upon which Islamophobia rests, are drawn from a mix of accurate and inaccurate, reflective and constructed, representations and misrepresentations.[14]

Populist politics is adept at manipulating inchoate anxiety and prejudice-shaped fear. Today attention is on Islam and Muslims to an unprecedented degree. Correlatively Islamophobia 'has become a focus of real concern for both the Muslim recipient of prejudiced negativity and the wider society in respect of the widespread anxiety, even fear, at the presence of Muslims'.[15]

To be sure, perceptions of Islam, and concerns about Islamic ideology and Islamist activities are of ongoing concern across the entire globe, for Muslims and non-Muslims alike. Antipathy towards Islam, long-standing from many quarters, not only seems to be increasing but is also evolving into a dominant element of political discourse and party political policies of containment and discrimination. This is occurring in many countries that have heretofore promoted policies of tolerance, openness and diversity. And even where other sorts of diversities – ethnic, gender, racial and so on – are yet affirmed, with respect to Islam and Muslims the door of liberality and acceptance closes.[16] Not only are minarets banned in one place, forms of Muslim clothing are proscribed in others. And much of the reference in Trump's inaugural speech to 'reclaiming our borders' was to the notion of keeping out unwanted aliens – including especially suspect Muslims. For the unspoken inference is that Muslims, as such, cannot be trusted. It would seem, for example, that within the orbit of present American politics, it is Muslims who have replaced the communist bogey of half a century ago. But that observation is of little comfort and underplays the deeper issue of Islamophobia per se.

On the one hand, Islam, or rather Muslim leaders and spokespeople in different parts of the world, produce much rhetoric concerning peaceful coexistence and membership in the global community. Yet on the other hand there are Islamist ideologues who foment virulent policies of opposition to the secular West and to Zionism and, in some cases, also to Christianity – or at least to some Christian churches and related organizations. Such active opposition may be directed against Israel, and may even produce a negative response to Judaism, Quranic injunctions to the contrary notwithstanding. It certainly has produced an overriding and alarmingly growing negative response to Jews as such.[17] The emergence – in some respects, the re-emergence – in recent years of the Islamic State, or Caliphate, with its undisputed horrific atrocities and extermination of various Muslims and non-Muslims as targeted enemies, has meant that the peace-oriented interpretations and lifestyle expressions of Islam, as followed by many millions across the globe, are in danger of being overshadowed. Even in the face of knowing peace-loving Muslim individuals, Muslims everywhere are often too readily perceived as harbingers of hate towards any who are not like them. Fear is thus generalized. Correlatively, there is increasing report of Muslim individuals and communities at the receiving end of expressions and actions of hate and rejection. And certainly, as we advance into the twenty-first century, it seems that horrifying headlines provide an incessant reminder of the widespread presence of extreme forms of Islam. Such attention-grabbing headlines are part of any terrorist or extremist project, for communicating the message is as much a tool of terrorism as is the destruction wrought by the violent act itself. As Alex Schmid notes, communication is one of the 'five conceptual lenses' whereby terrorism may be helpfully analysed and understood.[18]

An internet perusal will quickly disclose headlined reports of Muslim extremists committing gross acts such as beheading foreign hostages. Whether it is yet another account of an extrajudicial beheading – an American journalist, a British aid-worker, a volunteer convoy driver – by agents of the Islamic State (ISIS/ISIL); or the act of Boko Haram beheading a Nigerian officer for 'serving the State instead of Allah';[19] or the execution of a French mountaineer, also beheaded, by an Algerian affiliate of the Islamic State;[20] or reports of Syrian rebels beheading Christians, among other atrocities – the list could go on and on – the cumulative effect is inevitable: hostile reactions, whether by way of threat or act, emerge. So Muslims with no link to the extremists find themselves targeted. Muslims in Oklahoma are threatened with beheading. A mosque in Texas is firebombed, many others are vandalized. The website of the Council for American-Islamic Relations (CAIR) records the many such Islamophobic actions that take place within the United States.[21] And with such headlines and reportage, there comes the inevitable result of much media commentary and too many people tending to equate 'extreme' with 'mainstream', thereby tarring all Muslims with the same brush of hostile accusation and so subject to a subsequent Islamophobic response.

Paradoxically, extremist Muslims thrive on Islamophobia. For its hostile rejection of Muslims and Islam reinforces Islamist rhetoric of a godless siege being waged against the true believers of Islam. It thus aids the normalizing of their own extreme jihadist response to it. In light of this, the upsurge in aggressive anti-Muslim rhetoric and acts within the United States of America – a society that historically has been marked by the acceptance of religious otherness and diversity – is disturbingly marked. Such attitudes and actions are being increasingly repeated in other otherwise liberal and open Western societies. Examples cited above will be long eclipsed by yet other incidents. The actions of an increasingly reactionary extremism emanating from many non-Muslim quarters target not just the Islamist extremists themselves, but often any Muslims anywhere. This is where the phenomenon of Islamophobia comes into focus. It is not just a version of racial prejudice, nor a response to any extremism as such. It is an extremism in and of itself – an extremism that targets Muslims per se on the basis of their religious identity and nothing else. To that extent it is an example of the reactive co-radicalization discussed in the previous chapter.

There is in fact today a wide context of Islamophobic extremism that manifests forms of mutually reactive co-radicalization. For example, in Thailand there have been instances in recent years of reactionary Buddhist extremism in response to a perception of the danger posed by Islam and Muslims.[22] A Buddhist culture, confronted with the spectre of so-called 'jihadi terrorism', responds with forms of violent behaviour that *prima facie* runs counter to predominant religious teachings and sensibilities.[23] But such an apparently paradoxical shift from a religious predilection for peace to a religiously sanctioned reaction of violence is not so uncommon. Extremist organizations in countries with Buddhist majority populations have instigated confrontations and deadly riots against minority Muslim populations in recent years. There are anti-Muslim groups in Myanmar (Burma), Thailand and Sri Lanka which have found sympathizers in and among Buddhist monastics, householders and political leaders. In many postcolonial contexts, Muslims have become the targets of majority Buddhist populations in the wake of new forms of Buddhist nationalism. The reality today is that this scenario is broadly found in other societies as well. In Africa, radical Islamic groups like al-Qaeda and al-Shabab are increasing efforts to stoke and actively support African Muslim hostility towards their Christian counterparts.[24] And after the Nigerian security forces killed the founder of Boko Haram in 2009, 'al-Qaeda in the Islamic Maghreb (AQIM) issued a statement of condolence and offered to give Muslims training and weapons to fight Christians in Nigeria. The statement read in part: "We are ready to train your people in weapons, and give you whatever support we can in men, arms and munitions to enable you to defend our people in Nigeria".'[25] And, equally, today there are individuals and organizations in the West, especially in Germany and the United Kingdom, whose declared mission is to confront and demolish the foundations of Islam in a polemical war of words, if not also direct actions. Some of these organizations and individuals are scouring Africa, under the guise of providing support for persecuted Christians, organizing seminars on confrontational polemics and distributing inflammatory literature demonizing Islam and Muslims. They are stoking fear and hatred amongst Christians towards all Muslims. They are actively fomenting Islamophobia. They give evidence of Christian fundamentalism heading towards an active extremism.

Anti-Islamic prejudice and action

The common basis for Islamophobia is the rejection of religious and cultural diversity, with Islam and Muslims in the frame. Previously identified racially and culturally as Arabs, Turks, Asians or whoever, Muslims were – and often still are – depicted within

Western rhetoric as, among other things, exotic, violent, fanatic, hostile, strict, dishonest, duplicitous, medieval, despotic and evil.[26] It was just such identifiers that journalists and cartoonists at the French satirical magazine *Charlie Hebdo* constantly relied upon in their inflammatory pieces. As a result of the attack on them in January 2015, there was wide condemnation not only for their murders but also for what was claimed to be an attack by Islamist extremists on freedom of speech per se as valued and practiced in a modern civilized society. But how civil is a society that perpetuates anti-Islamic prejudice under the guise of free speech, so allowing the unfettered growth of Islamophobia in both attitude and action? Is being anti-Muslim wholly allowable on the basis of free speech?[27] For free speech was at the heart of Pastor Terry Jones's attempt to burn copies of the Qur'an in 2010, which he subsequently did in 2011. This blatant Islamophobic action sparked worldwide protests from Muslims, and even led to a number of deaths. However, as has been pointed out, the treating of Islamophobic attitudes and actions as something other than a form of racism, so therefore not subject to the proscriptions and sanctions that nowadays any racist attitude and action is subject to, and instead moving the discourse of Islamophobia into the realm of free speech, 'the debate is shifted to absolve perpetrators of Islamophobia of sentiments that would otherwise be considered abhorrent'.[28]

The fact that Islamophobia is a form of extremism is reinforced by, for example, the rising wider sociopolitical acceptance within the United Kingdom and Western Europe of right-wing groups with an anti-Islamic agenda such as the English Defence League, the UK Independence Party, the Netherlands' Party for Freedom, the Sweden Democrats and Germany's PEGIDA. On the other side of the world, in Australia there is the Australian Liberty Alliance which presents an anti-Islam platform – 'Islam is a problem and if we don't take steps to put laws in place to protect our culture and our society, then we are going to lose our freedom.'[29] The 'Restore Australia' party would ban Islam entirely.[30] Its leader is quite open on the matter: 'We believe that Islam is not compatible with Australian society, and under our constitution it is actually illegal for anyone to be a supporter of Islam.'[31] And groups such as the United Patriots Front and Reclaim Australia also see Islam as having no place in the country – where, according to the 2011 Census, Muslims make up only around 2.2 per cent of the total population. Australian senator Pauline Hansen is a long-time opponent of Islam. In late 2016 her call to ban Muslims entering Australia was picked up and endorsed by a local television celebrity, sparking fierce discussion and debate. The president of the Islamic Society of Toowoomba, Queensland, whose mosque has been destroyed by arson attacks twice in recent years, has complained that the 'irresponsible predominately anti-Muslim and also anti-Asian rhetoric of Ms Hanson is likely to have a significant impact on Australia's reputation as a peaceful egalitarian nation in the Asia-Pacific region' and he called upon the Australian prime minister to condemn publicly her extremist and hate-mongering views.[32] The *Australian Muslim Times* report noted that Australian Muslims 'have reacted with alarm at the blatant hate speech with vilification of Islam and demonisation of Muslims by extremist and racist politicians and media celebrities'.[33]

Religion and Extremism

The platform of anti-Islamic sentiment in North America is extensive and, under the new administration of Donald Trump, likely to increase. Islamophobia is not just a problem of disquiet with a particular religious 'other', but is manifesting as a disruption to the recent tradition of liberal, pluralist and inclusive sociopolitical values. It is a cipher for a deep-seated and growing form of extremism in its own right, an extremism that bears many of the hallmarks of the analysis of fundamentalism, as outlined above, in the way it is formed, fomented and expressed. The ultimate outworking of far-right views contained at the core of extreme right-wing political parties and movements is seen in and through a virulent hatred of Islam and Muslims. And this has increasing attraction for a largely ignorant, and certainly concerned, middle ground. And, even before Trump, it is disturbing to learn that there has been a purposeful campaign to 'form a political culture that not only formulates, then justifies, United States foreign and economic policies but also produces campaigns to ensure these policies are integrated into the American mainstream easily so as to solicit its support'.[34] The intention of this campaign is unashamedly anti-Islam and anti-Muslim. The consequence of such an unfettered, even actively facilitated, Islamophobic culture already is one of 'war, torture, kidnappings, incarcerations, executions, surveillance, entrapment and the curtailing of civil liberties, not to mention the harassment, discrimination, hate-speech, and acts of criminal violence experienced by Muslims, and others unfortunate enough to be mistaken as Muslims'.[35]

To reiterate, anxiety about the current state of affairs vis-à-vis relations with the world of Islam underlies increasing concern about Islam and the presence of Muslims within Western societies, thus fuelling the reaction of Islamophobia that results in acts of discrimination, vilification and even violence. Muslims in some situations become the target of policies that seek to contain the visibility of Islam in society and limit Muslims' access to the public sphere and society's institutions. Islamophobia simply names a particular type of negative prejudicial response towards Islam and Muslims based on an underlying fear of them. And Islamophobia is measureable. For instance a group of researchers in the United States tested for fear-related attitudes towards Islam and Muslims.[36] A sampling of 223 undergraduates showed that Republicans rated higher than non-Republicans and that those with at least one Muslim friend rated lower than those without. Islamophobia thrives on ignorance and avoidance of real engagement with the 'other'; indeed it is premised on a denial of the other. It is a combination of ignorance of Islam – its diversities and the realities of Islamism in relation to other ideological perspectives that exist within Islam – and the ways in which Islam is imaged within and by media perception, and so the consciousness of a non-Muslim population, that feeds and fosters the generalized fear of Islam and Muslims. The ignorance I refer to is found in at least four modalities, namely innocent, blind, dismissive and culpable. Let's take a closer look at these.

Ignorance and Islamophobia

Innocent ignorance, or ignorance *simpliciter*, refers to situations of a naïve 'not-knowing'. This is the case with regard to a direct and unequivocal 'don't know' response when a question of knowledge or perception is raised. However, this form of ignorance provides opportunity for correction and learning through gaining information and education. It implies no intentional prejudice on the part of the one who is innocently ignorant, simply that there is something they just don't know but with a little application can come to know. On the other hand, blind ignorance is something born of an intellectual incapability or cognitive barrier that effectively prevents any 'seeing' or 'knowing' other than what has been dictated by the worldview perspectives already held, or of knowledge presumed to be sufficient and so not requiring anything further. This results in the response of 'can't know' or 'don't need to know', because it is outside the field of interest or awareness. Or the response is one of: 'There is nothing I need to know' – on the grounds that the knowledge already held requires nothing further. Either way, knowledge and understanding of the 'other' are so utterly proscribed that no alternative perspective or image is admissible. Here the notion of applying a corrective, or a new learning, through gaining and processing new information is ruled out. In this situation any educational process, if attempted, will require sustained and careful execution to effect any real change. Nevertheless, even if such change is unwelcome or resisted, this mode is basically that of a cognitive inertia that, in principle, can be overcome. Arguably this type of ignorance yields to changes in social ordering and cultural life as happened in such momentous events of the twentieth century within, for example, the United States in respect of the civil rights movement, or South Africa in eventual response to both internal agitation and worldwide condemnation of apartheid.

However, there is yet a third kind of ignorance that goes beyond even that occasioned by the blinding effect of a limited perspective and a resistant or closed mind. This is what might be called 'dismissive ignorance'. It is the attitude and response of simply dismissing as irrelevant the presentation of any countering evidence or knowledge so as to avoid any challenge to, or rethinking of, a position or judgement held. It comes to the fore in respect of issues and debates where there is a measure of contestation or difference in opinion and conclusion. Dismissive ignorance is then expressed with lines such as 'I don't know; nobody knows'; with a corollary deprecation of any suggestion that someone might indeed know. It thus excuses the avoidance of addressing the issue in question. Finally, perhaps as an extension of dismissive ignorance, yet subtly different, there is culpable ignorance. This is 'active ignoring'. It is the deliberate refusal to know. It is the avoidance of the challenge to cognitive change; the reinforcement of a prejudicial perspective by deliberately shunning any evidence, argument or perspective to the contrary. Such ignorance issues in an active denial of alternative possibilities; in the out-of-hand rejection of options presented for alternate ways of thinking, understanding and interpreting. It prefers the already-held fixed position as a final word on a matter, irrespective of any suggestion or evidence to the contrary. Culpable ignorance thus discounts objective evidence and critical objectivity in favour of trumpeting its own 'alternative facts'. This modality goes hand-in-glove with the attitude and mindset that harbours most forms of fundamentalism or extremism. It produces an intentional 'I don't want to know' type of response. It is resistant to any information contrary to its own; it is inimical to educational process; it treats cognitive change as in effect, if not actually, treasonable.

Perceptions of Islam: Image and imagination

The distortions of perception derived from ignorance, of whatever kind, continue to impact upon the world in ways that now make the issue of addressing rising Islamophobia urgent. To do so requires, among other things, to reflect on the factors that shape and influence non-Muslim perceptions of Islam. This allows us to begin to see where the viewing of Islam as inherently extreme comes from, and so what it is that feeds the reactionary extremism of Islamophobia. The answer, for the most part, lies in the dominant portrayal of Islam through popular media, both secular and religious, together with much contemporary political discourse that has imbibed it. It is very often the imaginative construct of Islam as shaped by media images which drive Islamophobia, for such portrayals tend to conflate the extreme elements with the normative whole. It goes without saying that the primary, and for many the only, exposure to Islam is via television news coverage, newspaper reportage, and cinematic presentation with, for some, little more than hearsay gleaned from like-minded individuals, friends or family whose own source has been no more than a media diet. Added to that is the ubiquitous presence of mobile phone and other digital communications technology with its instant replay of photo-image, text message, Instagram and Twitter comment. All too often these media project images of Islam that are little more than stereotypes. Nonetheless it is the stereotypical image that powerfully influences the formation of imagination both for the individual and also the collective or common communal perception. And the image so formed reinforces the stereotype. A self-fulfilling and self-perpetuating feedback loop is in operation. In this regard the predominance of visual image, in a video age, hardly needs to be stressed. But, as well, the impact of the printed word – whether in newspaper, news journal, popular book or tract– contributes significantly to the image-making effect of the media. So what gives form and content to the image-shaping so conveyed? What constitutes the substance of the image held in the imagination? Given the incontrovertible pervasiveness of the media in the process of image-formation – and even allowing for the recognition that there is more than a grain of truth in the adage that 'the medium is the message' – what gives the image its content?

Perceptions of Islam within the popular Western consciousness are arguably shaped by dominant political forces at play. This is the two-edged sword of the predominance of political material as the source and focus of much media coverage, and the filtering effect of editorial choice and decision-making by those who control the media. Whether intentional or not, the selection of material, the way it is presented – the casting of the news – will reflect prior assumptions and agendas of a broadly political nature. Arguably all editing, all redaction, is a political act in the sense of not being undertaken in a cognitive vacuum. Rather it is guided by consideration of desired effects or the dictates of subtext message, propaganda and the like. Despite any profession of the objective neutrality of a reporter, and the supposed neutral objectivity of the camera – which 'never lies' – the outcome, in terms of presented image, necessarily yields to the language of the report and the angle of the camera shot (the more graphic, stark or dramatic, the more likely it will be aired or printed). This undoubtedly implies, even in a broad sense of the term, that there is a dimension of political domination in the image product, which is then projected through the media. But what does this mean, really?

Too often the image of Islam projected via the media lacks an authentically critical framework for interpretation, although there are also some very good exceptions to this observation, including the contributions of some excellent Muslim public intellectuals and commentators such as Waleed Aly in Australia, and Reza Aslan and Seyyed Hossain Nasr in the United States of America, for example. Nevertheless, certain hostile right-wing news channels and commentators carry great sway and influence. They manifest an almost palpable prejudicial and negative perspective of Islam and Muslims. The image portrayed is thus often contextually loose. That is, it lacks appropriately situating context that would enable considered critical understanding. Or it is just 'loose' in the sense of presenting only a simplistic – an often assumed and likely false or misleading – contextual point of reference. Thus, that which feeds the collective imagination and which in turn holds, embellishes, and draws upon the image for a variety of other purposes, lacks appropriate contextual reference markers to enable fuller and appropriately nuanced comprehension. Alternatively, such context as may be given is so limited and biased as to be actively misleading. Certainly, for the most part, it would be true to say that the projection and reception of the image of Islam is conducted with a bare minimum, if any, attention paid to proper contextual factors. Of course, good investigative journalists and reputable news reporters will defend their locating of reportage in context. I am not saying that good contextualizing of the image does not happen at all. Only that the predominant image of Islam that seems to prevail in popular and political discourse does not, in fact, come with an appropriate or authentic hermeneutical guide. Thus, for example, Islam is too frequently and falsely perceived as a monolithic entity; as an avaricious self-aggrandizing religious culture per se; as non-self-critical or reflective; as archaic, time-locked and irredeemably Middle Eastern. So the image of Islam is not rooted in sound contextual appreciation and understanding, and this results in a religiously skewed image of Islam.

In short, Islam is not usually portrayed or perceived as a religion or spiritual pathway, or certainly not portrayed in a balanced way as such. It is rarely presented on its own terms as *din* (the Arabic term more or less referring to the essential *idea* of Islam as religion). Islam is not normally portrayed as being at heart an encompassing spiritual orientation, inherently holistic in its outlook and application. Rather, the idea of religion that is seemingly and usually attached by Western media to the term 'Islam' is itself often skewed or conceptually twisted, emphasizing its sociopolitical aspect without due reference to the intrinsic and accompanying spiritual aspect, for it is both that make of it a religion. The image presented is thus off-centre, unbalanced so as to reinforce negative, even false, representations. The politico-juristic elements of Islam are over-stressed in comparison with the theological and pietistic dimensions; the pragmatics of Islamic programmes or Islamist agendas predominate over an awareness of Muslim ethical sensibilities and reflections. And the underlying and deeper raison d'être for any given Islamic action is thereby lost to view. The religious depth is trivialized: the picture remaining is two-dimensional. Thus the image of Islam that emerges, to the extent it is presented as religious, is all too often that of an ideologically oppositional 'religious other'. Islam is portrayed as the necessary de facto oppositional religion to Christianity, and vice versa. Muslims are portrayed as de facto oppositional, religiously and politically to a secular society and often also to Christians, as well as to Jews and other religions and their followers. And the vice versa is promoted: secular society, and these other religions, are urged to recognize Islam as inherently antithetical and so a threatening other. Islam is presented as the ideological rival par excellence to the West, indeed the world. The rhetoric of some Islamists can certainly reinforce this. Religious exclusivism – the sense of uniqueness, even superiority – which naturally adheres to most religions without doubt finds expression within Islamic ideology. It is quite clearly taken up and reinforced by various extremists and hard-line advocates, providing grounds for a sense of inherent oppositional positioning. But this is by no means the full story of Islam and its relation to other religions and societies.

The Western image of Islam is largely the product of the image-making process I have analysed so far. Islam is regarded as no friendly rival as in a competing sports team. Rather this 'rival' is so completely 'other' that the prospect of confrontation is couched in dramatic terms and fearful expectation. Thus Islam is portrayed as the 'Great Threat'; the ultimate opponent in a climatic and apocalyptic clash of civilizations; the historical antithesis to the West's thesis. As Beverly Milton-Edwards notes, Islam is falsely positioned as an inherent threat 'because Muslims are portrayed as harbouring monolithic consensual values that violently clash with those of the West ... Muslims – irrespective of their location – are represented as hostile and aggressive, and fringe dwellers in the Western context'.[37] Religious extremists of variant Christian types, for example, will transmute the antithesis to an antichrist image. Islam is then portrayed, ideologically, as the great contemporary satanic opponent to an idealized Judeo-Christian West. And ironically, the *vice versa* holds: to many in the Islamic world it is the West that is the demonic opposition, with America itself identified as the Great Satan. But such ideological oppositions are little more than mirror images of extremely fundamentalist and exclusivist religious postures that are indicative of the extent to which Islam is presented in terms of a sociologically misrepresented image. Islam is deemed to be, in a variety of ways, 'out of control'.

Such representations produce the view of this religion having an aura of inner conflict and lack of concerted direction for its own good, sociopolitically speaking. This viewpoint is echoed in the comments made from time to time that Islam needs, or is yet to have, its own 'Reformation' – as if somehow that would usher in an acceptable 'reformed' Muslim faith, one which a secular world could presumably better accommodate. This, of course, misreads Islam both historically and in the contemporary context. There is great social, political and ideological variety throughout the world of Islam, and much diversity in respect of localized political expression and difference in the way specific issues and agendas occupy the energies of Muslims. This diversity does not mean Islam is a threat by virtue of being, in some vague sense, out of control as a sociopolitical entity. Indeed the countervailing impetus to unity within the worldwide Islamic community, which acts as an internal check and corrective upon some of the more volatile elements, is not to be misread as suggesting the possibility that Islam may yet become the monolith it is feared to be already. Rather, it suggests that the dialectic implied in the tension between the ideal of an overarching unity of the Islamic community, and the variegated reality of it in practice only reflects the fact of Islam being an authentic and complex religio-political entity. Nevertheless, fear and hostility towards Islam are today rampant and require our attention. I suggest, as one of many lines of approach or elements to be considered, that Islamophobia may be understood to be a product, in part at least, of the twin correlated forces of ignorance and misinformed imagination. In this regard, Stefanie Wright draws attention to the disturbing level of Islamophobia present in the media and political discourse of the United States.[38]

Media and political discourse

Despite a long history of presence with the United States, Islam and Muslims are regarded 'as both foreign and antithetical to American civilisation', especially by Republicans.[39] Wright reports that a study undertaken in 2011 showed that 'one-third of self-identified Republicans believed that Muslims want to establish Shari'a as the law of the land' and she suggests that to challenge Islamophobia effectively would require 'an understanding not only of the production of anti-Muslim and anti-Islamic narratives, but of the production of the cultural contexts in which they are deemed credible'.[40] In other words, the answer to Islamophobia requires, first, to discern, then confront, the very prejudices and worldview contexts that promote it. And to large measure these are themselves bound up with extremist, largely Christian, religious fundamentalism and ideologies. Wright herself probes deeply into the historical and political legacy of response to, and perceptions of, Muslim presence in America, noting even 'how America's Founding Fathers invoked Islam as they sought to define the institutional character of their fledgling nation'.[41] She concludes that the twenty-first-century phenomenon of American's fear of Muslims needs to be understood not only against the backdrop of 9/11 and the resultant 'War on Terror' but also in light of 'anti-Muslim sentiments' that 'echo and reproduce aspects of a far older discursive tradition about Islam'.[42] These show that 'cultural tropes and stereotypes about Islam have changed rather little in the United States over time'.[43] These include the now standard view that Islam is inherently antithetical to democracy. This is a view that resonates today especially in Europe. Islamophobia may be a particular contemporary issue; it is also a deep-seated and long-standing one. It manifests in respect of violence against Muslims in Sweden[44] and elsewhere such as France which, proportionally, has the largest Muslim minority in Europe.[45] Others, especially northern European countries, have recently experienced an upsurge in Islamophobic acts and allied public discourse and political rhetoric, some of which also has a long-standing pedigree.[46]

Religion and Extremism

This pedigree goes back to the very inception of Islam in history when Islam first rubbed up against Christianity and Judaism. The nature of the relationship between Islam and Christianity has ever been marked by three fundamental dynamics: mutual antipathy, mutual affinity and mutual inquiry. The first, antipathy, has been typically predominant, especially as the two faiths most often engaged with one another in the context of political and at times military encounters and clashes. It emerged also as a mark of the relationship of Islam to Jews and Judaism, albeit for many years ameliorated by rabbinical quiescence and the context of Jews within the abode of Islam living in dhimmitude. With respect to Christian–Muslim relations, the epoch of the crusades stands out, of course. However, from early on, as Islam shaped up to be a genuinely alternative theistic religion, Christian reactions were largely negative with many regarding the new faith as heresy and heaping all sorts of negative opprobrium onto it. Such portrayals and assessments exist even today. Within both the Muslim world and many Christian communities today and among other religious and non-religious communities as well, levels of antipathy towards Islam and Muslims are increasing. So, just when modern media and communications can enable the free flow of information and ideas as never before, thus ostensibly enabling dialogue and deeper mutual appreciation and understanding each of the other, it is the voices of resistance, rejection and prejudicial stereotyping that nevertheless dominate. Just as the rewards of the modern dialogical age might be reaped, there appears within quarters of both Christianity and Islam, as well as Judaism, ever-increasing strident expressions of religious particularity and exclusivism that eschew any positive relationship with the 'other'. This constitutes a contemporary inter-religious paradox and challenge par excellence, for it lies at the heart of Islamophobia.

Conclusion

Evidence of a growing and deepening Islamophobia worldwide is incontrovertible.[47] Incessant headlines featuring acts of Muslim extremists lead irrefutably to too much media commentary and too many people simplistically equating 'extreme' with 'mainstream'. This results in tarring all Muslims with the same brush of hostile intent and, furthermore, projecting a hostile response on to all Muslims anywhere, without differentiation. This is the substance of the generalized fear of Muslims. And some commentators tout Islam as being inherently more violent than Christianity and Judaism. This is a reductionist approach that essentializes Islam as intrinsically violent and threatening, one that deliberately ignores the great diversity and variety within Islam 'in order to present Islam as the terror' par excellence, to be feared.[48] Certainly, much scholarship has been applied in recent times 'to establishing, describing, and demonstrating a direct causal link between Islam and terrorism'.[49] But in the absence of drawing a proper distinction it is Islam itself, and not Islamic extremism, which is 'repeatedly cited as hostile to the modern project and the progressive liberal values associated with modernity'.[50] A targeted concern is transmuted to a generalized fear.

Islamophobia does not just name an attitudinal stance. It applies also to sets of enacted exclusionary reactions, often drawing on religious imagery for inspiration and justification. And, as we have seen, Islamophobia can manifest as a form of extremism every bit as abhorrent and problematic as the Islamist extremism that ostensibly provoked it. As previously expressed, there is nothing wrong or irrational about fearing a declared enemy who seeks you harm. In the context of Islamic extremists, one can legitimately abjure their policy platforms and obnoxious rhetoric, and rightly decry their manifest ignorance and simplification of who they are targeting as their enemy. Antipathy to Muslim extremism is not by itself Islamophobic. Rather, the issue with Islamophobia 'is its essentializing and universalizing quality, which casts Islam itself and all Muslims as real or potential enemies'.[51] Many Muslims in Western countries experience a process that has been described as 'the progression of "garden-variety" prejudice, through to xenophobia and finally "chimera" in which the demonised out-group becomes associated with fantastical and monstrous attributes'.[52] Today, disturbingly, extremist denouncements and calls advocating and justifying exclusionary or eliminative actions against the threatening 'other' of Islam are increasingly tolerated. They are becoming normalized. Fear of the 'other', of difference and diversity, is the root problem. It is expressed as hostile antipathy that feeds religious extremism. It lies, indeed, at the heart of the extremism that is Islamophobia.

CHAPTER 10
CONCLUSION

The underlying thesis of this book is that the religious extremism which confronts the world today is largely an expression of diversity rejection. In this chapter I draw upon the preceding discussions and attempt to arrive at an overall conclusion concerning religion and extremism and point to a way ahead. What can we do about religious extremism? Are there better ways of responding to it than what seems to be today's currency of extreme reaction – attempts at elimination, immigrant and refugee exclusion and making war? Following the introductory discussion in Chapter 1, we explored perceptions of, and responses to, religious diversity and plurality. These are often treated as synonymous, though strictly speaking they are not. One references variety and differentiation, and the other, numerical quantity. But often, when it comes to religion, they tend to go together and so are treated as elements of the same basic issue: dealing with the 'other' – coping, or not, with that which is 'not us'. The various paradigms of conceptual framing, and differing patterns of response, include those that affirm diversity, those that try to 'contain and constrain' it in some inclusive way and those that manifest rejection. It is the last, we saw, that leads into motifs and tropes of exclusion linked to the point where fundamentalism becomes assertive and then extreme, as its inherent absolutism hardens, to the stage of enacting terrorist events or other violence. To the extent any religious community eschews diversity within, and rejects diversity without, it manifests forms of absolutism. This is the essence of religious extremism and its allied exclusion of any diversity to which it negatively reacts. As an outcome of extremism, religious terrorism can be seen to derive from fundamentalism which, in turn, can be thought of as an ideology of absolutism. An ideology provides the framework of presuppositions, underlying values and cognitive orientations without which the extreme behaviours would be rightly judged as nothing more than criminal and/or purely pathological. It is ideology that makes the difference. It provides a rationalizing context for otherwise criminal-minded and psycho-pathologically oriented individuals to act as they please. Thus, qua an extremist ideology, religion inevitably becomes linked to violence. In this regard, Mark Juergensmeyer is quite blunt in his assessment:

> Religion seems to be connected with violence virtually everywhere … Religion is crucial … since it gives moral justifications for killings and provides images of cosmic war that allow activists to believe that they are waging spiritual scenarios. This does not mean that religion causes violence … (rather) … religion often provides the mores and symbols that make possible bloodshed – even catastrophic acts of terrorism.[1]

Religion and Extremism

Ideologies of religious extremism are adept at providing forms of justification for actions and rationalization of views and attitudes, for there is 'no need ... to compromise one's goals in a struggle that has been waged in divine time and with the promise of heaven's rewards. There is no need ... to contend with society's laws and limitations when one is obeying a higher authority'.[2]

While ideology enables us to speak of this or that extremism as being the product of a particular worldview that includes, in the case of religion, a certain line of interpretation and application of religious beliefs and axioms, the specific actions of individual extremists may bear but tangential reference to the underlying ideology. At the same time, there are always many within an extremist camp for whom the respective ideology is everything. And there are many in between the poles of those who are primarily ideologically driven and those for whom any extreme ideology is but a cover or excuse for otherwise criminal behaviour. Investigating these sorts of differences and factors belongs to other disciplines than the ones I have utilized here – psychology, criminology and sociology, for example. My approach is more philosophical and phenomenological: probing what constitutes the structure of ideas, values and perspectives that allows for the emergence of extreme religious ideologies. Any given religious extremism is but one ideological position within the range of intellectual – or theological – perspectives of the religion to which it belongs. And it needs to be remembered that not all fundamentalist groups necessarily become impositional. And if they do, they may not necessarily resort to violence and terrorism in the attempt to achieve their aims. Nevertheless, Charles Selengut points out that 'so long as religion is about commitment to an absolute truth and a commitment to a sacred history, faithful women and men will be willing soldiers in the battles for God'.[3]

In general terms, religion is about commitment to that which is conceived as 'absolute' – in the case of theistic religions, this is deity or God. But there is also a more specific way in which the motif of 'absolute' impacts religious sensibility, one which lies at the root of what we commonly refer to as fundamentalism. This is the notion of 'religious absolutism' that closes off any provisionality or interrogation of the way in which the absolute is conceived and the way response to this is prescribed. For although the motif of 'the absolute' is arguably normative for religion, for most religions – and in particular the three we are concerned with here – there is also a measure of provisionality and an allowance of appropriate interrogation. For it is only so that the great traditions of interpretation, and the great debates concerning meaning and definitions, that thread throughout the histories of these religions was able to take place. And what often passes for a 'liberal' or 'open' stance within these faiths is no more that the appreciative recognition that all religious language, perception and so belief and doctrine, are provisional and subject always to being questioned, critiqued and rethought. Religious absolutism, however, refers to the stance of an utter commitment to an absolute religious truth; a commitment to an ideological construct that holds to a specific set of religious beliefs, teachings, values and worldview absolutely and without any possibility of question or critique. Indeed, it is by virtue of religious absolutism that 'religion can bring about a moral attitude that legitimates violence and contributes to the ideologies, symbols and rituals that accompany violent deeds'.[4]

Conclusion

As noted already, 'absolutism' is perhaps a more apposite term for what has hitherto been discussed as 'fundamentalism', although for the purposes of wider discussion we cannot but use the term as it has such wide coinage. In so doing, the aim is to tease out an understanding of the relationship between fundamentalism and extremism, and the propensity for terror to which these may lead. As we have seen, the process (i.e. radicalization) by which an individual or a group become extremist in thinking, rhetoric and behaviours, involves many factors of which, crucially, ideology is one. A fundamentalist ideology involves a combination of absolute attitudes, values, presuppositions and judgements that yield a certain religio-political perspective and results in a set of totalizing claims. Fundamentalism is both a specifically focused mindset and a certain kind of narrow worldview. It has a modus operandi indicative of absolutism, which can apply to just about any sphere of human activity. As a 'source of an unreal picture of the truth about the matter to which it pertains ... fundamentalisms have reared their ugly heads in every field of human endeavor throughout history and have been particularly noticeable in the fields of religion and ethics'.[5] Thus, grounded in absolutism, fundamentalism may be regarded as producing 'a psychopathology and Orthodoxy ... in whatever field or discipline ... in which one encounters it'.[6] Indeed, as a 'psychological pathology' fundamentalism 'can shape and take possession of the framework of thought and action in any arena of life, and particularly any ideology'.[7]

For the most part the extremists of a religion are fundamentalists, as defined in Chapter 3. But the reverse is not necessarily the case: a religious fundamentalist is not necessarily an extremist or at least not the sort likely to engage in violent acts. Passive fundamentalists, for example, do not. Assertive fundamentalism sets the scene for religious extremism that leads into the impositional fundamentalism that may certainly yield violent behaviours. And clearly some do. Further, David Guinn has observed that 'no system of law has been able to fully address the potential for religious violence'.[8] Religious extremism and violence are the products of a form of religious absolutism that needs to be understood and addressed as a particular type of ideology. Thus religious extremism may be viewed as an ideology of fundamentalism – meaning here something more than the theological origins of the term within a Christian orbit. Fundamentalism, as we saw, comprises a series of key factors analysed in terms of a progression of paired factors constituting features which are further subgrouped into phases. Thus we are able to distinguish between passive, assertive and impositional forms of fundamentalism. Passive fundamentalism amounts to a sincerely held, but not impinging or imposing upon anyone else, set of beliefs. These exist within the marketplace of non-threatening religious ideological options. But then comes the more rigid and insistent view of some groups whose style and approach identifies them as being in the middle 'assertive', even 'hard-line', phase. This is often marked by a sense of withdrawal – as into communities or compounds, or in other ways absenting themselves from wider 'secular' society – and by expressions of being necessarily oppositional. Such fundamentalism is inherently 'over against' the wider religious tradition with which it is otherwise identified, or opposes ideologically the status quo of the society from which it withdraws. Religious history – especially that of Christianity – is replete with such sectarian groups.

Religion and Extremism

It is the last phase of the fundamentalist paradigm that involves violence and terrorizing extremism of one sort or another. This is where the ideological hardening that is manifest in the second phase becomes distinctly impositional, even aggressively so. For extremist violence 'is not merely the preoccupation of militant extremists on the fringes of civilization. It is perpetuated by zealous groups and individuals from within major religions of our time, and, perhaps even more devastating, in the name of religion within the most developed and advanced societies on our planet'.[9] In broad terms, the ideological developmental sequence goes something like this. Within the assertive phase there emerges an assertion of identity that combines both an ideological exclusivity – the sense of inherent opposition – and at the same time a strong sense that the ideological polity carries with it an inclusive dimension. That is to say, all alternative views are excluded and at the same time all are meant, in theory if not yet in actuality, to be included within the purview of the fundamentalist's worldview. It is this seemingly paradoxical juxtaposition that accounts for the phenomenon of aggressive Christian fundamentalist evangelicalism, for example. All other religions are necessarily false, and the resolution is that, in the end, all should join the fundamentalist's camp. Along with this distinctive assertion of identity there is often a strong expression of condemnation of all that is 'other'. Social intercourse with non-believers is forbidden, even contact with former family and especially with any who have exited the group. For these are 'apostates' – those who eschew their God-given birthright and for whom sanctions will apply, even, in some cases, death. At the very least, contact with them will be prohibited. In this context it is easy to see how the ideological values of a specific extreme fundamentalism become applied: all threatening, even problematic 'otherness' is utterly negated and the superiority of self-identity of the fundamentalist group, and its ideology, is asserted absolutely.

By now the second phase has given way to the third: assertion yields to imposition. Religious fundamentalism – whether that of a religious group, society or even a nation-state – has become extreme. No quarter is given to the possibility of alternative viewpoints or identities as admissible. One religious community or society imposes itself on not just an 'other' – in the sense of a total 'other' religion – but often especially upon variants and diversities within its own religious milieu. Christian Europe has known the bloody wars of rivalry as Protestants and Catholics took impositional turnabout. Today in some places there are Muslims who likewise display forms of profound intolerance of Islamic variation, with the mutual destruction of persons and property. The elimination of a Muslim 'other' simply by virtue of their 'otherness', whatever form that may take, is as much a feature of our daily news as any strife reported between Muslims and non-Muslims. So in this third phase there emerges very clear and explicit justification for the sanctioning of the imposition of viewpoint, ideology and interpretation upon the included constituency – and the legitimation of violence in the achievement of that. With these factors in place, the final feature of ideological development from a benign religious fundamentalism to an enacted religious extremism is complete. The contempt of the denied 'other' is manifest in terms of policy and action and, in some instances, a terrorizing event is carried out in order to further the extremist's ideological aims and purposes. This may involve symbolic actions, including the destruction of property, where human targets are indirect casualties. As has been remarked in relation to the fundamentalist worldview, 'Violence is always the product of such worldviews. Whether it is violation of the truth, or violation of persons, property, and appropriate procedures for human social and juridical order, it is violence.'[10]

The violent behaviours in which religious extremists indulge are by no means random or arbitrary. There is a very particular logic and rationale that applies. 'The groups and individuals engaged in violence construct and maintain a social and theological reality in which killing and mayhem are legitimated.'[11] They generally take action against that which is perceived to be a threat or danger and regard any responsive measure as 'an ethical and moral act'[12]. This applies to extremist movements, groups and individuals within all three religions – especially when their religious 'other' is perceived as the threat. It is a feature of Islamophobic and reactive extremism. It is not a feature that is manifested by just one religion. And in each case there is a context of approval and reward: 'Muslim suicide bombers are considered by their communities as sacred martyrs who will go immediately to a joyous afterlife. Christian antiabortion activists who have bombed clinics and murdered providers are considered religious saints and heroes in their extremist worlds. Some messianic Zionists saw Yigal Amir as a true patriot for murdering Yitzhak Rabin and foiling the return of sacred land.'[13]

There are, of course, religious groups and movements other than extremists from within any religion who wish to influence society, to advocate policy and values, to effect change in accord with their agendas. But they are nowhere near terrorism or even extremism. They lie outside the fundamentalist paradigm for they do not express religious absolutism as such, even though they may profess to hold to certain guiding truths or values as absolute. They advocate; they do not impose. The desire for change, and active participation in sociopolitical processes, does not by itself equate with fundamentalism, let alone terrorism. It is not religious activism per se which is at issue, rather activist impositional fundamentalism expressing the rejection of religious diversity. This contrasts with ideologies of toleration and inclusivism which have been significant cultural markers in the West since the middle of the twentieth century but which are now increasingly challenged and threatened.

From the more theoretical discussions of the first three chapters, Chapter 4 moved to an examination of scriptural texts – the Bible and the Qur'an. Within them there are 'toxic texts' that provide a fund of ostensibly divine support for extremism found in Judaism, Christianity and Islam. The assumption often applied is that 'a straight line can be drawn from the text to violent behavior',[14] whether in providing a direct model for violent acts or as justification for other forms and instances of violence. As Charles Selengut has observed, 'history and sacred texts are not [only] something about the past but guides to current action and responsibilities'.[15] Thus, for example, with respect to those Jewish fundamentalists who wish to see the Temple rebuilt, 'the Beit Hamikdash, the ancient center of the Jewish cult in Jerusalem destroyed two thousand years ago, remains a holy site worth defending in a holy war'.[16] Equally, however, for Muslims 'the very same site, the Haram al-Sharif, is known as the place where Muhammad ascended to heaven and is similarly to be defended by any means'.[17] History and geography intertwine with the different textual references providing differing perceptions, apprehensions and resultant ideological perspectives that, in this case, directly clash. But the point is made: religious ideologies are grounded in the respective religious texts and their varying interpretations and applications.

Tim Winter has wryly noted that even though 'Abraham famously greeted strangers with the word "Peace" (e.g. Qur'an 51:25; Gen 18:1–5) the three religions which trace their pedigree back to him have found numerous ways of sacralizing the warrior's calling'.[18] The underlying thread of all three – Judaism, Christianity and Islam – is the fact that all are centred on a belief in the Absolute: the Deity who has given revelation as recorded in a holy scripture. Religious absolutism, however, focuses on select motifs, models, tropes and values from a perspective that these are to be treated as unyieldingly absolute with no dimension of contextual relativity or alternative interpretation admissible. This is, of course, the root of fundamentalism – hence the observation that what has been discussed as 'fundamentalism' can be also spoken of as the outworking of religious absolutism. As Juergensmeyer notes, such absolutism can be seen 'especially in the notion of cosmic war' in which, significantly, 'a satanic enemy cannot be transformed; it can only be destroyed'.[19]

Very often it is religion, or a sympathetic religious community, that 'contributes to the organizational structure of terrorist groups, directly or indirectly'.[20] And there is a great supportive fund of extremist rhetoric that gives a clue to the ideological source of the extreme acts. As Collins notes, 'biblical narratives have been a factor in the Zionist movement in Israel, shaping the imagination even of secular, socialist Zionists and providing powerful precedents for right-wing militants', and the Puritans of America's New England 'applied the biblical texts about … conquest to their own situation, casting the Native American Indians (sic) in the role of the Canaanites and Amalekites'.[21] Such judgements were applied elsewhere as, for example, in the case of South Africa with the Boers who 'applied the story of the Exodus to their situation under British rule', and later when 'black liberationists … applied it to their situation under the Boers'.[22] There have been numerous ways in which biblical – and Quranic – texts have been used to legitimate violence and terrorizing behaviours, with perhaps the model of Phineas taking a lead. Timothy Beal makes a salutary point:

> Although seldom recognized as such, radical white supremacist culture in the US is in many respects a *textual* culture. More precisely, it is a *biblical* culture. Its primary text is the Christian Bible, accompanied by a vast apocrypha of sermon transcripts and recordings, biblical commentaries, Bible study aids, and hagiographies, all of which are widely circulated.[23]

Furthermore, there is a particular religio-cultural trope of the West which has ever privileged Christianity. It is derived from the view of the second-century convert to Christianity, Marcion, who drew a 'distinction between the God of the Old Testament as responsible for violence and vengeance and the God of the New Testament as a God of mercy and love'.[24] This dichotomous view has probably held greater sway than is typically realized. For, as biblical scholars have noted, of more concern 'than studies of violence in the Bible that ignore the New Testament are those that lift up the New Testament as somehow containing the antidote for Old Testament violence'.[25] Although in his life Marcion's views were rejected by Christian leaders, and in the end he was regarded as a heretic, some modern cultural theorists, such as René Girard, who advocate a deep connection between religion and violence, have tended to take 'a triumphalist reading of Christian Scripture' and so promote a Marcionite prejudice.[26] Thus Christians are excused; Jews get the blame. Although Girard offered 'a universal theory that could explain the direct connection between religion and violence in primitive as well as modern cultures … based not on scarcity in human society or on human aggression, but on the concepts of sacrifice and scapegoating', this perspective has been largely rejected.[27]

In commenting that 'there is no one psychology of religious terrorists', James Jones notes that, as with religion itself, 'religiously motivated terrorism is a multidimensional, multidetermined phenomenon … no one unitary explanation for religious behavior can ever be sufficient'.[28] He goes on to observe that religious extremism and allied acts of violence and terrorism are

> characterized by certain psychological themes … teachings and texts that evoke shame and humiliation; an apocalyptic vision impatient with ambiguity, which presents a polarized view of the world; a drive for godly rule and complete purification (involving the control of gender relations and sexuality); a ritualization of violence and violent imagery; a deep desire for union with God; and the sanctification of violence.[29]

And these themes are not only psychological in content; they are very much component elements of an ideological perspective that is undergirded by absolutism. Thus, 'it makes theoretical as well as empirical sense that a person who envisions God as wrathful and punitive would also be more inclined towards a rigid dichotomizing of the world and have less capacity for empathy – traits that appear to characterize many religiously motivated terrorists'.[30] As Keith Ward usefully points out, an intolerant perspective in relation to rejecting diversity 'uses religion to give alleged "moral" support to the real causes of intolerance – hatred of those perceived or imagined to be oppressors or threats to one's own welfare'.[31] And in respect of the extremism of the CI movement and others in the United States, Karen Armstrong notes that 'there is a religious patina to … these extremist groups, who use the language of faith to express fears, anxieties and enthusiasms that are widespread, though not openly expressed, in the mainstream'.[32]

Today we are confronted with new forms of an old issue. Religious extremism is not itself something new, but it is causing new waves of concern and stirring up confused and confusing reactions that, as we explored in Chapters 8 and 9 above – in respect of mutual extremism and Islamophobia – is bringing some new twists. Globally we are seeing a religio-political lurch to the fascist right. In Turkey the evidence of impositional opportunism in wake of the failed coup of 15 July 2016 is incontrovertible, with a raft of human rights violations and other abuses catalogued.[33] The Turkish president and his supporters wasted no time in their thinly veiled attempt to neutralize all opposition, both secular neo-nationalist and liberal-Muslim. This latter includes the Hizmet movement associated with Fethullah Gülen on the basis of confessions extracted by torture. The closing down of a free press and the silencing of voices of opposition – voices that reflect diversity – is a stock-in-trade tool of fascist totalitarian regimes. Such tactics are now increasingly evident in countries that purport to be modern secular democracies, even with a distinct dominant religious identity. Strategies of disinformation – the proclamation of 'alternative facts' – and the avoidance of critical questions coupled with manifest contradictions promulgated by the dominant government agencies and the president do not seem restricted to the current situation of Turkey. Arguably they emerged as part of the behavioural pattern of the new US administration, at least in its first days and weeks of power. And in both cases, the leadership is supported by a groundswell of religious fundamentalism and extremism.

Kevin Clements, professor at the National Centre for Peace and Conflict Studies at the University of Otago, New Zealand, and chair of the International Advisory Board of the Global Peace Index of the Institute for Economics and Peace,[34] in an early 2017 communique commented:

> The most fundamental challenge to global peace lies in the global retreat from tolerant cosmopolitanism to intolerant atavistic nationalism, growing racial prejudice, anti-immigrant and refugee sentiment, Euroskepticism, homophobia and Islamophobia. These are the correlates of radical right movements all around the world and they are very closely correlated with the racism, sexism, Islamophobia and intolerance to outsiders that propelled Donald Trump to victory in the United States.[35]

As observant as this remark is, Clements has left religious extremism as such off the list, other than indirectly referencing in respect of Islamophobia. For underlying much of the contentiousness and substance of these issues there is, in fact, a matrix of religious beliefs, worldviews, teachings and perspectives that are in themselves illiberal and exclusionary. Such religion is opposed to the acceptance of gender diversities and homosexuality in particular (so homophobia), at times privileging the religious superiority of one race over all others (so racial prejudice and racism) and preferring racial, ethnic and social purity on distinctly religious grounds (so a retreat from tolerant cosmopolitanism) with often the promotion of a religio-nationalist identity (so both intolerant atavistic nationalism and increasing scepticism by some of the EU). As discussed above, the reaction to Islam produces both a fear of Muslims (Islamophobia) as well as providing an example of the reactive co-radicalization of mutual extremism.

The ideology of religious extremism is not confined to one religion alone. Violence that is fomented by extremists of any religion can be viewed sociologically as an attempt 'to achieve specific goals deemed appropriate and necessary in particular religious worldviews … where sacred texts and traditions continue to hold people's pious allegiance'.³⁶ Religious extremists portray themselves as 'true believers' or 'holy warriors', or suchlike, and may even be upheld as such by a wider supportive constituency. Such extremists 'operate in an alternative reality in which killings, murder, and suicide are just and reasonable' where, for example, ethical values 'of moral relativism, tolerance, pluralism, and compromise, so much part of the Western modern Enlightenment tradition' are eschewed.³⁷ Extremists of all three religions we have examined equally eschew such values; they are all antithetical to the toleration, let alone acceptance, of a wide range of diverse 'others'. And, of course, religions are much more than their extremists, even though where religion is 'involved in processes of peace building' they 'are often left out of the journalistic or cinematic frame'.³⁸ Bad news always trumps good news, and religion is too often associated with the bad and overlooked for all the good that flows from it.

Jolyon Mitchell notes that when religion features in film, documentary and news media it is most often 'linked with acts of violence'.³⁹ Indeed, he avers that violence inspired by religion 'is a recurring narrative'.⁴⁰ Furthermore, 'stories about religiously motivated violence, specifically the Crusades, continue to circulate even hundreds of years after they actually happened'.⁴¹ Thus, arguably, a constant diet of image and story where religion is seen to be fomenting violence is a chief contributing factor 'to the common trope within the public sphere that religious belief leads to violence'.⁴² In other words, in secular societies today there is a widely imbibed trope of prejudicial bias that acts as a cultural Petri dish. All it requires is an act of religious violence to occur, and a virus of presupposition about a religion – virtually any religion – being inherently extreme or otherwise threateningly obnoxious roars into life. Furthermore, in an era where reality and virtual reality increasingly intersect, it is the power of narrative that drives perception and response with often confused and even counterproductive outcomes. For example, recent suggestions from the new US administration that it wishes to concentrate on radical Islamic extremism,⁴³ thereby ignoring all other forms of extremism, blatantly manifests the dismissive and culpable ignorance that underlies much Islamophobia and fuels the fires of extreme reactions against Islam. Attending to one religious extremism only will likely be counterproductive and serve to give licence to other – especially in this case, Islamophobic and white supremacist – extremisms. However, although interest in religious extremism may reflect the observation that 'religion has given terrorism a remarkable power',⁴⁴ in the end it is not enough simply to describe and critically discuss the phenomenon of religious extremism and all that it entails. To be sure, it is usefully instructive and informative to engage in analysis and reflection on the nature and extent of this extremism. But a key pressing question is: What can we do about it? Such a pragmatic concern is the focus of political leadership and wider societal interest. It was articulated by the question posed by Donald Trump in the lead-up to his election as president of the United States – 'What the hell is going on?'

Religious extremism certainly poses a vexatious contemporary problem of global proportions and significance. The challenge is to find a way through to the advocacy of a potential resolution. In this regard it is worth noting that, in recent years, much attention has been paid by many countries to the issue of countering violent extremism (CVE) – a term that embraces more than just religious extremism. However, it certainly recognizes that Islamism is not the only challenging extremism needing to be countered. CVE has become a field of both academic study and practitioner engagement, with wide international support and involvement. It typically has two dimensions – the application of a security apparatus to detect and thwart violent extremist acts before they take place, and engagement with communities from which extremists emerge. This latter is with respect to both supporting the security dimension and also promoting dialogue and education with the aim of undercutting the appeal of extremist ideologies and claims. Thus far the attention of such strategies has been primarily with Islamic extremists and Muslim communities. Is this adequate? Given the anti-Muslim extremisms driving Islamophobia and the evidence of reactive or mutual extremisms in response to negative perceptions of and reactions to Islam, should not similar strategies be applied to other religious extremists and their communities? At this juncture it is worth being reminded that such extremisms are born of religious fundamentalism and that fundamentalist ideologies and expressions of extremism precede and undergird any allied violent behaviour. There is much rhetoric – speech-act behaviours – that is high on the danger scale of extremism on account of the depth of hateful antipathy it involves. There is often, too, an implicit – sometimes explicit – call to oppose, derogate and reject the targets of the rhetoric. Words can themselves wound. They can incite. They foment. They express underlying values and beliefs that are inimical to positive appreciation, preferring instead the rejection of diversity, however that may be exercised, and its accompanying schadenfreude.

The particular thrust of my own research and reflection suggests that, when it comes to religious extremism, the underlying problem of the rejection of diversity – the eliminative denial of differing 'others' or of that which presents alterities and alternatives to a status quo – needs to be addressed, both ideologically and practically. So the specific issue we face is that of combating diversity rejection. This is, at heart, the issue of human beings learning to live together in peaceful productive relationships not simply in spite of, but in positive affirmation and appreciation for, the rich diversity – including religious – of the identity and make-up of individuals and societies. The capacity for peaceful coexistence in a context of mutual acceptance and respect is premised on the capacity to assert some form of pluralism: to affirm diversity. Hence the possibility that religions may counter religious extremism via the route of affirming religious diversity is something that needs to be explored further and actively promoted. Juergensmeyer suggests that 'some assertion of moderation in religion's passion, and some acknowledgement of religion in elevating the spiritual and moral values of public life' are both needed in order to end religious violence and that, indeed, 'the cure for religious violence may ultimately lie in a renewed appreciation for religion itself'.[45]

The answer to the problem of religious extremism will not be found by looking outside of religion and its ideological structures, but looking to religion and into its ideologies. If extremism is a manifestation of the rejection of diversity as I have argued, and rejection flows from an ideology of exclusivism resulting in exclusionary stances, then addressing exclusivism would be a good place to start. A rather sharp question is thus posed: Is there a proper way of speaking of exclusive religion, or of religion in terms of exclusive identity, without necessarily falling into the pit of exclusivist extremism? The critical contrast to be addressed may be stated thus: exclusive religion as a matter of identity articulation on the one hand and religious exclusivism as a governing ideological set on the other. Exclusivity of identity is a requirement when it comes, for example, to matters of inter-religious relational engagement. Interlocutors need to know who they are and that their respective identities are indeed mutually exclusive. Otherwise dialogue would effectively collapse. To that extent, being 'exclusively' who we are is a necessary mark of identity uniqueness that provides the requisite measure of distinction upon which all relational intercourse is founded. 'Exclusiveness' is here a cipher for ontological differentiation in the realm of religion. Such 'exclusive religion' is not a cipher for the exclusionary stance of religious exclusivism. All religion is exclusive, in the sense of that which is uniquely itself, and, unless it holds to a rigid exclusionary identity, manifests a capacity to recognize, at least, the fact of other religions and engage in some sort of relation with them. As such, religion, while 'exclusive', implicitly validates the variety of religious 'otherness' for only so can any form of mutual acknowledgement and communication take place. The ideological perspective of *exclusivism*, however, is intent on invalidating such otherness. Religious *exclusivism* plays into the hands of ideological extremism. But exclusive *religion* allows for the integrity of difference and otherness and thereby the possibility of interfaith relations and inter-religious dialogue.

Thus affirmation of a particular, unique and so exclusive religious identity does neither necessarily entail, nor require, a denial of alterity. An affirmation of the natural exclusivity of one's religious identity that, at the same time, upholds the validation of religious variety and so the validity of religious others is a sine qua non of any religious diversity affirmation. A self-understanding of being a unique and valid member of a diverse community of faith needs to be asserted as inherent to one's own religious identity. At the same time this needs to be acknowledged as being the case with the religious identities of others too. For such a perspective stands in contrast to the paradigm of religious exclusivism that is a specific marker of highly conservative or fundamentalist religion. Indeed, it is from within this religious ideological perspective that the rejection of diversity, and so the extremisms that manifest it, spring. To reiterate, religious exclusivity is not the same as religious exclusivism: the one refers to identity uniqueness, the other to an excluding attitude and ideology. The former can be positively, or at least neutrally, disposed towards the fact of religious diversity and plurality, and indeed of engagement with the 'other', the latter quite clearly is not. It seems that, especially in the context of inter-religious engagement and dialogue, if religious identity is not to succumb to syncretistic blurring or relativist reduction then some measure of exclusivity must necessarily apply. Religious identity, in being discrete, must – as with any discrete identity – incorporate a measure of the 'exclusive' if only as a marker of, or a synonym for, being 'unique', for uniqueness is a necessary element of identity per se. In which case, the paradigm of exclusivism, so long virtually automatically eschewed by all except, supposedly, fundamentalists, needs to be rehabilitated – or at least given a more nuanced attention so as to admit the distinction between exclusion (qua the behaviours of 'excluding') and exclusive (qua the mark of distinctiveness). On the one hand a measure of exclusivity is logically required for clarity of identity, and clarity of identity is a necessary prerequisite for dialogical engagement. Yet, on the other hand, when taken to an extreme, exclusivity of identity militates against any sort of dialogical rapport by becoming exclusionary – and that is a hallmark of extreme religious fundamentalism. So the distinctive contemporary challenge is to clarify the exclusivity that adheres to proper religious identity as something distinct from the exclusion of religious exclusivism that is inimical of any validation of the 'other'.

The exclusivist absolutism of diversity rejection is at the root of religious extremism. There is a simplistic logic of theistic extremism premised on an absolute expectation, namely, create the right condition and God will ensure the right outcome. The divine response to a human initiative is guaranteed when the initiative is to honour without compromising the will of God. This is the logic of absolutism that underlies the exclusivist identity of religious extremism and the exclusionary thrust of extremist ideology and actions. In respect of Islam, Tim Winter notes that alongside the contrast of *Dar al-Islam* and *Dar al-Harb* (the Abode of War), there is another category, namely *Dar al-Sulh*, or House of Treaty which reflects 'the Prophet's practice of concluding truces with non-Muslim powers'.[46] At the level of international relations, diversity was acknowledged and accepted, with appropriate relational intercourse taking place. And a key Christian intellectual in the high Middle Ages, St Thomas Aquinas, once wrote: 'The immense diversity and pluriformity of this creation more perfectly represents God than any one creature alone or by itself'.[47] It is the way of diversity affirmation that effectively combats exclusivist rejection and, in so doing, neutralizes religious extremism.

NOTES

INTRODUCTION

1 HRH The Prince of Wales, 'Thought for the Day', *BBC Radio 4*, 22 December 2016. Available online: http://www.express.co.uk/news/royal/746345/Prince-Charles-Radio-4-Thought-for-the-Day-religious-threats (accessed 27 December 2016).
2 Tariq Ali, *The Clash of Fundamentalisms; Crusades, Jihads and Modernity* (London: Verso, 2002).
3 Private communication as received by the author.
4 Among the notable 'classics' on this, see, for example, Sigmund Freud, *Totem and Taboo* (New York: Moffat, Yard, 1919) and René Girard, *Violence and the Sacred* (Baltimore: John Hopkins University Press, 1977).
5 Gideon Aran and Ron E. Hassner, 'Religious Violence in Judaism: Past and Present', *Terrorism and Political Violence* 25 no. 3 (2013): 356.
6 For examples illustrating this view, see Samuel Huntington, *The Clash of Civilizations* (New York: Touchstone, 1996); Raphael Israeli, *Islamikaze* (London: Taylor & Francis, 2003) and Bruce Hoffman, *Holy Terror: The Implications of Terrorism Motivated by a Religious Imperative* (Santa Monica, CA: Rand Corp, 1993).
7 Aran and Hassner, 'Religious Violence in Judaism', 356. see also Robert Pape, *Dying to Win: The Strategic Logic of Suicide Terrorism* (New York: Random House, 2005).
8 Aran and Hassner, 'Religious Violence in Judaism', 356.
9 Kille, D. Andrew. '"The Bible Made Me Do it": Text, Interpretation, and Violence', in *The Destructive Power of Religion: Violence in Judaism, Christianity, and Islam*. Volume 1, *Sacred Scriptures, Ideology, and Violence*, ed. J. Harold Ellens (Westport, CT: Praeger, 2004), 56.
10 Ibid., 60.
11 Aran and Hassner, 'Religious Violence in Judaism', 357. see also Scott Appleby, *The Ambivalence of the Sacred: Religion, Violence and Reconciliation* (Lanham, MD: Rowman & Littlefield, 2000); Mark Juergensmeyer, *Terror in the Mind of God: The Global Rise of Religious Violence*, 3rd edition (Berkeley: University of California Press, 2003); Martin Marty and Scott Appleby (eds.), *Fundamentalisms Observed* (Chicago: University of Chicago Press, 1991).
12 See David Bromley and J. Gordon Melton, eds., *Cults, Religion and Violence* (Cambridge: Cambridge University Press, 2002).
13 This was in fact an erroneous assumption as New Zealand has ever been a secular society: 'New Zealand has no official or established religion'. *Statement on Religious Diversity in Aotearoa New Zealand* (Wellington: Human Rights Commission, 2009), 3.
14 Brian Tamaki, cited in news report, 'Lockout Sparks Unholy Row', *New Zealand Herald*, Tuesday, 29 May 2007, A3.
15 Gary Bouma, *Australian Soul: Religion and Spirituality in the Twenty-first Century* (Melbourne: Cambridge University Press, 2006), 5.
16 David C. Rapoport, 'The Fourth Wave: September 11 in the History of Terrorism', *Current History* 100, no. 650 (2001): 419–24.
17 Aran and Hassner, 'Religious Violence in Judaism', 361.

Notes

18 Ibid.
19 'Settlements – Facts on the Ground', Geoff Witte of the Washington Post, as reproduced in the *New Zealand Herald*, 4 January 2017, A18.
20 Aran and Hassner, 'Religious Violence in Judaism', 361.
21 David Fisher and Brian Wicker, eds., *Just War on Terror? A Christian and Muslim Response* (Farnham: Ashgate, 2010), 5.
22 Keith Ward, *Is Religion Dangerous?* (Oxford: Lion, 2006), 36.
23 Ibid., 36.
24 Ibid., 64.
25 John J. Shepherd, 'Self-Critical Children of Abraham? Roots of Violence and Extremism in Judaism, Christianity and Islam', in *Islam & the West post 9/11*, ed. Ron Geaves, Theodore Gabriel, Yvonne Haddad and Jane Idleman Smith (Aldershot: Ashgate, 2004), 27.
26 Ward, *Is Religion Dangerous?* 81.
27 Ibid.; cf. Karen Armstrong, *Fields of Blood: Religion and the History of Violence* (London: Bodley Head, 2014).
28 Ward, *Is Religion Dangerous?* 81.
29 Ibid.
30 Ibid.
31 Armstrong, *Fields of Blood*, 323.
32 Shepherd, 'Self-Critical Children of Abraham?' 42.
33 Ibid.
34 Gilles Kepel, *The Revenge of God: The Resurgence of Islam, Christianity and Judaism in the Modern World* (Cambridge: Polity Press, 1994).
35 Youssef M. Choueiri, *Islamic Fundamentalism, 3rd Edition: The Story of Islamist Movements* (London: Continuum, 2010), 7.
36 Ibid.
37 Ron Geaves, *Aspects of Islam* (London: Darton, Longman & Todd, 2005), 190.
38 Charles Kimball, *When Religion Becomes Evil* (New York: HarperSanFrancisco, 2003).
39 Jonathan Matusitz, *Symbolism in Terrorism: Motivation, Communication, and Behavior* (Lanham, MD: Rowan & Littlefield, 2015), 133.
40 Ibid.
41 Ibid.
42 Ibid.

ACCOMMODATING DIVERSITY: PARADIGMS AND PATTERNS

1 Gary Bouma, *Australian Soul: Religion and Spirituality in the Twenty-first Century* (Melbourne: Cambridge University Press, 2006), 1.
2 David Harvey, *The Condition of Postmodernity* (Malden, MA: Blackwell, 1990), 10.
3 Ibid., 12.
4 Ibid., 10.
5 Ibid.
6 Ibid., 20.
7 Ibid., 30.
8 Stanley J. Grenz, *A Primer on Postmodernism* (Grand Rapids: Wm B. Eerdmans, 1996), 81.
9 Ibid.
10 Ibid.
11 Steven Connor, *Postmodernist Culture: An Introduction to Theories of the Contemporary* (Oxford: Blackwell, 1992), 9.

Notes

12 Jean-François Lyotard, *The Postmodern Condition: A Report on Knowledge*, trans. Geoff Bennington and Brian Massumi (Manchester: Manchester University Press, 1984).
13 Harvey, *The Condition of Postmodernity*, 9.
14 David Ray Griffin, William A. Beardslee and Joe Holland, *Varieties of Postmodern Theology* (New York: SUNY, 1989), xii.
15 Alvin Toffler, *Future Shock* (New York: Random House, 1970).
16 Frederic Jameson, *Postmodernism or, the Cultural Logic of Late Capitalism* (Durham, NC: Duke University Press, 1994), ix.
17 Here we may simply note the range of perspectives from Wittgenstein's notion of language games; Saussure's view of language as social convention; the structuralist critique of a Levi-Straus; and the rethinking of the hermeneutical task by, for example, such seminal scholars as Dilthey, Heidegger and Gadamer.
18 Grenz, *A Primer on Postmodernism*, 81.
19 See, for example, Ernest Gellner, *Postmodernism, Reason and Religion* (London: Routledge, 1992).
20 See Harvey, *The Condition of Postmodernity*, 113ff.
21 Kenneth Cracknell, *Considering Dialogue: Theological Themes in Interfaith Relations, 1970-1980* (London: British Council of Churches, 1981).
22 Cf. Douglas Pratt, 'Pluralism and Interreligious Engagement: The Contexts of Dialogue', in *A Faithful Presence: Essays for Kenneth Cragg*, ed. David Thomas with Clare Amos (London: Melisende Press, 2003), 402–18; 'Contextual Paradigms for Interfaith Relations', *Current Dialogue* N42 (December 2003): 3–9.
23 S. J. Samartha, *Courage for Dialogue: Ecumenical Issues in Inter-religious Relationships* (Geneva: WCC Publications, 1981), 100.
24 S. Wesley Ariarajah, *Not without My Neighbour: Issues in Interfaith Relations*, Risk Book Series No. 85 (Geneva: WCC Publications, 1999), 22.
25 The term 'fundamentalism' is problematic, yet it is widely used to denote forms of narrow and hard-line religious perspectives and identities. See below for a detailed critique and discussion.
26 Bouma, *Australian Soul*, 5.
27 Ibid.
28 Douglas Pratt, 'Pluralism and Interreligious Engagement'; see also: Douglas Pratt, 'Contextual Paradigms for Interfaith Relations', *Current Dialogue* 42 (December 2003): 3–9.
29 John Hick, *The Rainbow of Faiths* (London: SCM Press, 1995), 15.
30 John Hick, *God and the Universe of Faiths: Essays in the Philosophy of Religion* (London: Palgrave Macmillan, 1988), 131.
31 Ibid., 139.
32 Ibid., 137.
33 John Hick, *The Metaphor of God Incarnate* (London: SCM Press, 1993), 140.
34 John Hick, *The Myth of God Incarnate* (London: SCM Press, 1977), 181.
35 Hick, *Metaphor*, 140.
36 See for example, John B. Cobb, *Beyond Dialogue* (Philadelphia: Fortress Press, 1982). see also Leonard Swidler, John B. Cobb, Paul F. Knitter and Monika K. Hellwig, *Death or Dialogue?* (London: SCM Press, 1990).
37 Cf. S. Wesley Ariarajah, *Hindus and Christians: A Century of Protestant Ecumenical Thought* (Amsterdam and Grand Rapids, MI: Editions Rodopi and Wm B. Eerdmans, 1991), 178.
38 Ibid.
39 Mark Heim, *Salvations: Truth and Difference in Religion* (Maryknoll, NY: Orbis Books, 1995); Mark Heim, *The Depth of the Riches: A Trinitarian Theology of Religious Ends* (Grand Rapids, MI: Wm. B. Eerdmans, 2001).

Notes

40 Paul F. Knitter, *Without Buddha I Could Not Be a Christian* (Oxford: Oneworld, 2013).
41 See Paul F. Knitter, *No Other Name? A Critical Survey of Christian Attitudes toward the World Religions* (Maryknoll, NY: Orbis Books, 1985).
42 Ariarajah, *Hindus and Christians*, 177.
43 Cf. Ninian Smart, *The World's Religions: Old Traditions and Modern Transformations* (Cambridge: Cambridge University Press, 1989); Douglas Pratt, *Religion: A First Encounter* (Auckland: Longmans, 1993).
44 Hans Küng, *Global Responsibility: In Search of a New World Ethic* (London: SCM Press, 1991).
45 Paul F. Knitter, *One Earth Many Religions: Multifaith Dialogue & Global Responsibility* (Maryknoll, NY: Orbis Books, 1995).
46 Samartha, *Courage for Dialogue*; S. J. Samartha, *One Christ, Many Religions: Toward a Revised Christology* (Maryknoll, NY: Orbis Books, 1991).
47 Diogenes Allen, *Christian Belief in a Postmodern World* (Louisville, KY: Westminster/John Knox Press, 1989), 187.
48 Raimundo Panikkar, *The Unknown Christ of Hinduism* (Maryknoll, NY: Orbis Books, 1981).

DIVERSITY RESISTED: EXCLUSION AND FUNDAMENTALISM

1 Mark Juergensmeyer, *Terror in the Mind of God: The Global Rise of Religious Violence* (Berkeley: University of California Press, 2000), 248.
2 Ibid.
3 Ibid.
4 See Douglas Pratt, 'Religious Fundamentalism: A Paradigm for Terrorism?' in *International Terrorism: New Zealand Perspectives*, ed. Rachel Barrowman. (Wellington: Institute of Policy Studies, Victoria University of Wellington, 2005), 31–52; Douglas Pratt, 'Terrorism and Religious Fundamentalism: Prospects for a Predictive Paradigm'. *Marburg Journal of Religion* 11, no. 1 (June 2006), pp.11. Online journal available at: http://web.uni-marburg.de/religionswissenschaft/journal/mjr/.
5 Bryan Gilling, ed., *"Be Ye Separate": Fundamentalism and the New Zealand Experience* (Red Beach: Colcom Press, 1992), xi.
6 'Material identification' is a technical philosophical term that is relevant here as it denotes a certain mode of equivalence in distinction from other modes – for example, it contrasts with the mode of equivalence (effective identity) that obtains with inclusivism.
7 Diana L. Eck, *Encountering God: A Spiritual Journey from Bozeman to Banares* (Boston: Beacon Press, 1993), 174.
8 See, for example, Alan Race and Paul Hedges, *Christian Approaches to Other Faiths* (London: SCM Press, 2008); Paul Hedges, *Controversies in Interreligious Dialogue and the Theology of Religions* (London: SCM Press, 2010).
9 Cf. Paul F. Knitter, *No Other Name? A Critical Survey of Christian Attitudes toward the World Religions* (Maryknoll, NY: Orbis Books, 1985), 122–23; Alan Race, *Christians and Religious Pluralism* (London: SCM Press, 1993), 10–11.
10 'Outside the Church there is no salvation'.
11 John Hick, *God and the Universe of Faiths*. Revised ed. (London: Collins, 1977), 121.
12 W. A. Visser t'Hooft, *No Other Name: The Choice between Syncretism and Christian Universalism* (London: SCM Press, 1963), 88.
13 Ibid., 95.

14 J. Harold Ellens, 'Introduction', *The Destructive Power of Religion: Violence in Judaism, Christianity, and Islam*. Volume 1, *Sacred Scriptures, Ideology, and Religion*, ed. J. Harold Ellens (Westport, CT: Praeger, 2004), 7.
15 LeRoy H. Aden, 'The Role of Self-Justification in Violence' in *The Destructive Power of Religion: Violence in Judaism, Christianity, and Islam*. Volume 2, *Religion, Psychology, and Violence*, ed. J. Harold Ellens (Westport, CT: Praeger, 2004), 252.
16 Juergensmeyer, *Terror in the Mind of God*, 186.
17 Ibid., 188.
18 Keith Ward, *What the Bible Really Teaches: A Challenge for Fundamentalists* (London: SPCK, 2004), 1.
19 See Martin E. Marty, *Fundamentalisms Compared: The Charles Strong Memorial Lecture 1989* (Underdale, South Australia: Australian Association for the Study of Religions, 1989), 8.
20 J. Harold Ellens, 'Fundamentalism, Orthodoxy, and Violence', in *The Destructive Power of Religion: Violence in Judaism, Christianity, and Islam*. Volume 4, *Contemporary Views on Spirituality and Violence*, ed. J. Harold Ellens (Westport, CT: Praeger, 2004), 119.
21 Ibid.
22 See, for example, the ISIS magazine publication *Dabiq* which is available for download from various internet sites.
23 Ellens, 'Fundamentalism, Orthodoxy, and Violence', 119.
24 Ibid, 120.
25 See for example: Ernest R. Sandeen, *The Roots of Fundamentalism: British and American Millenarianism, 1800–1930* (Chicago: University of Chicago Press, 1970); James Barr, *Fundamentalism* (London: SCM Press, 1977); George M. Marsden, *Understanding Fundamentalism and Evangelicalism* (Grand Rapids, MI: W. B. Eerdmans, 1991); John Shelby Spong, *Rescuing the Bible from Fundamentalism* (San Francisco: HarperSanFrancisco, 1991).
26 See for example: Santosh C. Saha (ed.), *Religious Fundamentalism in the Contemporary World: Critical Social and Political Issues* (Lanham, MD: Lexington Books, 2004); Lionel Caplan, *Studies in Religious Fundamentalism* (Basingstoke: Macmillan, 1987); Bruce B. Lawrence, *Defenders of God: The Fundamentalist Revolt against the Modern Age* (San Francisco: Harper and Row, 1989); David Westerlund, *Questioning the Secular State: The Worldwide Resurgence of Religion in Politics* (London: Hurst, 1996); Leonard Weinberg and Ami Pedahzur (eds.), *Religious Fundamentalism and Political Extremism* (Portland, OR: Frank Cass, 2004); Gilles Kepel, *The Revenge of God: The Resurgence of Islam, Christianity and Judaism in the Modern World* (Cambridge: Polity Press, 1994).
27 See Martin E. Marty and R. Scott Appleby (eds.), *The Fundamentalism Project* (Chicago: University of Chicago Press, 1991); Martin E. Marty and R. Scott Appleby (eds.), *Fundamentalisms Observed* (Chicago: University of Chicago Press, 1991); Martin E. Marty and R. Scott Appleby (eds.), *Fundamentalisms and the State: Remaking Politics, Economies, and Militance* (Chicago: University of Chicago Press, 1993); Martin E. Marty and R. Scott Appleby (eds.), *Accounting for Fundamentalisms: The Dynamic Character of Movements* (Chicago: University of Chicago Press, 1994); Martin E. Marty and R. Scott Appleby (eds.), *Fundamentalisms Comprehended* (Chicago: University of Chicago Press, 1995).
28 See for example: Joseph E. B. Lumbard (ed.), *Islam, Fundamentalism, and the Betrayal of Tradition* (Bloomington, IN.: World Wisdom, 2004); Beverley Milton-Edwards, *Islamic Fundamentalism since 1945* (New York: Routledge, 2005); Bassam Tibi, *The Challenge of Fundamentalism: Political Islam and the New World Disorder* (Berkeley: University of California Press, 2002); Mahmud A. Faksh, *The Future of Islam in the Middle East: Fundamentalism in Egypt, Algeria, and Saudi Arabia* (Westport, CT: Praeger, 1997); Ahmad Mawsilili, *Moderate and Radical Islamic Fundamentalism: The Quest for*

Notes

Modernity, Legitimacy, and the Islamic State (Gainesville: University Press of Florida, 1999); Mansoor Moaddel and Kamran Talattof (eds.), *Contemporary Debates in Islam: An Anthology of Modernist and Fundamentalist Thought* (Basingstoke: Macmillan Press, 2004); Lawrence Davidson, *Islamic Fundamentalism: An Introduction* (Westport, CT: Greenwood Press, 2003).

29 Marty, *Fundamentalisms Compared*, 1.
30 Ibid., 7.
31 Ibid., 8.
32 Cf. Douglas Pratt, 'Fundamentalism, Exclusivism, and Religious Extremism', in *Understanding Interreligious Relations*, ed. D. Cheetham, D. Pratt and D. Thomas (Oxford: Oxford University Press, 2013), 241–60.
33 Mark Adam Elliott, 'Retribution and Agency in the Dead Sea Scrolls and the Teaching of Jesus', in *The Destructive Power of Religion: Violence in Judaism, Christianity, and Islam*. Volume 1, *Sacred Scriptures, Ideology, and Violence*, ed. J. Harold Ellens, (Westport, CT: Praeger, 2004), 207.

TEXTS OF TERROR: SCRIPTURAL MOTIFS FOR EXTREMISM

1 Phyllis Trible, *Texts of Terror: Literary-Feminist Readings of Biblical Narratives* (Philadelphia, PA: Fortress Press, 1984).
2 John J. Collins, *Does the Bible Justify Violence?* (Minneapolis: Fortress Press, 2004), 14.
3 Simon John De Vries, 'Human Sacrifice in the Old Testament: In Ritual and in Warfare', in *The Destructive Power of Religion: Violence in Judaism, Christianity, and Islam*. Volume 1, *Sacred Scriptures, Ideology, and Religion*, ed. J. Harold Ellens (Westport, CT: Praeger, 2004), 99.
4 Ibid., 100.
5 Both these counter-texts speak of beating 'swords into ploughshares, and their spears into pruning hooks' in an eschatological vision wherein 'nation shall not lift up sword against nation, neither shall they learn war anymore' (Isa. 2.4, RSV).
6 Cf. Ricardo J. Quinones, 'The Cain–Abel Syndrome: In Theory and in History', in *The Destructive Power of Religion: Violence in Judaism, Christianity, and Islam*. Volume 3, *Models and Cases of Violence in Religion*, ed. J. Harold Ellens (Westport, CT: Praeger, 2004), 81–125; cf. James G. Williams, *The Bible, Violence, and the Sword* (Valley Forge, PA: Trinity Press International, 1991) for another perspective on the Cain–Abel narrative. see also James L. Kugel, *How to Read the Bible: A Guide to Scripture, Then and Now* (New York: Free Press, 2007).
7 See Elliott Horowitz, 'Genesis 34 and the Legacies of Biblical Violence', in *The Blackwell Companion to Religion and Violence*, ed. Andrew R. Murphy (Malden, MA: Wiley-Blackwell, 2011), 163–82.
8 Quinones, 'The Cain–Abel Syndrome', 166.
9 Cited in Horowitz, 'Genesis 34', 170.
10 Ibid., 165.
11 Trible, *Texts of Terror*, xiii.
12 Ibid., 1.
13 Gideon Aran and Ron E. Hassner, 'Religious Violence in Judaism: Past and Present', *Terrorism and Political Violence* 25, no. 3 (2013): 367.
14 Ibid.
15 Ibid.
16 Ibid

17 Ibid., 369.
18 Ibid.
19 Ibid., 368.
20 John J. Collins, 'The Zeal of Phinehas, the Bible, and the Legitimation of Violence', in *The Destructive Power of Religion: Violence in Judaism, Christianity, and Islam*. Volume 1, *Sacred Scriptures, Ideology, and Violence*, ed. J. Harold Ellens (Westport, CT: Praeger, 2004), 13; cf. Susan Niditch, *War in the Hebrew Bible: A Study in the Ethics of Violence* (New York: Oxford University Press, 1993), 28–89. Note: the term herem carries at least two meanings, one of which is destruction, as discussed; the other is a 'softer' meaning of 'censure' or 'excommunication'.
21 Collins, *Does the Bible Justify*, 5.
22 Collins, 'The Zeal of Phinehas', 15; cf. Niditch, *War in the Hebrew Bible*, 56–77.
23 Collins, 'The Zeal of Phinehas', 15.
24 Collins, *Does the Bible Justify*, 11.
25 Ibid., 18.
26 Ibid.
27 Ibid., 11.
28 Raymund Schwager SJ, *Must there be Scapegoats? Violence and Redemption in the Bible* (New York: Crossroads Publishing, 2000), 76.
29 Aran and Hassner, 'Religious Violence in Judaism', 371.
30 Ibid.
31 Ibid.
32 Keith Ward, *Is Religion Dangerous?* (Oxford: Lion, 2006), 113.
33 Ibid., 114.
34 Shelly Matthews and E. Leigh Gibson, eds., *Violence in the New Testament* (New York: T & T Clark, 2005), 2.
35 Ibid., 4.
36 Ibid.
37 J. Harold Ellens, 'The Violent Jesus', in *The Destructive Power of Religion: Violence in Judaism, Christianity, and Islam*. Volume 3, *Models and Cases of Violence in Religion*, ed. J. Harold Ellens (Westport, CT: Praeger, 2004), 34.
38 Perry Schmidt-Leukel, 'Christianity and the Religious Other', in *Understanding Interreligious Relations*, ed. D. Cheetham, D. Pratt and D. Thomas (Oxford: Oxford University Press, 2013), 119.
39 Ibid., 123.
40 See for example: Pieter G. R. de Villiers and Jan Willem van Henten, eds., *Coping with Violence in the New Testament* (Leiden and Boston: Brill, 2012); Philip L. Tite, *Conceiving Peace and Violence: A New Testament Legacy* (Lanham, MD: University Press of America, 2004).
41 Beverly Milton-Edwards, 'Islam and Violence', in *The Blackwell Companion to Religion and Violence*, ed. Andrew R. Murphy (Malden, MA: Wiley-Blackwell, 2011), 187.
42 Abdullah Yusuf Ali, *Holy Qur'an. Text, Translation, and Commentary* (Al-Murgab, Kuwait: That Es-Salasil Publishing, n.d.). All Quranic citations are from this version.
43 Patrick Sookhdeo, *Understanding Islamic Terrorism: The Islamic Doctrine of War* (Wiltshire: Isaac Publishing, 2004), 28.
44 Ibid.
45 See also: Reuven Firestone, *Jihad: The Origin of Holy War in Islam* (New York: Oxford University Press, 1999), 67–91, for a distinction of four kinds of war verses, namely, non-militant verses, verses giving restrictions on fighting, verses expressing conflict between God's command and the reaction of Muhammad's followers and verses which strongly advocate war on behalf of Islam.
46 Sura 5.85.

Notes

47 J. Harold Ellens, 'Introduction: Toxic Texts', in *The Destructive Power of Religion: Violence in Judaism, Christianity, and Islam. Volume 3, Models and Cases of Violence in Religion*, ed. J. Harold Ellens (Westport, CT: Praeger, 2004), 2.
48 Collins, *Does the Bible Justify Violence?* 32.
49 Ibid., 33.
50 Collins, 'The Zeal of Phinehas', 21.
51 Ibid.
52 Ibid., 23.

THE JEWISH EXPERIENCE OF EXTREMISM

1 Gideon Aran and Ron E. Hassner, 'Religious Violence in Judaism: Past and Present', *Terrorism and Political Violence* 25, no. 3 (2013): 362.
2 Ibid.
3 Ibid., 363. see also Ami Pedahzur and Arie Perliger, *Jewish Terrorism in Israel* (New York: Columbia University Press, 2011).
4 Emmanual Sivan, Gabriel Almond and Scott Appleby, *Strong Religion* (Chicago: University of Chicago Press, 2000); cf. Aran and Hassner, 'Religious Violence in Judaism', 363; also Gideon Aran, 'Religiosity and Super-Religiosity: Measures of Radical Religion', *Numen* 60 (2013): 155–94.
5 See Aran and Hassner, 'Religious Violence in Judaism', 363.
6 Samuel C. Heilman and Menachem Friedman, 'Religious Fundamentalism and Religious Jews: The Case of the Haredem', in *Fundamentalisms Observed*, ed. Martin E. Marty and R. Scott Appleby (Chicago: The University of Chicago Press, 1991), 197–264.
7 Aran and Hassner, 'Religious Violence in Judaism', 364.
8 Ibid. See also: Gideon Aran, 'Jewish Zionist Fundamentalism: The Bloc of the Faithful in Israel (Gush Emunim)', in *Fundamentalisms Observed*, ed. Martin E. Marty and R. Scott Appleby (Chicago: The University of Chicago Press, 1991), 265–344.
9 Aran and Hassner, 'Religious Violence in Judaism', 363.
10 Charles Selengut, 'The Sociology of Religious Violence', in *The Blackwell Companion to Religion and Violence*, ed. Andrew R. Murphy (Malden, MA: Wiley-Blackwell, 2011), 94.
11 Ibid.
12 Ibid.
13 Aran and Hassner, 'Religious Violence in Judaism', 356.
14 Ibid., 364.
15 Ibid.
16 Gideon Aran, 'Israeli-Jewish and American-Protestant Fundamentalist Violence: Contemporary Variations on an Ancient Theme', in *Religion and Terrorism: The Use of Violence in Abrahamic Monotheism*, ed. Veronica Ward and Richard Sherlock (Lanham, MD: Lexington Books, 2014), 106.
17 Ibid.
18 Ibid., 108.
19 Ibid.
20 Ibid.
21 Ibid., 109.
22 Ibid.
23 Aran and Hassner, 'Religious Violence in Judaism', 372.
24 Ibid., 373.
25 Ibid., 377.
26 Ibid.

27 Ibid., 378.
28 Ibid., 374.
29 Ibid., 375.
30 Ibid., 374.
31 Ibid., 375.
32 Ibid., 382.
33 Cf. David Biale, *Blood and Belief: The Circulation of a Symbol between Jews and Christians* (Berkeley: University of California Press, 2007).
34 Aran and Hassner, 'Religious Violence in Judaism', 388.
35 Ibid.
36 Ibid.
37 Ibid.
38 Ibid., 381.
39 Mark Juergensmeyer, *Terror in the Mind of God: The Global Rise of Religious Violence*, 3rd edition. Berkeley: University of California Press, 2003 (First edition, 2000), 52.
40 Ellen Posman, 'History, Humiliation, and Religious Violence', in *The Blackwell Companion to Religion and Violence*, ed. Andrew R. Murphy (Malden, MA: Wiley-Blackwell, 2011), 339.
41 Ibid, 336.
42 Elliott Horowitz, 'Genesis 34 and the Legacies of Biblical Violence' in *The Blackwell Companion to Religion and Violence*, ed. Andrew R. Murphy (Malden, MA: Wiley-Blackwell, 2011), 176.
43 Aran and Hassner, 'Religious Violence in Judaism', 357.
44 Juergensmeyer, *Terror in the Mind of God*, 54.
45 Ibid.
46 Ibid., 55.
47 Ibid., 57.
48 Aran and Hassner, 'Religious Violence in Judaism', 358.
49 Ibid.
50 Ibid., 359.
51 Ibid.
52 Ibid., 360.
53 Juergensmeyer, *Terror in the Mind of God*, 47.
54 Amir's context, reasoning and action echo the assassination of India's Mahatma Gandhi in January 1948.
55 Ibid., 48.
56 Aran and Hassner, 'Religious Violence in Judaism', 360.
57 Ibid.
58 Ibid.
59 Juergensmeyer, *Terror in the Mind of God*, 44.
60 Ibid., 47.
61 Ibid., 46.
62 Aran and Hassner, 'Religious Violence in Judaism', 388.
63 Ibid.
64 Ibid.
65 Ibid.
66 Ibid., 389.
67 Ibid.
68 Ibid.
69 Ibid., 390.
70 Ibid., 394.
71 Ibid.

Notes

72 Ibid., 395.
73 Ibid.
74 Ibid.
75 Ibid., 396.
76 Ibid., 365.
77 Ibid., 391.
78 Ibid.
79 Ibid., 364.
80 Ibid., 391.
81 Ibid., 356.
82 Ibid., 357.
83 Ibid., 393.
84 Ibid.

FORMS OF CHRISTIAN EXTREMISM

1 Pieter G. R. de Villiers and Jan Willem van Henten, eds., *Coping with Violence in the New Testament* (Leiden and Boston: Brill, 2012), ix.
2 Ibid.
3 Jonathan Matusitz, *Symbolism in Terrorism: Motivation, Communication, and Behavior* (Lanham, MD: Rowan & Littlefield, 2015), 155.
4 Ibid.
5 Ibid.
6 John J. Collins, *Does the Bible Justify Violence?* (Minneapolis: Fortress Press, 2004), 23.
7 Ibid.
8 Ibid., 27.
9 Gnosticism came in many varieties and featured a radical dualism (a concept of the cosmic order being constituted by a realm of Goodness, or Light, forever battling with a realm of Evil, or Darkness) wherein salvation was believed to be effected by the reception of a special 'saving' knowledge mediated by a special 'teacher'.
10 Marcionism is a gnostic variant attributed to a wealthy convert called Marcion who formed his own church and devised his own, very limited, canon of scripture.
11 Montanism refers to a Christian apocalyptic movement in the late second century.
12 Jonathan Ebel, 'Christianity and Violence', in *The Blackwell Companion to Religion and Violence*, ed. Andrew R. Murphy (Malden, MA: Wiley-Blackwell, 2011), 154.
13 Ibid., 155.
14 Ibid.
15 Ibid., 156.
16 The expression of normative orthodox Christian belief in Jesus as fully human and fully divine promulgated at an ecumenical council held in 481 at the town of Chalcedon within the eastern Roman Empire.
17 That is, commandments and behavioural prescriptions found in the book of Leviticus.
18 William C. Placher, *A History of Christian Theology: An Introduction* (Philadelphia, PA: Westminster Press, 1983), 190.
19 John J. Collins, 'The Zeal of Phinehas, the Bible, and the Legitimation of Violence', in *The Destructive Power of Religion: Violence in Judaism, Christianity, and Islam*. Volume 1, *Sacred Scriptures, Ideology, and Violence*, ed. J. Harold Ellens (Westport, CT: Praeger, 2004), 20; cf. Michael Walzer, *Exodus and Revelation*, (New York: Basic Books, 1984), 3–4.
20 Ebel, 'Christianity and Violence', 149.

21 Ibid.
22 A term encompassing various groups of Christian dissidents, but in particular refers to a large group of dissenters in the twelfth and thirteenth centuries which posed a serious challenge to the authority of the Church.
23 The Taborites were an extreme group of the followers of the early reformer, John Hus. They named their fortified stronghold after Mount Tabor (hence their name) and applied force to support their viewpoint, abjuring rational theology of any kind. They successfully fought off a series of papal armies intent on bringing them to heel, as had Augustine in respect of the Donatists several centuries previously.
24 See Douglas Pratt, with Piet Naudé, 'South Speaks to South: A New Zealand Response to the *kerygma* of Belhar', *Ned Geref Teologiese Tydskrif* 44, nos. 3 and 4 (September and December 2003): 421–32.
25 Specific detail need not concern us; suffice to say this group took steps to impose its will and vision upon the electorate in an underhand manner.
26 Matusitz, *Symbolism in Terrorism*, 159.
27 Mattais Gardell, *Gods of the Blood: The Pagan Revival and White Separatism* (Durham, NC: Duke University Press, 2003), 118.
28 Gardell, *Gods of the Blood*, 121.
29 Ibid., 126.
30 Ibid. Note: by 'Israel' is meant the 'true' Aryan Israel, not the Jewish state.
31 Ibid., 118.
32 Timothy K. Beal, 'The White Supremacist Bible and the Phineas Priesthood', in *Sanctified Aggression: Legacies of Biblical and Post-biblical Vocabularies of Violence*, ed. Jonneke Bekkenkamp and Yvonne Sherwood (London: T & T Clark, 2003), 120.
33 Richard Kelly Hoskins, *Vigilantes for Christendom: The Story of the Phineas Priesthood* (Lynchburg, VA: Virginia Publishing, 1990), 213; cited in Beal, 'The White Supremacist Bible', 123.
34 Beal, 'The White Supremacist Bible', 123.
35 Ibid., 121.
36 Ibid., 129.
37 Ibid.
38 Ibid.
39 Ibid., 130.
40 Ibid.
41 Eugene V. Gallagher, 'God and Country: Revolution as a Religious Imperative on the Radical Right', *Terrorism and Political Violence* 9, no. 3 (1997): 63.
42 Ibid.
43 Ibid., 65.
44 Ibid.
45 Ibid.
46 Ibid., 67.
47 Cf. Chester L. Quarles, *The Ku Klux Klan and Related American Racialist and Antisemitic Organisations: A History and Analysis* (Jefferson, NC: McFarland, 1999).
48 Cf. Christopher Tyerman, *Fighting for Christendom: Holy War and the Crusades* (Oxford: Oxford University Press, 2004); Joseph Perez, *The Spanish Inquisition: A History* (London: Profile Books, 2004).
49 Gideon Aran, 'Israeli-Jewish and American-Protestant Fundamentalist Violence: Contemporary Variations on an Ancient Theme', in *Religion and Terrorism: The Use of Violence in Abrahamic Monotheism*, ed. Veronica Ward and Richard Sherlock (Lanham, MD: Lexington Books), 106.

Notes

TRAJECTORIES OF ISLAMIC EXTREMISM

1. David Cook, 'Jihad and Martyrdom in Classical and Contemporary Islam', in *The Blackwell Companion to Religion and Violence*, ed. Andrew R. Murphy (Malden, MA: Wiley-Blackwell, 2011), 287.
2. Ibid.
3. Rafiq Zakaria, *The Struggle within Islam: The Conflict between Religion and Politics* (London: Penguin, 1989), 114.
4. Ibid., 157.
5. Ibid., 164.
6. Sami Zubaida, *Islam: The People and the State: Political Ideas and Movements in the Middle East* (London: I. B. Taurus, 1993), 38.
7. Andrew Rippin, *Muslims: Their Religious Beliefs and Practices*, Volume 2, *The Contemporary Period* (London: Routledge, 1993), 16.
8. Tim Winter, 'Terrorism and Islamic Theologies of Religiously-Sanctioned War', in *Just War on Terror? A Christian and Muslim Response*, ed. David Fisher and Brian Wicker (Farnham: Ashgate, 2010), 17. Indeed, Winter points out that the very meaning of the Arabic word *hamas*, which is also the acronym for the main Palestinian Muslim extremist movement opposed to Israel, is 'zealotry'.
9. Akbar S. Ahmed, *Living Islam* (London: BBC Books, 1993), 128.
10. Beverly Milton-Edwards, 'Islam and Violence', in *The Blackwell Companion to Religion and Violence*, ed. Andrew R. Murphy (Malden, MA: Wiley-Blackwell, 2011), 183.
11. Ibid., 187; cf. B. Lewis, *The Crisis of Islam: Holy War and Unholy Terror* (New York: Modern Library, 2003), 164.
12. Rippin, *Muslims*, 28ff.
13. William Shepard, 'Islam and Ideology: Towards a Typology', *International Journal of Middle East Studies* 19 (1987): 307–36.
14. Douglas Pratt, *The Challenge of Islam: Encounters in Interfaith Dialogue* (Abingdon: Routledge Revivals, 2017), 148–60.
15. Karen Armstrong, *Fields of Blood: Religion and the History of Violence* (London: Bodley Head, 2014), 314.
16. Ibid.
17. Winter, 'Terrorism and Islamic Theologies', 17.
18. Pete Lentini, *Neojihadism: Towards a New Understanding of Terrorism and Extremism?* (Northampton, MA: Edward Elgar Publishing, 2013), 16.
19. Ibrahim A. Karawan, *The Islamist Impasse*, International Institute for Strategic Studies, Adelphi Paper 314 (London: Oxford University Press, 1997), 7.
20. John L. Esposito, *Islam: The Straight Path*, Expanded Edition (Oxford: Oxford University Press, 1994), 163.
21. James P. Piscatori, *Islam in a World of Nation-States* (Cambridge: Cambridge University Press, 1994), 32.
22. Rippin, *Muslims*, 30.
23. Mahmud A. Faksh, *The Future of Islam in the Middle East: Fundamentalism in Egypt, Algeria, and Saudi Arabia* (Westport, CT: Praeger, 1997), 33.
24. Karawan, *The Islamist Impasse*, 13.
25. Faksh, *The Future of Islam*, 33.
26. Ibid., 31.
27. Ibid., 5.
28. Ibid., 8.
29. Ibid., 10.

30 Ibid., 11.
31 See for example Patrick Cockburn, *The Rise of Islamic State: ISIS and the New Sunni Revolution* (London and New York: Verso, 2015); Abdel Bari Atwan, *Islamic State: The Digital Caliphate* (London: Saqi Books, 2015); Michael Weiss and Hassan Hassan, *ISIS: Inside the Army of Terror* (New York: Regan Arts, 2015).
32 Faksh, *The Future of Islam*, 31.
33 Bassam Tibi, *The Challenge of Fundamentalism: Political Islam and the New World Disorder*, Updated Edition (Berkeley: University of California Press, 2002), iv.
34 Tibi, *The Challenge of Fundamentalism*, iv.
35 Esposito, *Islam: The Straight Path*, 152.
36 Ron Geaves, *Aspects of Islam* (London: Darton, Longman & Todd, 2005), 221.
37 See Ron Geaves, *Islam Today* (London: Continuum, 2010), 89.
38 Tibi, *The Challenge of Fundamentalism*, iv.
39 Ibid., xxii.
40 Ibid., xxvii.
41 Ibid., 20.
42 Ibid., 3.
43 Ibid., 14 – material in brackets added for clarity of meaning.
44 Ibid., 143.
45 Ibid.
46 Ibid., 155.
47 Ibid.
48 John L. Esposito, *The Islamic Threat: Myth or Reality?* 2nd edition (New York: Oxford University Press, 1995), 19.
49 Geaves, *Islam Today*, 88.
50 Ibid., 95.
51 Ibid., 94.
52 See for example, Youssef M. Choueiri, *Islamic Fundamentalism, 3rd Edition: The Story of Islamist Movements* (London and New York: Continuum, 2010).
53 Bruce Lincoln, *Holy Terrors: Thinking about Religion after September 11* (Chicago and London: University of Chicago Press, 2003), 15.
54 Ibid.

MUTUAL EXTREMISM: REACTIVE CO-RADICALIZATION

1 See Anna Halafoff, 'Encounter as Conflict: Interfaith Peace-Building', in *Understanding Interreligious Relations*, ed. D. Cheetham, D. Pratt and D. Thomas (Oxford: Oxford University Press, 2013), 262–80.
2 Tanja Ellingsen, 'Toward a Revival of Religion and Religious Clashes?' *Terrorism and Political Violence* 14, no. 3 (2005): 305–32; Susanna Pearce, 'Religious Rage: A Quantitative Analysis of the Intensity of Religious Conflicts', *Terrorism and Political Violence* 14, no. 3 (2005): 333–52.
3 Clark McCauley and Sophia Moskalenko, 'Mechanisms of Political Radicalization: Pathways toward Terrorism', *Terrorism and Political Violence* 20, no. 3 (2008): 416.
4 Anja Dalgaard-Nielsen, 'Violent Radicalization in Europe: What We Know and What We Do Not Know', *Studies in Conflict and Terrorism* 33, no. 9 (2010): 797–814.
5 Pete Lentini, 'The Transference of Neojihadism: Towards a Process Theory of Transnational Radicalisation', *Proceedings of the 2008 GTREC International Conference, 26–27 November* (Melbourne: Monash University Global Terrorism Research Centre, 2009), 1–32.

Notes

6 See Douglas Pratt, 'Religious Identity and the Denial of Alterity: Plurality and the Problem of Exclusivism', in *The Relation of Philosophy to Religion Today*, ed. Paolo Diego Bubbio and Philip Andrew Quadrio (Newcastle-upon-Tyne: Cambridge Scholars Publishing, 2011), 201–15.

7 Anna Halafoff, 'Riots, Mass Casualties, and Religious Hatred: Countering Anticosmopolitan Terror through Intercultural and Interreligious Understanding', in *Controversies in Contemporary Religion: Education, Law, Politics, Society, and Spirituality*, ed. Paul Hedges (Santa Barbara, CA: Praeger, 2014), 297.

8 Breivik's 1518 page 'manifesto' has the title *2083 – A European Declaration of Independence* in which he asserts that 'the fear of Islam is all but irrational' and claims to address topics 'related to historical events and aspects of past and current Islamic Imperialism'. The manifesto, a compilation from multiple sources, is available as a pdf download via a Google search.

9 Jean-Francois Mayer, 'In the Shadow of the Minaret: Origins and Implications of a Citizens' Initiative', in *The Swiss Minaret Ban: Islam in Question*, ed. Patrick Haenni and Stephane Lathion, trans., Tom Genrich (Fribourg: Religiscope, 2011), 8.

10 For a fuller discussion, see Douglas Pratt, 'Swiss Shock: Minaret Rejection, European Values, and the Challenge of Tolerant Neutrality', *Politics, Religion & Ideology* 14, no. 2 (2013): 193–207.

11 Douglas Pratt, *The Church and Other Faiths: The World Council of Churches, the Vatican, and Interreligious Dialogue* (Bern: Peter Lang, 2010), 20.

12 The far-right SVP (Schweizerischen Volkspartei) and the right-leaning EDU (Eidgenössischen Demokratischen Union).

13 Mayer, 'In the Shadow of the Minaret', 10.

14 Samuel M. Behloul, 'Minarett-Initiative. Im Spannungsfeld zwischen Abwehr-Reflex und impliziter Anerkennung nuer gesellschaftlicher Fakten', in *Streit um das Minarett: Zusammenleben in der religiöse pluralistischen Gesellschaft*, ed. Mathias Tanner, Felix Müller, Frank Mathwig and Wolfgang Lienemann (Zürich: Theologischer Verlag, 2009), 106 (my translation).

15 Ibid., 109.

16 Wolfgang Lienemann, 'Argumente für ein Minaret-Verbot? Eine kritische Analyze', in *Streit um das Minarett: Zusammenleben in der religiöse pluralistischen Gesellschaft*, ed. Mathias Tanner, Felix Müller, Frank Mathwig and Wolfgang Lienemann (Zürich: Theologischer Verlag, 2009), 129 (my translation).

17 Ibid., 130.

18 For a contemporary critical discussion of Breivik and the wider context of his actions, see Sindre Bangstad, *Anders Breivik and the Rise of Islamophobia* (London: Zed Books, 2014).

19 Egil Asprem, 'The Birth of Counterjihadist Terrorism: Reflections on Some Unspoken Dimensions of 22 July 2011', *The Pomegranate* 13, no. 1 (2011): 17.

20 Ibid.

21 *De Laude Novae Militiae – Pauperes Commilitones Christi Temlique Solomnici*

22 Asprem, 'The Birth of Counterjihadist Terrorism', 17.

23 Notably the Dutch PVV, the Sweden Democrats, the Norwegian Peoples' Party, the True Finns and the Hungarian Jobbik party.

24 Asprem, 'The Birth of Counterjihadist Terrorism', 19.

25 Ibid.

26 See Mark Juergensmeyer, 'Why Breivik Was a Christian Terrorist', *Huffington Post*, 27 July 2011 at: http://www.huffingtonpost.com/mark-juergensmeyer/why-breivik-was-a-christi_b_910443.html (accessed 10 February 2015); 'Is Norway's Suspected Murderer a Christian Terrorist?' *Religion Despatches*, 24 July 2011 at: http://www.religiondispatches.org/archive/politics/4910/is_norway%E2%80%99s_suspected_murderer_anders_breivik_a_christian_terrorist/ (accessed 10 February 2015).

27 Cited in Asprem, 'The Birth of Counterjihadist Terrorism', 22.

28 Anders Behring Breivik, *2083 – A European Declaration of Independence* (Self-published pdf document, 2011), 1361.
29 Ibid.
30 Cf. Asprem, 'The Birth of Counterjihadist Terrorism', 28.
31 Umberto Eco, *Foucault's Pendulum* (New York: Ballantine Books, 1989), 56.
32 Asprem, 'The Birth of Counterjihadist Terrorism', 30.
33 Angela Charlton. 'Far-Right Anger, Violence Thrive on Europe's Edges', *Sunday Star Times* (New Zealand), 7 August 2011: A13.
34 Paul Holmes, 'A Crime beyond Punishment', *Weekend Herald* (New Zealand), 6 August 2011: A19.
35 Tapu Misa, 'How to Live up to Freedom's Ideals', *New Zealand Herald*, 1 August 2011: A11.
36 Ibid.
37 Cf. Douglas Pratt, 'Islamophobia as Reactive Co-radicalization', *Islam and Christian–Muslim Relations* 26, no. 2 (April 2015): 205–18.
38 See for example, 'Quebec Mosque Shooting: Student Charged with Six Counts of Murder over Gun Attack in Mosque', *The Telegraph News* at: http://www.telegraph.co.uk/news/2017/01/30/quebec-mosque-shooting-two-students-arrested-gun-attack-mosque/ (accessed 1 February 2017).
39 See also, Douglas Pratt, 'Reactive Co-radicalization: Religious Extremism as Mutual Discontent', *Journal for the Academic Study of Religion* 28, no. 1 (2015): 3–23.
40 Martha C. Nussbaum, *The New Religious Intolerance: Overcoming the Politics of Fear in an Anxious Age* (Cambridge, MA: The Belknap Press, 2012), 2.
41 Ibid., 6.
42 Ibid., 48.
43 Ibid., 23.
44 Ibid., 244.
45 Douglas Pratt, 'The Persistence and Problem of Religion: Modernity Continuity and Diversity', *ARSReview* 25, no. 3 (2102): 285.

EXTREMISM AND ISLAMOPHOBIA

1 Donald Trump, Inaugural Address, as prepared for delivery. Online at: http://edition.cnn.com/2017/01/20/politics/trump-inaugural-address/index.html (accessed 21 January 2017).
2 Ibid.
3 Ibid. This rhetorical question ('What the hell is going on?') was a recurring trope of Mr Trump's campaign rhetoric.
4 See Douglas Pratt and Rachel Woodlock, eds., *Fear of Muslims? International Perspectives on Islamophobia* (Switzerland: Springer International, 2016); see also S. Sayyid, 'A Measure of Islamophobia', *Islamophobia Studies Journal* 2, no. 1 (Spring 2014): 10–25.
5 World Islamic Front Statement, 'Jihad against Jews and Crusaders'. Online at https://fas.org/irp/world/para/docs/980223-fatwa.htm (accessed 21 February 2017). see also Pete Lentini, *Neojihadism: Towards a New Understanding of Terrorism and Extremism?* (Northampton, MA: Edward Elgar Publishing, 2013).
6 Christopher Allen, *Islamophobia* (Farnham: Ashgate, 2010), 80.
7 Jocelyne Cesari, 'Islamophobia in the West: A Comparison between Europe and the United States', in *Islamophobia: The Challenge of Pluralism in the 21st Century*, ed. John L. Esposito and Ibrahim Kalin (Oxford: Oxford University Press, 2011), 21.
8 The Runnymede Trust, *Islamophobia: A Challenge for Us All; Report of the Runnymede Trust Commission on British Muslims and Islamophobia* (London: Runnymede Trust, 1997). Online at: http://goo.gl/o80ksA (accessed 22 January 2017).

Notes

9 Christopher Allen and Jørgen S. Nielsen, *Summary report on Islamophobia in the EU after 11 September 2001* (Vienna: European Monitoring Centre on Racism and Xenophobia, 2002).
10 Ihsan Yilmaz, 'The Nature of Islamophobia: Some Key Features', in *Fear of Muslims? International Perspectives on Islamophobia*, ed. Douglas Pratt and Rachel Woodlock (Switzerland: Springer International, 2016), 20.
11 Ibid., 19.
12 Ibid., 23.
13 For instance, the shooting dead of six Sikh worshippers, and wounding four others, at the Oak Creek Gurdwara, Wisconsin, on 5 August 2012. Online at: http://edition.cnn.com/2012/08/05/us/wisconsin-temple-shooting/ (accessed 15 February 2017).
14 Pratt and Woodlock, *Fear of Muslims?* 3.
15 Yilmaz, 'The Nature of Islamophobia', 19.
16 Cf. Hatem Bazian, 'National Entry–Exit Registration System: Arabs, Muslims, and Southeast Asians and Post-9/11 "Security Measures"', *Islamophobia Studies Journal* 2, no. 1 (Spring 2014): 82–98.
17 Douglas Pratt, 'Muslim-Jewish Relations: Some Islamic Paradigms', *Islam and Christian–Muslim Relations* 21, no. 1 (2010): 11–21.
18 Alex Schmid, 'Frameworks for Conceptualizing Terrorism', *Terrorism and Political Violence* 16, no. 2 (2004): 197–221.
19 'Boko Haram Members Behead Nigerian Airforce Officer'. Available at: http://dailypost.ng/2014/07/23 (Accessed 13 October 2014).
20 'French Hostage Herve Gourdel Beheaded in Algeria'. Available at: http://www.bbc.com/news/world-africa-29352537 (Accessed 13 October 2014).
21 See www.cair.com (accessed 1 February 2017).
22 'Straying from the Middle Way: Extremist Buddhist Monks Target Religious Minorities', *TIME*, 20 June 2013. Available at: http://world.time.com/2013/06/20/extremist-buddhist-monks-fight-oppression-with-violence/ (accessed 10 February 2015).
23 See Virginie Andre, 'Neojihadism and YouTube: Patani Militant Propaganda Dissemination and Radicalization', *Asian Security* 8, no. 1 (2012): 27–53; Virginie Andre, 'The Janus Face of New Media Propaganda: The Case of Patani Neojihadist YouTube Warfare and its Islamophobic Effect on Cyber-Actors', *Islam and Christian–Muslim Relations* 25, no. 3 (2014): 335–56.
24 Cf. John Azumah, *The Legacy of Arab-Islam in Africa: A Quest for Inter-religious Dialogue* (Oxford: Oneworld, 2001).
25 John Azumah, 'Boko Haram in Retrospect', *Islam and Christian–Muslim Relations* 26, no. 1 (2015): 33–52.
26 Peter Gottschalk and Gabriel Greenberg, *Islamophobia: Making Muslims the Enemy* (Lanham, MD: Rowman & Littlefield, 2008).
27 See, for example, Erich Kolig, ed., *Freedom of Speech and Islam* (Farnham: Ashgate, 2014).
28 Pratt and Woodlock, *Fear of Muslims?* 6.
29 Grant Taylor, 'Anti-Islam Party Takes First Steps'. https://au.news.yahoo.com/thewest/wa/a/29902634/anti-islam-party-australian-liberty-alliance-takes-first-steps/ (accessed 11 February 2016).
30 Bianca Hall, 'Restore Australia: The Party that Would Ban Islam', *The Age* 1 January 2016. http://www.smh.com.au/federal-politics/political-news/restore-australia-the-party-that-would-ban-islam-20160101-glxsfh.html (accessed 11 February 2016).
31 Ibid.
32 'Call on PM to Publicly Condemn Islamophobia', *Australian Muslim Times*. Available at: http://www.amust.com.au/2016/08/call-on-pm-to-publicly-condemn-islamophobia/ (accessed 5 August 2016).

33 Ibid.
34 Stephen Sheehi, *Islamophobia: The Ideological Campaign against Muslims* (Atlanta GA: Clarity Press, 2011); see also Corey Saylor, 'The U.S. Islamophobia Network: Its Funding and Impact', *Islamophobia Studies Journal* 2, no.1 (Spring 2014): 99–118.
35 Pratt and Woodlock, *Fear of Muslims?* 7; see also Ajahat Ali, Eli Clifton, Matthew Duss, Lee Fang, Scott Keyes and Faiz Shakir, *Fear, Inc. The Roots of the Islamophobia Network in America* (Washington, DC: Center for American Progress, 2011).
36 Sherman A. Lee, Jeffrey A. Gibbons, John M. Thompson and Hussan S. Timani, 'The Islamophobia Scale: Instrument Development and Initial Validation', *International Journal for the Psychology of Religion* 19 (2009): 92–105.
37 Beverly Milton-Edwards, 'Islam and Violence', in *The Blackwell Companion to Religion and Violence*, ed. Andrew R. Murphy (Malden, MA: Wiley-Blackwell, 2011), 186.
38 Stefanie Wright, 'Reproducing Fear: Islamophobia in the United States', in *Fear of Muslims? International Perspectives on Islamophobia*, ed. Douglas Pratt and Rachel Woodlock (Switzerland: Springer International, 2016), 45–65; see also Juan Cole, 'Islamophobia and American Foreign Policy Rhetoric: The Bush Years and after', in *Islamophobia: The Challenge of Pluralism in the 21st Century*, ed. John L. Esposito and Ibrahim Kalin (Oxford: Oxford University Press, 2011), 127–42.
39 Wright, 'Reproducing Fear', 46.
40 Ibid.
41 Ibid., 48.
42 Ibid., 61.
43 Ibid.
44 Göran Larsson and Simon Stjenreholm, 'Islamophobia in Sweden: Muslim Advocacy and Hate-Crime Statistics', in Pratt and Woodlock, ed., *Fear of Muslims?* 153–66; see also Sam Cherribi, 'An Obsession Renewed: Islamophobia in the Netherlands, Austria, and Germany', in Esposito and Kalin, ed., *Islamophobia*, 47–62.
45 Natalie Doyle, 'The Fear of Islam: French Context and Reaction', in Pratt and Woodlock, ed., *Fear of Muslims?* 167–90.
46 See, for example, Sindre Bangstad, 'Norwegian Right-Wing Discourses: Extremism post-Utøya', in Pratt and Woodlock, ed., *Fear of Muslims?* 231–50.
47 See for example, George Morgan and Scott Poynting, eds., *Global Islamophobia: Muslims and Moral Panic in the West* (Farnham: Ashgate 2012).
48 Beverly Milton-Edwards, 'Islam and Violence', in *The Blackwell Companion to Religion and Violence*, ed. Andrew R. Murphy (Malden, MA: Wiley-Blackwell, 2011), 185; cf. Tariq Ali, *The Clash of Fundamentalisms: Crusades, Jihads and Modernity* (London: Verso, 2002).
49 Milton-Edwards, 'Islam and Violence', 188.
50 Ibid., 190.
51 Andrew J. Shryock, 'Attack of the Islamophobes: Religious War (and Peace) in Arab/Muslim Detroit', in *Islamophobia in America: The Anatomy of Intolerance*, ed. Carl W. Ernst (New York: Palgrave Macmillan, 2013), 143–73.
52 Pratt and Woodlock, *Fear of Muslims?* 9; cf. Raymond Taras, *Xenophobia and Islamophobia in Europe* (Edinburgh: Edinburgh University Press, 2012), 10.

CONCLUSION

1 Mark Juergensmeyer, *Terror in the Mind of God: The Global Rise of Religious Violence*, 3rd edition (Berkeley: University of California Press, 2003), xi.
2 Ibid., 221.

Notes

3 Charles Selengut, 'The Sociology of Religious Violence', in *The Blackwell Companion to Religion and Violence*, ed. Andrew R. Murphy (Malden, MA: Wiley-Blackwell, 2011), 96.
4 Jan Willem van Henten, 'Religion, Bible and Violence', in *Coping with Violence in the New Testament*, ed. Pieter G. R. de Villiers and Jan Willem van Henten (Leiden and Boston: Brill, 2012), 15.
5 J. Harold Ellens, 'Fundamentalism, Orthodoxy, and Violence', in *The Destructive Power of Religion: Violence in Judaism, Christianity, and Islam*. Volume 4, *Contemporary Views on Spirituality and Violence*, ed. J. Harold Ellens (Westport, CT: Praeger, 2004), 121.
6 Ibid., 120.
7 Ibid., 140.
8 David E. Guinn, 'Religion, Law, and Violence', in *The Blackwell Companion to Religion and Violence*, ed. Andrew R. Murphy (Malden, MA: Wiley-Blackwell, 2011), 109.
9 P. de Villiers and J. van Henten, eds., *Coping with Violence in the New Testament*, ix.
10 Ellens, 'Fundamentalism, Orthodoxy, and Violence', 122. Ellens (see Note 5 above for bibliographical detail) discusses various Protestant, Catholic, Jewish and Muslim forms of violence (pp. 125–32) as well as other religious fundamentalisms (pp. 132–40).
11 Selengut, 'The Sociology of Religious Violence', 89.
12 Ibid.
13 Ibid., 90.
14 D. Andrew Kille, '"The Bible Made Me Do It": Text, Interpretation, and Violence', in *The Destructive Power of Religion: Violence in Judaism, Christianity, and Islam*. Volume 1, *Sacred Scriptures, Ideology, and Violence*, ed. J. Harold Ellens (Westport, CT: Praeger, 2004), 55. Kille notes an illustrative bumper sticker popular in parts of the United States: 'God Said It. I Believe It. That Settles It'.
15 Selengut, 'The Sociology of Religious Violence', 93.
16 Ibid.
17 Ibid. See also on these points, Gershon Gorenberg, *The End of Days: Fundamentalism and the Struggle for the Temple Mount* (New York: Free Press, 2000).
18 Tim Winter, 'Terrorism and Islamic Theologies of Religiously-Sanctioned War', in *Just War on Terror? A Christian and Muslim Response*, ed. David Fisher and Brian Wicker (Farnham: Ashgate, 2010), 9.
19 Juergensmeyer, *Terror in the Mind of God*, 220.
20 J. van Henten, 'Religion, Bible and Violence', 15.
21 John J. Collins, 'The Zeal of Phinehas, the Bible, and the Legitimation of Violence', in *The Destructive Power of Religion: Violence in Judaism, Christianity, and Islam*. Volume 1, *Sacred Scriptures, Ideology, and Violence*, ed. J. Harold Ellens (Westport, CT: Praeger, 2004), 20.
22 Ibid.
23 Timothy K. Beal, 'The White Supremacist Bible and the Phineas Priesthood', in *Sanctified Aggression: Legacies of Biblical and Post-biblical Vocabularies of Violence*, ed. Jonneke Bekkenkamp and Yvonne Sherwood (London: T & T Clark, 2003), 130.
24 Shelly Matthews and E. Leigh Gibson, eds., *Violence in the New Testament* (New York: T & T Clark, 2005), 1.
25 Ibid., 3.
26 Ibid.
27 J. van Henten, 'Religion, Bible and Violence', 8.
28 James W. Jones, 'Sacred Terror: The Psychology of Contemporary Religious Terrorism', in *The Blackwell Companion to Religion and Violence*, ed. Andrew R. Murphy (Malden, MA: Wiley-Blackwell, 2011), 293.
29 Ibid.
30 Ibid., 301; cf. James W. Jones, *Blood that Cries Out from the Earth: The Psychology of Religious Terrorism* (New York: Oxford University Press, 2008).

Notes

31 Keith Ward, *Is Religion Dangerous?* (Oxford: Lion, 2006), 38.
32 Karen Armstrong, *Fields of Blood: Religion and the History of Violence* (London: Bodley Head, 2014), 312.
33 See for example the report of the Alliance of Shared Values, *The Failed Military Coup in Turkey & the Mass Purges: A Civil Society Perspective* (New York: Alliance of Shared Values, 2016).
34 See http://economicsandpeace.org/ (Accessed 2 February 2017).
35 Kevin Clements, private pre-released communique for VUW-IGPS *Policy Quarterly*, February 2017 edition.
36 Selengut, 'The Sociology of Religious Violence', 96.
37 Ibid.
38 Jolyon Mitchell, 'Mediating Religious Violence', in *The Blackwell Companion to Religion and Violence*, ed. Andrew R. Murphy (Malden, MA: Wiley-Blackwell, 2011), 113.
39 Ibid.
40 Ibid.
41 Ibid., 119.
42 Ibid., 122.
43 3 February 2017; various news sources.
44 Juergensmeyer, *Terror in the Mind of God*, 221.
45 Ibid., 249.
46 Winter, 'Terrorism and Islamic Theologies', 15.
47 *Summa Theologica* 1.47.1.

BIBLIOGRAPHY

Aden, LeRoy H. 'The Role of Self-Justification in Violence'. In *The Destructive Power of Religion: Violence in Judaism, Christianity, and Islam*. Volume 2, *Religion, Psychology, and Violence*, edited by J. Harold Ellens, 251–63. Westport, CT: Praeger , 2004.
Ahmed, Akbar S. *Living Islam*. London: BBC Books, 1993.
Ali, Abdullah Yusuf. *Holy Qur'an. Text, Translation, and Commentary*. Al-Murgab, Kuwait: That Es-Salasil Publishing, n.d.
Ali, Ajahat, Eli Clifton, Matthew Duss, Lee Fang, Scott Keyes and Faiz Shakir. *Fear, Inc. The Roots of the Islamophobia Network in America*. Washington, DC: Center for American Progress, 2011.
Ali, Tariq. *The Clash of Fundamentalisms: Crusades, Jihads and Modernity*. London: Verso, 2002.
Allen, Christopher. *Islamophobia*. Farnham: Ashgate, 2010.
Allen, Christopher, and Jørgen S. Nielsen. *Summary Report on Islamophobia in the EU after 11 September 2001*. Vienna: European Monitoring Centre on Racism and Xenophobia, 2002.
Allen, Diogenes. *Christian Belief in a Postmodern World*. Louisville, KY: Westminster/John Knox Press, 1989.
Alliance of Shared Values. *The Failed Military Coup in Turkey & the Mass Purges: A Civil Society Perspective*. New York: Alliance of Shared Values, 2016.
Andre, Virginie. 'Neojihadism and YouTube: Patani Militant Propaganda Dissemination and Radicalization'. *Asian Security* 8, no. 1 (2012): 27–53.
Andre, Virginie. 'The Janus Face of New Media Propaganda: The Case of Patani Neojihadist YouTube Warfare and Its Islamophobic Effect on Cyber-Actors'. *Islam and Christian–Muslim Relations* 25, no. 3 (2014): 335–56.
Appleby, Scott. *The Ambivalence of the Sacred: Religion, Violence and Reconciliation*. Lanham, MD: Rowman & Littlefield, 2000.
Aran, Gideon. 'Jewish Zionist Fundamentalism: The Bloc of the Faithful in Israel (Gush Emunim)'. In *Fundamentalisms Observed*, edited by Martin E. Marty and R. Scott Appleby, 265–344. Chicago: University of Chicago Press, 1991.
Aran, Gideon. 'Religiosity and Super-Religiosity: Measures of Radical Religion'. *Numen* 60 (2013): 155–94.
Aran, Gideon. 'Israeli-Jewish and American-Protestant Fundamentalist Violence: Contemporary Variations on an Ancient Theme'. In *Religion and Terrorism: The Use of Violence in Abrahamic Monotheism,* edited by Veronica Ward and Richard Sherlock, 103–18. Lanham, MD: Lexington Books, 2014.
Aran, Gideon, and Ron E. Hassner. 'Religious Violence in Judaism: Past and Present'. *Terrorism and Political Violence* 25, no. 3 (2013): 355–405.
Ariarajah, S. Wesley. *Hindus and Christians: A Century of Protestant Ecumenical Thought*. Amsterdam and Grand Rapids, MI: Editions Rodopi and Wm B. Eerdmans, 1991.
Ariarajah, S. Wesley. *Not without My Neighbour: Issues in Interfaith Relations*. Risk Book Series No. 85. Geneva: WCC Publications, 1999.
Armstrong, Karen. *Fields of Blood: Religion and the History of Violence*. London: Bodley Head, 2014.
Asprem, Egil. 'The Birth of Counterjihadist Terrorism: Reflections on Some Unspoken Dimensions of 22 July 2011'. *The Pomegranate* 13, no. 1 (2011): 17–32.
Atwan, Abdel Bari. *Islamic State: The Digital Caliphate*. London: Saqi Books, 2015.

Bibliography

Azumah, John. *The Legacy of Arab-Islam in Africa: A Quest for Inter-religious Dialogue*. Oxford: Oneworld, 2001.
Azumah, John. 'Boko Haram in Retrospect'. *Islam and Christian–Muslim Relations* 26, no. 1 (2015): 33–52.
Bangstad, Sindre. *Anders Breivik and the Rise of Islamophobia*. London: Zed Books, 2014.
Bangstad, Sindre. 'Norwegian Right-Wing Discourses: Extremism Post-Utøya'. In *Fear of Muslims? International Perspectives on Islamophobia*, edited by Douglas Pratt and Rachel Woodlock, 231–50. Switzerland: Springer International, 2016.
Barkun, Michael. *Religion and the Racist Right: The Origin of the Christian Identity Movement*. Chapel Hill: University of North Carolina Press, 1994.
Barr, James. *Fundamentalism*. London: SCM Press, 1977.
Bazian, Hatem. 'National Entry–Exit Registration System: Arabs, Muslims, and Southeast Asians and Post-9/11 "Security Measures"'. *Islamophobia Studies Journal* 2, no. 1 (Spring 2014): 82–98.
Beal, Timothy K. 'The White Supremacist Bible and the Phineas Priesthood'. In *Sanctified Aggression: Legacies of Biblical and Post-biblical Vocabularies of Violence*, edited by Jonneke Bekkenkamp and Yvonne Sherwood, 120–31. London: T & T Clark, 2003.
Behloul, Samuel M. 'Minarett-Initiative. Im Spannungsfeld zwischen Abwehr-Reflex und impliziter Anerkennung nuer gesellschaftlicher Fakten'. In *Streit um das Minarett: Zusammenleben in der religiöse pluralistischen Gesellschaft*, edited by Mathias Tanner, Felix Müller, Frank Mathwig and Wolfgang Lienemann. Zürich: Theologischer Verlag, 2009.
Bekkenkamp, Jonneke, and Yvonne Sherwood. *Sanctified Aggression: Legacies of Biblical and Post-biblical Vocabularies of Violence*. London: T & T Clark, 2003.
Biale, David. *Blood and Belief: The Circulation of a Symbol between Jews and Christians*. Berkeley: University of California Press, 2007.
Bouma, Gary. *Australian Soul: Religion and Spirituality in the Twenty-First Century*. Melbourne: Cambridge University Press, 2006.
Breivik, Anders Behring. *2083 – A European Declaration of Independence*. Self-published pdf document, 2011.
Bromley, and J. Gordon Melton, eds. *Cults, Religion and Violence*. Cambridge: Cambridge University Press, 2002.
Caplan, Lionel. *Studies in Religious Fundamentalism*. Basingstoke: Macmillan, 1987.
Cesari, Jocelyne. 'Islamophobia in the West: A Comparison between Europe and the United States'. In *Islamophobia: The Challenge of Pluralism in the 21st Century*, edited by John L. Esposito and Ibrahim Kalin, 21–43. Oxford: Oxford University Press, 2011.
Cherribi, Sam. 'An Obsession Renewed: Islamophobia in the Netherlands, Austria, and Germany'. In *Islamophobia: The Challenge of Pluralism in the 21st Century*, edited by John L. Esposito and Ibrahim Kalin, 47–62. Oxford: Oxford University Press, 2011.
Choueiri, Youssef M. *Islamic Fundamentalism, 3rd Edition: The Story of Islamist Movements*. London: Continuum, 2010.
Cobb, John B. *Beyond Dialogue*. Philadelphia: Fortress Press, 1982.
Cockburn, Patrick. *The Rise of Islamic State: ISIS and the New Sunni Revolution*. London and New York: Verso, 2015.
Cole, Juan. 'Islamophobia and American Foreign Policy Rhetoric: The Bush Years and after'. In *Islamophobia: The Challenge of Pluralism in the 21st Century*, edited by John L. Esposito and Ibrahim Kalin, 127–42. Oxford: Oxford University Press, 2011.
Collins, John J. *Does the Bible Justify Violence?* Minneapolis: Fortress Press, 2004.
Collins, John J. 'The Zeal of Phinehas, the Bible, and the Legitimation of Violence'. In *The Destructive Power of Religion: Violence in Judaism, Christianity, and Islam*. Volume 1,

Bibliography

    Sacred Scriptures, Ideology, and Violence, edited by J. Harold Ellens, 11–33. Westport, CT: Praeger, 2004.

Connor, Steven. *Postmodernist Culture: An Introduction to Theories of the Contemporary*.Oxford: Blackwell, 1992.

Cook, David. 'Jihad and Martyrdom in Classical and Contemporary Islam'. In *The Blackwell Companion to Religion and Violence*, edited by Andrew R. Murphy, 282–91. Malden, MA: Wiley-Blackwell, 2011.

Cracknell, Kenneth. *Considering Dialogue: Theological Themes in Interfaith Relations, 1970–1980*. London: British Council of Churches, 1981.

Dalgaard-Nielsen, Anja. 'Violent Radicalization in Europe: What We Know and What We Do Not Know'. *Studies in Conflict and Terrorism* 33, no. 9 (2010): 797–814.

Davidson, Lawrence. *Islamic Fundamentalism: An Introduction*. Westport, CT: Greenwood Press, 2003.

de Villiers Pieter G. R., and Jan Willem van Henten, eds. *Coping with Violence in the New Testament*. Leiden and Boston: Brill, 2012.

de Vries, Simon John. 'Human Sacrifice in the Old Testament: In Ritual and in Warfare'. In *The Destructive Power of Religion: Violence in Judaism, Christianity, and Islam*. Volume 1, *Sacred Scriptures, Ideology, and Violence*, edited by J. Harold Ellens, 99–121. Westport, CT: Praeger, 2004.

Doyle, Natalie. 'The Fear of Islam: French Context and Reaction'. In *Fear of Muslims? International Perspectives on Islamophobia*, edited by Douglas Pratt and Rachel Woodlock, 167–90. Switzerland: Springer International, 2016.

Ebel, Jonathan. 'Christianity and Violence'. In *The Blackwell Companion to Religion and Violence*, edited by Andrew R. Murphy, 149–62. Malden, MA: Wiley-Blackwell, 2011.

Eck, Diana L. *Encountering God: A Spiritual Journey from Bozeman to Banares*. Boston: Beacon Press, 1993.

Eco, Umberto. *Foucault's Pendulum*. New York: Ballantine Books, 1989.

Eisen, Robert. *The Peace and Violence of Judaism*. New York: Oxford University Press, 2011.

Ellens, J. Harold, 'Fundamentalism, Orthodoxy, and Violence'. In *The Destructive Power of Religion: Violence in Judaism, Christianity, and Islam*. Volume 4, *Contemporary Views on Spirituality and Violence*, edited by J. Harold Ellens, 119–42. Westport, CT: Praeger, 2004.

Ellens, J. Harold, 'Introduction: Toxic Texts'. In *The Destructive Power of Religion: Violence in Judaism, Christianity, and Islam*. Volume 3, *Models and Cases of Violence in Religion*, edited by J. Harold Ellens, 1–13. Westport, CT: Praeger, 2004.

Ellens, J. Harold, 'The Violent Jesus'. In *The Destructive Power of Religion: Violence in Judaism, Christianity, and Islam*. Volume 3, *Models and Cases of Violence in Religion*, edited by J. Harold Ellens, 15–37. Westport, CT: Praeger, 2004.

Ellens, J. Harold, ed. *The Destructive Power of Religion: Violence in Judaism, Christianity, and Islam*. Volume 1, *Sacred Scriptures, Ideology, and Violence*. Westport, CT: Praeger, 2004.

Ellens, J. Harold, ed. *The Destructive Power of Religion: Violence in Judaism, Christianity, and Islam*. Volume 2, *Religion, Psychology, and Violence*. Westport, CT: Praeger, 2004.

Ellens, J. Harold, ed. *The Destructive Power of Religion: Violence in Judaism, Christianity, and Islam*. Volume 3, *Models and Cases of Violence in Religion*. Westport, CT: Praeger, 2004.

Ellens, J. Harold, ed. *The Destructive Power of Religion: Violence in Judaism, Christianity, and Islam*. Volume 4, *Contemporary Views on Spirituality and Violence*. Westport, CT: Praeger, 2004.

Ellingsen, Tanja. 'Toward a Revival of Religion and Religious Clashes?' *Terrorism and Political Violence* 14, no. 3 (2005): 305–32.

Elliott, Mark Adam. 'Retribution and Agency in the Dead Sea Scrolls and the Teaching of Jesus'. In *The Destructive Power of Religion: Violence in Judaism, Christianity, and Islam*. Volume

1, *Sacred Scriptures, Ideology, and Violence*, edited by J. Harold Ellens, 207–31. Westport, CT: Praeger, 2004.
Esposito, John L. *Islam: The Straight Path*. Expanded edition. Oxford: Oxford University Press, 1994.
Esposito, John L. *The Islamic Threat: Myth or Reality?* 2nd edition. New York: Oxford University Press, 1995.
Esposito, John L., and Ibrahim Kalin, eds. *Islamophobia: The Challenge of Pluralism in the 21st Century*. Oxford: Oxford University Press, 2011.
Faksh, Mahmud A. *The Future of Islam in the Middle East: Fundamentalism in Egypt, Algeria, and Saudi Arabia*. Westport, CT: Praeger, 1997.
Firestone, Reuven. 'Conceptions of Holy Wars in Biblical and Quranic Traditions', *Journal of Religious Ethics* 24, no. 1 (1996): 99–123
Firestone, Reuven. *Jihad: The Origin of Holy War in Islam*. New York: Oxford University Press, 1999.
Fisher, David, and Brian Wicker, eds. *Just War on Terror? A Christian and Muslim Response*. Farnham: Ashgate, 2010.
Freud, Sigmund. *Totem and Taboo*. New York: Moffat, Yard, 1919.
Gallagher, Eugene V. 'God and Country: Revolution as a Religious Imperative on the Radical Right'. *Terrorism and Political Violence* 9, no. 3 (1997): 63–79.
Gardell, Mattais. *Gods of the Blood: The Pagan Revival and White Separatism*. Durham, NC: Duke University Press, 2003.
Geaves, Ron. *Aspects of Islam*. London: Darton, Longman & Todd, 2005.
Geaves, Ron. *Islam Today*. London: Continuum, 2010.
Geaves, Ron, Theodore Gabriel, Yvonne Haddad and Jane Idleman Smith. *Islam & the West post 9/11*. Aldershot: Ashgate, 2004.
Gellner, Ernest. *Postmodernism, Reason and Religion*. London: Routledge, 1992.
Gilling, Bryan, ed. *"Be Ye Separate": Fundamentalism and the New Zealand Experience*. Red Beach: Colcom Press, 1992.
Girard, René. *Violence and the Sacred*. Baltimore: Johns Hopkins University Press, 1977.
Goldin, Simha, Yigal Levin and C. Michael Copeland. *The Ways of Jewish Martyrdom*. Turnhout: Brepols, 2008.
Gorenberg, Gershon. *The End of Days: Fundamentalism and the Struggle for the Temple Mount*. New York: Free Press, 2000.
Gottschalk, Peter, and Gabriel Greenberg. *Islamophobia: Making Muslims the Enemy*. Lanham, MD: Rowman & Littlefield, 2008.
Grenz, Stanley J. *A Primer on Postmodernism*. Grand Rapids: Wm B. Eerdmans, 1996.
Griffin, David Ray, William A. Beardslee and Joe Holland. *Varieties of Postmodern Theology*. New York: SUNY, 1989.
Guinn, David E. 'Religion, Law, and Violence', in *The Blackwell Companion to Religion and Violence*, edited by Andrew R. Murphy, 99–111. Malden, MA: Wiley-Blackwell, 2011.
Halafoff, Anna. 'Encounter as Conflict: Interfaith Peace-Building'. In *Understanding Interreligious Relations*, edited by D. Cheetham, D. Pratt and D. Thomas, 262–80. Oxford: Oxford University Press, 2013.
Halafoff, Anna. 'Riots, Mass Casualties, and Religious Hatred: Countering Anticosmopolitan Terror through Intercultural and Interreligious Understanding'. In *Controversies in Contemporary Religion: Education, Law, Politics, Society, and Spirituality*, edited by Paul Hedges, 293–312. Santa Barbara, CA: Praeger, 2014.
Harvey, David. *The Condition of Postmodernity*. Malden, MA: Blackwell, 1990.
Hassner, Ron E. *War on Sacred Grounds*. Ithaca, NY: Cornell University Press, 2009.
Hedges, Paul. *Controversies in Interreligious Dialogue and the Theology of Religions*. London: SCM Press, 2010.

Bibliography

Heilman, Samuel C., and Menachem Friedman. 'Religious Fundamentalism and Religious Jews: The Case of the Haredom'. In *Fundamentalisms Observed*, edited by Martin E. Marty and R. Scott Appleby, 197–264. Chicago: University of Chicago Press, 1991.

Heim, Mark. *Salvations: Truth and Difference in Religion*. Maryknoll, NY: Orbis Books, 1995.

Heim, Mark. *The Depth of the Riches: A Trinitarian Theology of Religious Ends*. Grand Rapids: Wm. B. Eerdmans, 2001.

Hick, John. *God and the Universe of Faiths*, revised edition. London: Collins, 1977.

Hick, John. *The Myth of God Incarnate*. London: SCM Press, 1977.

Hick, John. *God and the Universe of Faiths: Essays in the Philosophy of Religion*. London: Palgrave Macmillan, 1988.

Hick, John. *The Metaphor of God Incarnate*. London: SCM Press, 1993.

Hick, John. *The Rainbow of Faiths*. London: SCM Press, 1995.

Hoffman, Bruce. *Holy Terror: The Implications of Terrorism Motivated by a Religious Imperative*. Santa Monica, CA: Rand Corp, 1993.

Horowitz, Elliott. 'Genesis 34 and the Legacies of Biblical Violence'. In *The Blackwell Companion to Religion and Violence*, edited by Andrew R. Murphy, 163–82. Malden, MA: Wiley-Blackwell, 2011.

Hoskins, Richard Kelly. *Vigilantes of Christendom: The Story of the Phinehas Priesthood*. Lynchburg, VA: Virginia Publishing, 1990

Huntington, Samuel. *The Clash of Civilizations*. New York: Touchstone, 1996.

Israeli, Raphael. *Islamikaze*. London: Taylor & Francis, 2003.

Jameson, Frederic. *Postmodernism or, the Cultural Logic of Late Capitalism*. Durham, NC: Duke University Press, 1994.

Jones, James W. *Blood that Cries Out from the Earth: The Psychology of Religious Terrorism*. New York: Oxford University Press, 2008.

Jones, James W. 'Sacred Terror: The Psychology of Contemporary Religious Terrorism'. In *The Blackwell Companion to Religion and Violence*, edited by Andrew R. Murphy, 293–303. Malden, MA: Wiley-Blackwell, 2011.

Juergensmeyer, Mark. *Terror in the Mind of God: The Global Rise of Religious Violence*, 3rd edition. Berkeley: University of California Press, 2003. (First edition, 2000)

Juergensmeyer, Mark, Margo Kitts and Michael Jerryson, eds. *Oxford Handbook of Religion and Violence*. Oxford: Oxford University Press, 2013.

Kaplan, Jeffrey, *Radical Religion in America*. Syracuse, NY: Syracuse University Press, 1997.

Karawan, Ibrahim A. *The Islamist Impasse*. International Institute for Strategic Studies. Adelphi Paper 314. London: Oxford University Press, 1997.

Karpin, Michael, and Ina Friedman. *Murder in the Name of God: The Plot to Kill Yitzhak Rabin*. London: Granta Books, 2000.

Kepel, Gilles. *The Revenge of God: The Resurgence of Islam, Christianity and Judaism in the Modern World*. Cambridge: Polity Press, 1994.

Kille, D. Andrew. '"The Bible Made Me Do it": Text, Interpretation, and Violence'. In *The Destructive Power of Religion: Violence in Judaism, Christianity, and Islam*. Volume 1, *Sacred Scriptures, Ideology, and Violence*, edited by J. Harold Ellens, 55–73. Westport, CT: Praeger, 2004.

Kimball, Charles. *When Religion Becomes Evil*. New York: HarperSanFrancisco, 2003.

Knitter, Paul F. *No Other Name? A Critical Survey of Christian Attitudes toward the World Religions*. Maryknoll, NY: Orbis Books, 1985.

Knitter, Paul F. *One Earth Many Religions: Multifaith Dialogue & Global Responsibility*. Maryknoll, NY: Orbis Books, 1995.

Knitter, Paul F. *Without Buddha I Could Not Be a Christian*. Oxford: Oneworld, 2013.

Kolig, Erich, ed. *Freedom of Speech and Islam*. Farnham: Ashgate, 2014.

Kugel, James L. *How to Read the Bible: A Guide to Scripture, Then and Now*. New York: Free Press, 2007.
Küng, Hans. *Global Responsibility: In Search of a New World Ethic*. London: SCM Press, 1991.
Larsson, Göran, and Simon Stjenreholm. 'Islamophobia in Sweden: Muslim Advocacy and Hate-Crime Statistics'. In *Fear of Muslims? International Perspectives on Islamophobia*, edited by Douglas Pratt and Rachel Woodlock, 153–66. Switzerland: Springer International, 2016.
Lawrence, Bruce B. *Defenders of God: The Fundamentalist Revolt against the Modern Age*. San Francisco: Harper and Row, 1989.
Lee, Sherman A., Jeffrey A. Gibbons, John M. Thompson and Hussan S. Timani. 'The Islamophobia Scale: Instrument Development and Initial Validation'. *International Journal for the Psychology of Religion* 19 (2009): 92–105.
Lentini, Pete. 'The Transference of Neojihadism: Towards a Process Theory of Transnational Radicalisation'. In *Proceedings of the 2008 GTREC International Conference, 26–27 November*, 1–32. Melbourne: Monash University Global Terrorism Research Centre, 2009.
Lentini, Pete. *Neojihadism: Towards a New Understanding of Terrorism and Extremism?* Northampton, MA: Edward Elgar Publishing, 2013.
Lewis, Bernard. *The Crisis of Islam: Holy War and Unholy Terror*. New York: Modern Library, 2003.
Lewis, James, and Olav Hammer, eds. *The Invention of Sacred Tradition*. Cambridge: Cambridge University Press, 2007.
Lienemann, Wolfgang. 'Argumente für ein Minaret-Verbot? Eine kritische Analyze'. In *Streit um das Minarett: Zusammenleben in der religiöse pluralistischen Gesellschaft*, edited by Mathias Tanner, Felix Müller, Frank Mathwig and Wolfgang Lienemann. Zürich: Theologischer Verlag, 2009.
Lincoln, Bruce. *Holy Terrors: Thinking about Religion after September 11*. Chicago and London: University of Chicago Press, 2003.
Lumbard, Joseph E. B., ed. *Islam, Fundamentalism, and the Betrayal of Tradition*. Bloomington, IN: World Wisdom, 2004.
Lyotard, Jean-François. *The Postmodern Condition: A Report on Knowledge,* trans. Geoff Bennington and Brian Massumi. Manchester: Manchester University Press, 1984.
Marsden, George M. *Understanding Fundamentalism and Evangelicalism*. Grand Rapids, MI: W. B. Eerdmans, 1991.
Marty, Martin E. *Fundamentalisms Compared: The Charles Strong Memorial Lecture 1989*. Underdale, South Australia: Australian Association for the Study of Religions, 1989.
Marty, Martin, and Scott Appleby, eds. *The Fundamentalism Project*. Chicago: University of Chicago Press, 1991.
Marty, Martin, and Scott Appleby, eds. *Fundamentalisms Observed*. Chicago: University of Chicago Press, 1991.
Marty, Martin, and Scott Appleby, eds. *Fundamentalisms and the State: Remaking Politics, Economies, and Militance*. Chicago: University of Chicago Press, 1993.
Marty, Martin, and Scott Appleby, eds. *Accounting for Fundamentalisms: The Dynamic Character of Movements*. Chicago: University of Chicago Press, 1994.
Marty, Martin, and Scott Appleby, eds. *Fundamentalisms Comprehended*. Chicago: University of Chicago Press, 1995.
Matthews, Shelly, and E. Leigh Gibson, eds. *Violence in the New Testament*. New York: T & T Clark, 2005.
Matusitz, Jonathan. *Symbolism in Terrorism: Motivation, Communication, and Behavior*. Lanham, MD: Rowan & Littlefield, 2015.
Mawsilili, Ahmad. *Moderate and Radical Islamic Fundamentalism: The Quest for Modernity, Legitimacy, and the Islamic State*. Gainesville: University Press of Florida, 1999.

Bibliography

Mayer, Jean-Francois. 'In the Shadow of the Minaret: Origins and Implications of a Citizens' Initiative'. In *The Swiss Minaret Ban: Islam in Question,* edited by Patrick Haenni and Stephane Lathion, trans. Tom Genrich, 10–16. Fribourg: Religioscope 2011.

McCauley, Clark, and Sophia Moskalenko. 'Mechanisms of Political Radicalization: Pathways toward Terrorism'. *Terrorism and Political Violence* 20, no. 3 (2008): 415–33.

Milton-Edwards, Beverley. *Islamic Fundamentalism since 1945.* New York: Routledge, 2005.

Milton-Edwards, Beverley. 'Islam and Violence'. In *The Blackwell Companion to Religion and Violence,* edited by Andrew R. Murphy, 183–95. Malden, MA: Wiley-Blackwell, 2011.

Mitchell, Jolyon. 'Mediating Religious Violence'. In *The Blackwell Companion to Religion and Violence,* edited by Andrew R. Murphy, 112–24. Malden, MA: Wiley-Blackwell, 2011.

Moaddel, Mansoor, and Kamran Talattof, eds. *Contemporary Debates in Islam: An Anthology of Modernist and Fundamentalist Thought.* Basingstoke: Macmillan Press, 2004.

Morgan, George, and Scott Poynting, eds. *Global Islamophobia: Muslims and Moral Panic in the West.* Farnham: Ashgate 2012.

Murphy, Andrew R., ed. *The Blackwell Companion to Religion and Violence.* Malden, MA: Wiley-Blackwell, 2011.

Niditch, Susan. *War in the Hebrew Bible: A Study in the Ethics of Violence.* New York: Oxford University Press, 1993.

Nussbaum, Martha C. *The New Religious Intolerance: Overcoming the Politics of Fear in an Anxious Age.* Cambridge, MA: The Belknap Press, 2012.

Panikkar, Raimundo. *The Unknown Christ of Hinduism,* revised edition. Maryknoll, NY: Orbis Books, 1981.

Pape, Robert. *Dying to Win: The Strategic Logic of Suicide Terrorism.* New York: Random House, 2005.

Pearce, Susanna. 'Religious Rage: A Quantitative Analysis of the Intensity of Religious Conflicts'. *Terrorism and Political Violence* 14, no. 3 (2005): 333–52.

Pedahzur, Ami, and Arie Perliger. *Jewish Terrorism in Israel.* New York: Columbia University Press, 2011.

Perez, Joseph. *The Spanish Inquisition: A History.* London: Profile Books, 2004.

Peri, Yoram ed. *The Assassination of Yitzhak Rabin.* Palo Alto, CA: Stanford University Press, 2000.

Piscatori, James P. *Islam in a World of Nation-States.* Cambridge: Cambridge University Press, 1994.

Placher, William C. *A History of Christian Theology: An Introduction.* Philadelphia, PA: Westminster Press, 1983.

Posman, Ellen. 'History, Humiliation, and Religious Violence'. In *The Blackwell Companion to Religion and Violence,* edited by Andrew R. Murphy, 331–42. Malden, MA: Wiley-Blackwell, 2011.

Pratt, Douglas. *Religion: A First Encounter.* Auckland: Longmans, 1993.

Pratt, Douglas. 'Contextual Paradigms for Interfaith Relations', *Current Dialogue* 42 (December 2003): 3–9.

Pratt, Douglas. 'Pluralism and Interreligious Engagement: The Contexts of Dialogue'. In *A Faithful Presence: Essays for Kenneth Cragg,* edited by David Thomas with Clare Amos, 402–18. London: Melisende Press, 2003.

Pratt, Douglas. *The Challenge of Islam: Encounters in Interfaith Dialogue.* Abingdon: Routledge Revivals, 2017. (First published by Ashgate, 2005).

Pratt, Douglas. 'Religious Fundamentalism: A Paradigm for Terrorism?' In *International Terrorism: New Zealand Perspectives,* edited by Rachel Barrowman, 31–52. Wellington: Institute of Policy Studies, Victoria University of Wellington, 2005.

Bibliography

Pratt, Douglas. 'Terrorism and Religious Fundamentalism: Prospects for a Predictive Paradigm'. *Marburg Journal of Religion* 11, no. 1 (June 2006): 1–11. Online journal available at: http://web.uni-marburg.de/religionswissenschaft/journal/mjr/

Pratt, Douglas. 'Religious Fundamentalism: A Paradigm for Terrorism?' *Australian Religion Studies Review* 20, no. 2 (2007): 195–215.

Pratt, Douglas. *The Church and Other Faiths: The World Council of Churches, the Vatican, and Interreligious Dialogue*. Bern: Peter Lang, 2010.

Pratt, Douglas. 'Muslim-Jewish Relations: Some Islamic Paradigms'. *Islam and Christian–Muslim Relations* 21 no. 1 (2010): 11–21.

Pratt, Douglas. 'Religion and Terrorism: Christian Fundamentalism and Extremism'. *Terrorism and Political Violence* 22 no. 3 (2010): 438–56.

Pratt, Douglas. 'Religious Identity and the Denial of Alterity: Plurality and the Problem of Exclusivism'. In *The Relation of Philosophy to Religion Today*, edited by Paolo Diego Bubbio and Philip Andrew Quadrio, 201–15. Newcastle-upon-Tyne: Cambridge Scholars Publishing, 2011.

Pratt, Douglas. 'The Persistence and Problem of Religion: Modernity Continuity and Diversity'. *ARSReview* 25, no. 3 (2012): 273–92.

Pratt, Douglas. 'Fundamentalism, Exclusivism, and Religious Extremism'. In *Understanding Interreligious Relations*, edited by D. Cheetham, D. Pratt and D. Thomas, 241–60. Oxford: Oxford University Press, 2013.

Pratt, Douglas. 'Swiss Shock: Minaret Rejection, European Values, and the Challenge of Tolerant Neutrality'. *Politics, Religion & Ideology* 14, no. 2 (2013): 193–207.

Pratt, Douglas. 'Islamophobia as Reactive Co-radicalization'. *Islam and Christian–Muslim Relations* 26, no. 2 (April 2015): 205–18.

Pratt, Douglas. 'Reactive Co-radicalization: Religious Extremism as Mutual Discontent'. *Journal for the Academic Study of Religion* 28, no. 1 (2015): 3–23.

Pratt, Douglas, and Piet Naudé, 'South Speaks to South: A New Zealand Response to the *kerygma* of Belhar', *Ned Geref Teologiese Tydskrif* 44, nos. 3 and 4 (September and December 2003): 421–32.

Pratt, Douglas, and Rachel Woodlock, eds. *Fear of Muslims? International Perspectives on Islamophobia*. Switzerland: Springer International, 2016.

Quarles, Chester L. *The Ku Klux Klan and Related American Racialist and Antisemitic Organisations: A History and Analysis*. Jefferson, NC: McFarland, 1999.

Quarles, Chester L. *Christian Identity: The Aryan American Bloodline Religion*. Jefferson, NC: McFarland, 2004.

Quinones, Ricardo J. 'The Cain–Abel Syndrome: In Theory and in History'. In *The Destructive Power of Religion: Violence in Judaism, Christianity, and Islam*. Volume 3, *Models and Cases of Violence in Religion*, edited by J. Harold Ellens, 81–125. Westport, CT: Praeger, 2004.

Race, Alan. *Christians and Religious Pluralism*. London: SCM Press, 1993.

Race, Alan, and Paul M. Hedges. *Christian Approaches to Other Faiths*. London: SCM Press, 2008.

Rapoport, David C. 'The Fourth Wave: September 11 in the History of Terrorism'. *Current History* 100, no. 650 (2001): 419–24.

Reich, Walter, ed. *Origins of Terrorism: Psychologies, Ideologies, Theologies, States of Mind*. Washington, DC: Woodrow Wilson Centre Press, 1998.

Rippin, Andrew. *Muslims: Their Religious Beliefs and Practices*. Volume 2, *The Contemporary Period*. London: Routledge, 1993.

Rosenfeld, Jean E., ed. *Terrorism, Identity and Legitimacy: The Four Waves Theory and Political Violence*. London: Routledge, 2011.

Runnymede Trust, The. *Islamophobia: A Challenge for Us All; Report of the Runnymede Trust Commission on British Muslims and Islamophobia*. London: Runnymede Trust, 1997.

Bibliography

Saha, Santosh C., ed. *Religious Fundamentalism in the Contemporary World: Critical Social and Political Issues*. Lanham, MD: Lexington Books, 2004.

Samartha, S. J. *Courage for Dialogue: Ecumenical Issues in Inter-religious Relationships*. Geneva: WCC Publications, 1981.

Samartha, S. J. *One Christ, Many Religions: Toward a Revised Christology*. Maryknoll, NY: Orbis Books, 1991.

Sandeen, Ernest R. *The Roots of Fundamentalism: British and American Millenarianism, 1800–1930*. Chicago: University of Chicago Press, 1970.

Saylor, Corey. 'The U.S. Islamophobia Network: Its Funding and Impact'. *Islamophobia Studies Journal* 2, no. 1 (Spring 2014): 99–118.

Sayyid, S. 'A Measure of Islamophobia'. *Islamophobia Studies Journal* 2, no. 1 (Spring 2014): 10–25.

Schmid, Alex. 'Frameworks for Conceptualizing Terrorism'. *Terrorism and Political Violence* 16, no. 2 (2004): 197–221.

Schmidt-Leukel, Perry. 'Christianity and the Religious Other'. In *Understanding Interreligious Relations*, edited by D. Cheetham, D. Pratt and D. Thomas, 118–47. Oxford: Oxford University Press, 2013,

Schwager, Raymund, SJ. *Must there be Scapegoats? Violence and Redemption in the Bible*. New York: Crossroads Publishing, 2000.

Selengut, Charles. 'The Sociology of Religious Violence'. In *The Blackwell Companion to Religion and Violence*, edited by Andrew R. Murphy, 89–98. Malden, MA: Wiley-Blackwell, 2011.

Sheehi, Stephen. *Islamophobia: The Ideological Campaign against Muslims*. Atlanta, GA: Clarity Press, 2011.

Shepard, William. 'Islam and Ideology: Towards a Typology'. *International Journal of Middle East Studies* 19 (1987): 307–36.

Shepherd, John J. 'Self-Critical Children of Abraham? Roots of Violence and Extremism in Judaism, Christianity and Islam'. In *Islam & the West post 9/11*, edited by Ron Geaves, Theodore Gabriel, Yvonne Haddad and Jane Idleman Smith, 27–50. Aldershot: Ashgate, 2004.

Shryock, Andrew J. 'Attack of the Islamophobes: Religious War (and Peace) in Arab/Muslim Detroit'. In *Islamophobia in America: The Anatomy of Intolerance*, edited by Carl W. Ernst, 143–73. New York: Palgrave Macmillan, 2013.

Sivan, Emmanual, Gabriel Almond and Scott Appleby. *Strong Religion*. Chicago: University of Chicago Press, 2000.

Smart, Ninian. *The World's Religions: Old Traditions and Modern Transformations*. Cambridge: Cambridge University Press, 1989.

Sookhdeo, Patrick. *Understanding Islamic Terrorism: The Islamic Doctrine of War*. Wiltshire: Isaac Publishing, 2004.

Spong, John Shelby. *Rescuing the Bible from Fundamentalism*. San Francisco: HarperSanFrancisco, 1991.

Sprinzak, Ehud. *The Ascendance of Israel's Radical Right*. New York: Oxford University Press, 1991.

Statement on Religious Diversity in Aotearoa New Zealand. Wellington: Human Rights Commission, 2009.

Swidler, Leonard, John B. Cobb, Paul F. Knitter and Monika K. Hellwig. *Death or Dialogue?* London: SCM Press, 1990.

Taras, Raymond. *Xenophobia and Islamophobia in Europe*. Edinburgh: Edinburgh University Press, 2012.

Tibi, Bassam. *The Challenge of Fundamentalism: Political Islam and the New World Disorder*. Updated Edition. Berkeley: University of California Press, 2002.

Tite, Philip L. *Conceiving Peace and Violence: A New Testament Legacy*. Lanham, MD: University Press of America, 2004.

Toffler, Alvin. *Future Shock.* New York: Random House, 1970.
Trible, Phyllis. *Texts of Terror: Literary-Feminist Readings of Biblical Narratives.* Philadelphia, PA: Fortress Press, 1984.
Tyerman, Christopher. *Fighting for Christendom: Holy War and the Crusades.* Oxford: Oxford University Press, 2004.
van Henten, Jan Willem. 'Religion, Bible and Violence'. In *Coping with Violence in the New Testament,* edited by Pieter G. R. de Villiers and Jan Willem van Henten, 3–21. Leiden and Boston: Brill, 2012.
Visser t'Hooft, W. A. *No Other Name: The Choice between Syncretism and Christian Universalism.* London: SCM Press, 1963.
Walzer, Michael. *Exodus and Revelation.* New York: Basic Books, 1984.
Ward, Keith. *What the Bible Really Teaches: A Challenge for Fundamentalists.* London: SPCK, 2004.
Ward, Keith. *Is Religion Dangerous?* Oxford: Lion, 2006.
Ward, Veronica, and Richard Sherlock, eds. *Religion and Terrorism: The Use of Violence in Abrahamic Monotheism.* Lanham, MD: Lexington Books, 2014.
Weinberg, Leonard, and Ami Pedahzur, eds. *Religious Fundamentalism and Political Extremism.* Portland, OR: Frank Cass, 2004.
Weiss, Michael, and Hassan Hassan. *ISIS: Inside the Army of Terror.* New York: Regan Arts, 2015.
Wellman, James K., ed. *Belief and Bloodshed: Religion and Violence across Time and Tradition.* Lanham, MD: Rowman and Littlefield, 2007.
Westerlund, David. *Questioning the Secular State: The Worldwide Resurgence of Religion in Politics.* London: Hurst, 1996.
Williams, James G. *The Bible, Violence, and the Sword.* Valley Forge, PA: Trinity Press International, 1991.
Winter, Tim. 'Terrorism and Islamic Theologies of Religiously-Sanctioned War'. In *Just War on Terror? A Christian and Muslim Response,* edited by David Fisher and Brian Wicker, 9–24. Farnham: Ashgate, 2010.
Wright, Stefanie. 'Reproducing Fear: Islamophobia in the United States'. In *Fear of Muslims? International Perspectives on Islamophobia,* edited by Douglas Pratt and Rachel Woodlock, 45–65. Switzerland: Springer International, 2016.
Yilmaz, Ihsan. 'The Nature of Islamophobia: Some Key Features'. In *Fear of Muslims? International Perspectives on Islamophobia,* edited by Douglas Pratt and Rachel Woodlock, 19–29. Switzerland: Springer International, 2016.
Zakaria, Rafiq. *The Struggle within Islam: The Conflict between Religion and Politics.* London: Penguin, 1989.
Zubaida, Sami. *Islam: The People and the State: Political Ideas and Movements in the Middle East.* London: I. B. Taurus, 1993.

Newspaper reports and sundry other references

Charlton, Angela. 'Far-Right Anger, Violence Thrive on Europe's Edges'. *Sunday Star Times* (New Zealand), 7 August 2011: A13.
Holmes, Paul. 'A Crime beyond Punishment'. *Weekend Herald* (New Zealand), 6 August 2011: A19.
Lewis, Todd. 'Buddhist Extremism in Sri Lanka and Southeast Asia: Muslim Minorities, Nationalism, and Globalization'. Promotional material for lecture given at the *Alwaleed Bin Talal Center for Muslim-Christian Understanding, Georgetown University*, Washington DC, Wednesday, 22 October 2014.

Bibliography

Misa, Tapu. 'How to Live up to Freedom's Ideals'. *New Zealand Herald*, 1 August 2011: A11.
Tamaki, Brian, as cited in news report, 'Lockout Sparks Unholy Row'. *New Zealand Herald*, 29 May 2007: A3.
Witte, Geoff. 'Settlements – Facts on the Ground'. *New Zealand Herald*, 4 January 2017: A18.

Website references

'Boko Haram Members Behead Nigerian Airforce Officer'. Available at: http://dailypost.ng/2014/07/23 (accessed 13 October 2014).
'Call on PM to Publicly Condemn Islamophobia'. *Australian Muslim Times*. Available at: http://www.amust.com.au/2016/08/call-on-pm-to-publicly-condemn- hobia/ (accessed 5 August 2016).
Council for American-Islamic Relations (CAIR). Available at: www.cair.com (accessed 1 February 2017).
'French Hostage Herve Gourdel Beheaded in Algeria'. Available at: http://www.bbc.com/news/world-africa-29352537 (accessed 13 October 2014).
Hall, Bianca. 'Restore Australia: The Party that Would Ban Islam'. *The Age* 1 January 2016. http://www.smh.com.au/federal-politics/political-news/restore-australia-the-party-that-would-ban-islam-20160101-glxsfh.html (accessed 11 February 2016).
HRH The Prince of Wales. 'Thought for the Day'. *BBC Radio 4*, 22 December 2016. Available online: http://www.express.co.uk/news/royal/746345/Prince-Charles-Radio-4-Thought-for-the-Day-religious-threats (accessed 27 December 2016).
Juergensmeyer, Mark. 'Is Norway's Suspected Murderer a Christian Terrorist?' *Religion Despatches*, 24 July 2011. Available online: http://www.religiondispatches.org/archive/politics/4910/is_norway%E2%80%99s_suspected_murderer_anders_breivik_a_christian_terrorist/ (accessed 10 February 2015).
Juergensmeyer, Mark. 'Why Breivik Was a Christian Terrorist'. *Huffington Post*, 27 July 2011. Available online: http://www.huffingtonpost.com/mark-juergensmeyer/why-breivik-was-a-christi_b_910443.html (accessed 10 February 2015).
'Quebec Mosque Shooting: Student Charged with Six Counts of Murder over Gun Attack in Mosque'. *The Telegraph News*. Available at: http://www.telegraph.co.uk/news/2017/01/30/quebec-mosque-shooting-two-students-arrested-gun-attack-mosque/ (accessed 1 February 2017).
'Straying from the Middle Way: Extremist Buddhist Monks Target Religious Minorities'. *TIME* magazine, June 2013. Available at: http://world.time.com/2013/06/20/extremist-buddhist-monks-fight-oppression-with-violence/ (accessed 10 February 10 2015).
Taylor, Grant. 'Anti-Islam Party Takes First Steps'. https://au.news.yahoo.com/ thewest/wa/a/29902634/anti-islam-party-australian-liberty-alliance-takes-first-steps/ (accessed 11 February 2016).
Trump, Donald. Inaugural Address, as prepared for delivery. Available at: http://edition.cnn.com/2017/01/20/politics/trump-inaugural-address/index.html (accessed 21 January 2017).
'Wisconsin Temple Shooting', Available at: http://edition.cnn.com/2012/08/05/us/wisconsin-temple-shooting/ (accessed 15 February 2017)
World Islamic Front Statement, 'Jihad against Jews and Crusaders'. Online at https://fas.org/irp/world/para/docs/980223-fatwa.htm (accessed 21 February 2017).

INDEX

9/11 112–13, 123, 125, 135, 145

Aaron 56, 93
Abbasid 102
Abdulmutallab, Umar Farouk 100
Abel 91
Abraham 52, 54, 56, 154
abrogation 9, 50, 60–1
absolute 8–9, 11, 26, 33, 44, 47, 50–1, 63, 73, 82, 99, 113, 121, 150–1, 153–4, 160
absolutism 1, 7–9, 11, 36, 40, 42, 47–8, 50–1, 81, 89, 97, 103, 109, 149–51, 153–5, 160
acceptance 14, 88, 117–18, 129–30, 134, 136–7, 139, 156–8
Aden, LeRoy 36
Afghanistan 44, 46–7, 102, 106, 113
Africa 88, 138
aggression 5, 80, 88, 99, 123, 155
Ahmadiyya 121
Ahmed, Akbar 104
Ali, Tariq 2
Allah 47, 50–1, 100, 107, 137
Allen, Diogenes 27
al-Qaeda 8, 138
al-Shabab 107, 113, 138
alterity 35, 45, 95, 120, 129, 159
alt-right 2, 11
Aly, Waleed 143
America 2, 10, 37, 42, 52, 81, 88, 92, 110, 120, 133–4, 137, 140, 143–4, 145, 154
Amir, Yigal 75–6, 153
antipathy vi, 1, 114, 117–18, 120, 123, 127, 131, 136, 146–7, 158
antisemitism 60, 92–3, 129, 134
apartheid 18, 89, 141
apostate 81, 107, 112, 152
Aquinas, St Thomas 160
Aran, Gideon 4, 54, 66, 68–9, 80, 97
Armageddon 75, 91
Armstrong, Karen 10, 105, 155
Aryan Nations 90, 92–3
Asia 6, 102, 120, 139
Aslan, Reza 143
Asprem, Egil 124–5
Assassination 53, 67, 75–6, 78, 105, 125
asylum 28, 92, 121
Augustine, St 83–6, 89

Aum Shinrikyo 8
Australia 10, 110, 129, 133, 139, 143
Avrushmi, Yona 65

Baghdad 102
Balkans 122
Ban, the 55–7, 67
Bangalore 27
Bar Kochba 70, 72
Beal, Timothy 154
Beam, Louis 92
Beit Hamikdash 153
Belgium 128
Belhar Declaration 89
Berlin 18
Bible 9–10, 37, 49–59, 62, 70, 77–8, 89, 91, 93, 96, 126, 153–5
Bin Laden, Osama 109, 125, 134
Boko Haram 107, 109, 113, 137–8
Bouma, Gary 7, 13
Branch Davidian 96
Breivik, Anders 93, 119, 121, 124–31
British Israelite 90, 92, 95
Brothers, Richard 92
Buddhist extremists 2
Burkini 128, 135
Burqa 128
Butler, Richard 92

Cain 53, 91
Caliphate 2, 36, 101–2, 109, 113, 137
Calvin, John 86
Canada 128–9
Cathars 85, 89
Catholic 14, 23, 25–7, 34, 84, 87–9, 101, 152
Cesari, Jocelyne 134
Charlie Hebdo 139
Chechnya 113
Chosen People, the 9, 54, 92
Choueiri, Youssef M. 10
Christendom 14
Christ 9, 25–8, 37, 44, 48, 84, 91–2, 96, 124
Christian extremism 12, 50, 52, 56, 58–61, 63, 68, 81–97, 117, 126
Christian Identity movement (CI) 8, 90
Christianity vi, 1, 4, 6–7, 9, 17, 20–2, 25–8, 31, 33–7, 39, 48, 50–2, 57–8, 60, 81–91, 95–7, 99–101,

Index

107, 110, 117, 124–6, 130, 136, 144, 146, 151, 153–4
Christians 1, 4, 6, 8–9, 17, 22, 26, 28, 34, 48, 51, 58, 60–2, 71, 82–90, 102, 107, 125, 127, 137–8, 144, 155
Christmas 1–2, 100
Christology 85
Church, Protestant 25, 86, 90
Church, Roman Catholic 25–7, 88–9
Church, the 9, 26, 28, 34, 82–9, 117, 125
Civilization 16, 81, 102–4, 111, 114, 144, 152
Clements, Kevin 156
Cobb, John 21
Collins, John J. 52, 56, 62, 82, 154
communist 10, 136
Constantine 82–3, 86
contempt 45–7, 96, 102, 152
Cook, David 100
Cornwallis, Mary 53
Council for American-Islamic Relations (CAIR) 137
Council of Florence 34
Countering violent extremism (CVE) 157–5
Counter-jihadist 125
counterterrorism 78, 128
Cracknell, Kenneth 17
creation, the 14, 25, 28, 91, 107, 160
Cromwell, Oliver 87
Crusades 9, 87, 146, 157
Crusaders 3, 104, 107, 134
culture 15–16, 19, 94, 101, 103, 106, 108, 114, 127, 135, 138–40, 143, 154–5

Dalgard-Nielsen, Anja 119
Damascus 102
Dark Ages 91
Dead Sea Scrolls 70
Deity 11, 56, 150, 154
democracy 8, 68, 120, 122, 145
Descartes, René 15
destruction 2, 47, 53–6, 71–2, 75, 137, 152–3
Deuteronomy 56, 62–3
Devanandan, P. D. 27
Devil 36–7, 59, 91
Dhimmis 62
Dhimmitude 146
Dialogue, Inter-religious vi, 6–7, 17–18, 20, 23–4, 26, 28, 32–3, 35, 66, 146, 158–9
Diaspora 70, 79
Din rodef 76
Diocletian 82
discontent 72, 117–19, 131
discrimination 135–6, 140
dissimulation 53, 84
diversity vi–vii, 1–3, 6–7, 9, 11–13, 15, 17–20, 23–4, 28–9, 32–3, 47, 55, 83, 86–7, 91, 101, 111, 118–21, 128–31, 134, 136–8, 144, 146–4, 149, 153, 155–6, 158–60
Dome of the Rock 74–5
Donatists 84–5

Eco, Umberto 126
Egypt 55–6, 65, 102, 105, 109
elimination 2, 9–10, 55–6, 65, 89, 96, 121, 128, 149, 152
Ellens, J. Harold 4, 36–7, 59
Elliot, Mark 44
enemy 55, 70, 74, 82, 87–8, 99, 129, 134, 147, 154
England 2, 87, 110, 154
Enlightenment, the 13–16, 77, 136, 157
Esposito, John 106, 114
ethnic cleansing 9, 56
Europe 1, 10, 67, 71–2, 77, 87, 91, 99, 102, 104, 117, 120, 122–7, 130–1, 139, 145, 152
evangelical 10, 26, 106, 125, 152
evil 2, 11, 20, 36, 42, 62, 68, 72, 102, 113, 125, 139
exclusion 6, 9, 91, 115, 121, 149, 159–60
Exclusive Brethren 35, 44, 90
Exclusivism 1–2, 17–18, 22, 24, 29, 31–5, 43, 45, 47, 55, 95, 122, 144, 146, 158–60
Exodus 52, 55–7, 87, 154

factualism 42–3
fanaticism 5, 68, 87, 90, 99
Farquhar, J. N. 25
fascist vii, 10, 155–6
Fort Hood 100
France 110, 128, 135, 145
fundamentalism 2, 6–7, 9–11, 18, 29, 31–3, 35–51, 66, 80–2, 88–90, 94–5, 97, 103, 108–13, 115, 120, 122, 135, 138, 140–1, 145, 149–54, 156, 158, 160
  assertive 39, 42–5, 90, 95, 120, 149, 151
  impositional 39–40, 45–7, 50, 89–90, 120, 151, 153
  passive 39–42, 90, 120, 151
Fundamentalism Project, the 38

Gallagher, Eugene 94
Geaves, Ron 11, 110, 115
Geneva 86, 121
genocide 54–5
Germany 2, 110, 138–9
Girard, René 155
Gnosticism 83, 91
God 8–9, 14, 17, 20–1, 25, 27–8, 31, 34, 36–8, 43, 46–8, 50–62, 65, 68, 70, 72–6, 82–3, 86, 89, 91–4, 96, 99, 104–6, 108, 110, 114–15, 125, 133, 150, 152, 154–5, 160
Goldstein, Baruch 75–6
Grenz, Stanley 15–16
Guinn, David 151

Index

Gülen, Fethullah 156
Gush Emunim 66–7

Hadith 5
Halafoff, Anna 120
Hamas 66
Hansen, Pauline 139
Haram al-Sharif 153
Haredim 66, 79
Harvey, David 14
Hasan, Nidal Malik 100
Hassidism 72
Hassner, Ron 4, 54, 66, 68–9, 80
Hebrews 4, 44, 53, 73, 92
Heim, Mark 22
Heresy 5, 37, 83, 85, 100, 111, 146
Heretic 85–7, 155
Hermeneutic 13, 17, 19, 49, 60, 62, 89, 119, 129, 143
Heterodoxy 5, 85
Hick, John 20–1
Hilel, Michal 65–6
Hinduism 25–8, 31, 117
Hindutva 130
Holmes, Paul 127
Holocaust 10, 60, 67, 79
Holy war 11, 94, 153
Homogeneity 3, 13, 19, 28, 130
Homophobia 156
Hooft, Visser t' 34
Horowitz, Elliott 53, 73
Hoskins, Richard Kelly 91
Hume, David 15
Huntington, Samuel 104
Hus, John 86

Idaho 92
identity 5, 7, 10, 17–19, 22, 24, 26, 32–6, 38–9, 42–3, 47–8, 52, 56–7, 59, 63, 68, 72, 77, 79–83, 85–90, 93, 95, 99, 101–4, 107, 114, 120–3, 125–6, 130, 134–5, 138, 152, 156, 158–60
ideology vi, 2–4, 5–6, 10–12, 24, 28, 31, 33, 36, 39–40, 46–8, 50, 59, 67, 88–96, 100–2, 104–8, 110–14, 118–20, 124–6, 131, 135–6, 144, 149–52, 156, 158–60
idolatry 10, 55–6
ignorance 14, 34, 46, 106, 108, 133–5, 140–2, 145, 147, 157
imagination 31, 136, 142–3, 145, 154
immigrant 75, 127, 149, 156
immigration vi, 2, 28, 92, 121, 127, 136
imposition vi, 1–2, 4, 7, 14, 32, 39, 40, 45–8, 50, 66, 81, 83, 87, 89–90, 96, 102, 106–7, 109–10, 115, 117, 120, 128, 150–3, 155
inclusivism 7, 17–18, 24–8, 32–3, 43–5, 153

India 24–5, 27, 102, 117, 125, 130
Indonesia 34, 101
indwelling 40–1, 97, 126
inerrancy 37, 40–2
inquisition 61, 85
insurgency 35, 105
interfaith vi, vii, 6, 17, 24, 33, 118, 159
interpretation 4, 6–7, 9, 12, 16–19, 37, 41, 57–8, 61–3, 67, 81, 83, 85, 89, 94, 96, 100, 103, 105–6, 109, 111–12, 115, 137, 143, 150, 152, 154
intolerance 1, 111, 120, 128, 135, 152, 155–6
Iraq 1–2, 45, 102, 113
Iran 102, 108
Ireland 87
ISIS (Islamic State) 2–3, 8, 37, 90, 100, 106–7, 109, 113, 115, 137
Islam vi, 2–4, 7, 9, 22, 25, 27, 31, 34–9, 44, 47–51, 60–2, 67, 90, 97, 99–115, 119–31, 133–40, 142–7, 153–4, 156–8, 160
Islamic State 1–3, 7, 36–7, 44, 107, 109, 137
Islamism 99–100, 103–6, 108–9, 114–15, 133–4, 158
Islamist 8, 10, 37, 61, 93, 100, 103–12, 114, 134, 136–7, 139, 144, 147
Islamophobia 12, 117, 120, 123, 125, 127, 133–47, 155–8
Israel 8, 28, 44, 52–7, 61–2, 65, 67–8, 70–1, 73–5, 78–80, 90–4, 103–5, 107, 136, 154

Jahiliyya 106, 108–9
Jameson, Frederic 16
Japan 8
Jephthah 52, 54–5
Jericho 53, 55
Jerusalem 61, 65, 69, 74, 77, 92, 153
Jesus 2, 25, 27, 34, 37, 44, 52, 58–9, 83, 90, 92–3, 96
Jewish extremism 8, 12, 50, 52, 56, 58–9, 63, 66, 68, 70–6, 78–80, 117
Jews 1, 4, 9, 28, 44, 48, 50–1, 55, 58–61, 65–7, 70–80, 84–7, 90–3, 95, 107, 134, 137, 144, 146, 155
Jihad 105, 107, 109, 112–14, 120, 134
Jihadism 60, 102, 105, 120, 134, 138
Jones, James 155
Jones, Terry 139
Joshua 8, 53, 62
Judaism vi, 4, 9–10, 22, 27, 31, 34, 36, 48, 50–2, 57, 66, 68, 70–3, 76–80, 97, 104, 134, 137, 146, 153–4
Juergensmeyer, Mark 31, 36, 55, 74, 76, 125, 149, 154, 158
Justin Martyr 25, 82

Kabbalah 72, 74
Kahane, Meir 74–5
Kant, Immanuel 15

193

Index

Kashmir 113
Kepel, Gilles 10
Kimball, Charles 11
Knights Templar 124, 126
Knitter, Paul 22-3
Kraemer, Hendrikus 34
Ku Klux Klan (KKK) 89, 90, 92
Küng, Hans 23

Lebanon 65
Lederman, Israel 65
Lentini, Pete 105, 119
Lewis, Bernard 104
Libya 113
literalism 10, 32, 41, 50, 86, 89, 91
Logos 14, 25
London 106, 112
Luther, Martin 86
Lyotard, Jean-François 16

Maccabees 77
Madrasa 10
Madrid 112
Malaysia 101-2
Manhattan 74, 99
Marcion 154-5
Marcionism 83
Marty, Martin E. 38
Martyr 72, 75, 82, 84, 153
Martyrdom 62, 71-2, 82
Masada 70, 77
Massacre 52-4, 93, 120, 124-5
Matusitz, Jonathan 11
Mayer, Jean-Francois 122
McCauley, Clark 119
McVeigh, Timothy 93, 125
Mecca 2, 60-1
media 11, 74, 104, 111, 115, 119, 123, 125, 133, 137, 139, 140, 142-3, 145-6, 157
Medina 2, 9, 60-1, 103
Messiah 59, 71, 73-4
Messianism 66-7, 71-5, 77
Middle Ages 71-2, 86, 160
Middle East 1, 4, 55, 93, 100, 104, 107-8
militarism 77, 99
Millar, Glen 92
Milton-Edwards, Beverley 104, 144
Minaret 119-23, 128, 130, 136
Mishnah 69
Mitchell, Jolyon 157
modernity 13, 103, 110, 112, 146
modernism 13-16, 105, 114
Mohammed / Muhammad 2, 26, 51, 60, 103, 128, 153
Montanism 83

Moses 55, 57
Moskalenko, Sophia 119
Mosque 61, 75, 88, 107, 121, 124, 128, 135, 137, 139
Mughal Empire 102
Muslims 2, 8, 26, 28, 46, 48, 60-2, 67, 73, 84-5, 87-8, 95, 100-4, 106-7, 109-15, 119, 121-3, 125, 127-31, 133-40, 143-7, 152-3, 156
Muslim Brotherhood 109
Myanmar 117, 138
mysticism 71-2, 74

Napoleon 102
Nasr, Seyyed Hossain 143
Natan-Zada, Eden 65
nationalism 10, 68, 70, 78, 103, 108, 138, 156
National Socialism 91-2
New religious movement (NRM) 6
New Testament 50-2, 58-9, 81, 154-5
New Zealand 6, 90, 127, 156
Niagara 37
Nicea 83
Nigeria 44, 88, 102, 109, 113, 137-8
Niqab 128
North Korea 121
Norway 93, 119, 124, 129, 131, 133
Nussbaum, Martha 128-9

Odinism 125-6
Oklahoma 93, 96, 125, 137
Old Testament 51, 54, 68, 87, 92-3, 154-5
Open Brethren 35
Orthodox Judaism/Jews 10, 50, 65-7, 77-9
Orthodox (Eastern) Christianity 87-8
Oslo 124
otherness 3, 7, 24, 28, 34-5, 43, 45-6, 59, 88, 95, 120, 130, 134, 137, 152, 159
Ottoman Empire 72, 99, 102

Pagan 61, 126
Pakistan 10, 44, 68, 102
Palestine 67
Palestinian Authority, the 75-6
Palestinians 65-8, 73-5, 78
Panikkar, Raimundo 27
particularism 33, 108
Pashtun 113
peace 2, 4-5, 9, 23, 54, 57, 59, 61, 65, 73, 75-6, 80-1, 99, 113, 118, 137-8, 154, 156-7
persecution 1-2, 70, 72-3, 77-8, 82-4
Philistines 53, 55
Phineas 56-7, 62, 67-9, 93-4, 154
Phineas Priesthood (PP) 90-1, 93-4, 126
Pierce, William 92
Plague 54-5, 57
pluralism 7, 13, 17-24, 26, 32-4, 38, 111, 157-8

Index

plurality 13, 15, 17–20, 22–4, 33–4, 88, 120, 130, 149, 159
polity 43–4, 46, 77, 95, 152
Pope, G. U. 25
postmodernism 13, 15–17
postmodernity 7, 13
prejudice 4, 14, 122, 129, 133–6, 138–9, 141, 145, 147, 155–6
Prince Charles 1–2
Protestant 25, 34–5, 86–8, 90, 97, 101, 152
punishment 69–70, 76, 84, 86, 89, 93, 110

Quebec 128
Queensland 139
Qur'an 9, 47–51, 58, 60–1, 102, 108, 110, 112, 139, 153–4
Qutb, Sayyid 109

Rabin, Yitzhak 67, 75–6, 105, 153
racism 121–2, 135, 139, 156
Radicalization 117, 119, 121, 127–8, 133, 151
Rapoport, David C. 8
reactive co-radicalization 2, 8, 12, 117–31, 133, 138, 156
Reason, Age of 13
reconciliation 10, 80
redemption 70, 72–3, 75–6, 87, 91
reformation 83, 86–7, 144
rejection vi, 1, 3–4, 9, 11–13, 15–17, 21, 28–9, 32, 35, 47, 59–60, 65, 91, 103, 106, 113–14, 117–22, 128, 134, 137–8, 141, 146, 149, 153, 158–60
relativism 15, 19–20, 24, 157
revelation 14, 25, 34, 50, 58, 60, 63, 82, 110, 112, 154
rhetoric 6–7, 11, 19, 36–7, 39, 42, 44, 62, 67–8, 70, 78, 95, 101–2, 107, 109, 110, 113–14, 119, 125, 127–9, 131, 133, 136–7, 139, 144–5, 147, 151, 154, 158
Richter, Yehuda 65
Rippin, Andrew 103–6
Roman Empire 70, 82
Runnymede Trust 135
Russia 10

Sabbatai Sevi 72
Sabbath 79
Sadat, Anwar 105
Safavid Empire 102
salvation 9, 19, 26–8, 33–4, 46, 60, 74, 84, 89, 105
Samartha, Stanley 24
Satan 42, 62, 91, 94, 125, 144
Saudi Arabia 108, 121, 123
Schmid, Alex 137
Schmidt-Leukel, Perry 59
science 14, 104, 106
scripture 8, 32, 37, 43, 48–50, 52, 55, 56, 58–60, 62, 74, 84–5, 89, 112, 154–5

secularism 8, 10, 77, 104–5, 114, 118, 130
self-assertion 33, 45
self-superiority 45–6
Selengut, Charles 67, 150, 153
Shari'a 46, 104, 106–8, 110, 112, 124, 145
Shepard, William 105
Shepherd, John 9–10
Shi'a 45, 50, 101
Shoah 67
Sikh 8, 135
Sinai 65
Smart, Ninian 22
Somalia 102, 113
South Africa 89, 141, 154
Southeast Asia 2, 113
Spain 135
subjugation 46, 102
suicide 65, 75, 100, 112, 153, 157
Sunni 45, 50, 101
superiority 19–21, 34, 40, 46, 61, 75, 89, 92, 95, 144, 152, 156
supersession 9
supremacists 92
Sweden 139, 145
Swift, Wesley 91–2
Switzerland 121–3, 130
Swiss 119–23, 130
Syria 1–2, 107
Syrians 1

Tabernacle, Jewish 56–7, 93
Tabor 89
Taliban 44, 46–7, 90, 107, 113
Talmud 4, 69
Teitel, Yaakov 'Jack' 66
Temple, Jewish 56, 59, 62, 71, 73–4, 77, 124, 153
terrorism vi, 1, 6–8, 10–11, 31–2, 35–6, 39–40, 45, 47, 75, 81, 90–1, 95–7, 100, 105, 110–13, 118, 120, 124, 126–7, 133, 137–8, 146, 149–50, 153, 155, 157
terrorist 1, 3, 6, 8, 11, 32, 36, 40, 45, 47–8, 65–6, 74–5, 93, 95, 100, 105, 110, 113, 119, 124–7, 136–7, 149, 154–5
Texas 96, 100, 137
texts 5, 8–9, 11–12, 38, 49–63, 70–1, 74, 77–8, 80–1, 84, 96, 106, 126, 153–6
Tibi, Bassam 109, 111–12
tolerance 1, 22, 80, 87–8, 117, 123, 134, 136, 157
toleration 35, 79, 122, 153, 157
torture 9, 58, 61, 84–5, 89, 140, 156
treason 76, 84–5
Trible, Phyllis 49, 54
Trump, Donald 2, 133, 136, 140, 156–7
truth 11, 14, 16, 19, 22, 24–8, 32–4, 40–1, 43, 46–7, 51–2, 142, 150–1, 153

Index

Turkey 101–2, 122, 155–6
Tyranny 43–5, 96

Umayyad 102
Ummah 60, 101, 105, 108–9, 111
United Kingdom 113, 135, 138–9
United States 8, 52, 89–90, 93, 96, 121, 134, 137, 140–1, 143, 145, 155–7
Utøya 124

Vatican II 25
Vengeance 53, 72, 81–2, 154
Vienna 99
violence 2, 4–8, 10, 31–2, 36, 39, 44–7, 49, 51–5, 57–8, 60, 62–3, 65–74, 77–82, 85, 87, 89–90, 92–3, 96–7, 99, 104, 115, 117–20, 125, 129–30, 138, 140, 145, 149–58

Waco 96
Waldensians, the 86
war 6, 8, 10–11, 36, 44, 52–4, 60–1, 65, 67, 70, 73–4, 78–9, 81, 91, 94, 99, 102, 105, 109, 113, 117–18, 121, 124–5, 127, 133–4, 138, 140, 145, 149, 152–4
Ward, Keith 8–10, 58, 155
West, the vi, 13–14, 42, 71, 86, 88, 102, 105, 107, 109, 111, 113, 123, 129, 134–6, 138, 144, 153–4
West Bank, the 8, 65, 67, 74–7
Will (of God) 37, 51, 58, 68–9, 89, 99–100, 106, 108, 160
Winter, Tim 104–5, 154, 160
women 47, 53, 57, 93, 111, 128, 135, 150
World, the vi–vii, 1–4, 8, 13–16, 18, 20–3, 27–8, 35–6, 38, 42, 44, 61–2, 72–4, 76, 81, 90, 94–5, 97, 100–1, 103–5, 107, 109, 111–12, 117–18, 127–9, 133, 136, 139, 142, 144, 149, 156
World Council of Churches 19, 24, 88
World Islamic Front 134
Wright, Stefanie 145

Xenophobia 121–2, 127, 134–35, 147

Yeshiva 10, 66, 68, 74–5
Yilmaz, Ihsan 135
Yugoslavia 87

Zealot 62, 68–9, 77, 91, 93
Zealotry 56–7, 67–9, 73, 76, 97, 104
Ziegenbalg, Bartholomaus 25
Zionism 52, 67, 76–7, 79, 103, 104, 107, 136, 154
Zionists 67, 71, 78, 153–4
Zürich 121

www.ingramcontent.com/pod-product-compliance
Lightning Source LLC
Chambersburg PA
CBHW050139240426
43673CB00043B/1732